THE DEFINITIVE BROTHER JUNIPER

Dear Reader,

I've spent a year and a half working closely with Brother Juniper material and this book is the culmination of that effort and the capstone of the Brother Juniper Rejuvenation Project. Two years ago, the handful of existing Brother Juniper books were stuffed away in basements and used-book-sale bins gathering dust. The Brother Juniper cartoon was a sidenote on a few webpages and its digital existence amounted to two sentences on Wikipedia. Today Brother Juniper has his own website, email address, and Facebook page. He even tweets on Twitter occassionally. And today anyone on the planet can enjoy the Brother Juniper books via an *infinite* supply of high-quality print and digital formats.

After extensive pixel-level editing and remastering of the best possible source images, I present to you the "rejuvenated" Brother Juniper series. I hope you enjoy him as much as I do.

-A. Nicolai
Empty-Grave Publishing

PS - If you are interested in using Brother Juniper cartoons on your websites, newsletters, or just about anything else, feel free to email me at juniper@brotherjuniper.com for no-cost 300dpi print-quality vector or rasterized versions of your favorite cartoons.

For the Brother Juniper Rejuvenation Project, more cartoons, and information on other Brother Juniper books please visit us at www.brotherjuniper.com or on Facebook at www.facebook.com/BrotherJuniperProject/.

The Definitive Brother Juniper

by
Father Justin
'Fred' McCarthy

Empty-Grave Publishing
www.empty-grave.com

ISBN: 1620890135
ISBN-13: 978-1-62089-013-4

Author's Note

(From the first edition release of the first Brother Juniper book.)

Yes, Virginia, There Is a Brother Juniper

Almost everyone's heard of St. Francis. He's the saint who loved people - and birds, too. What most people don't know is that the good saint had a real-life follower, name of Brother Juniper, who was the original good-humor man. The little fellow was quicksilver . . . he was sunbeams in burlap. He showed people they could be merry and still save their souls in the process.

St. Francis so admired this brand of sanctity that he used to say, "Would that I had a whole forest of such Junipers." This volume is our humble effort to provide the saint with a grove, if not a forest, of Junipers.

We've simply lifted Brother Juniper, a historic comic, from his thirteenth-century Umbrian context, fattened him up a few pounds, and placed him in a twentieth-century publisher's showcase.

Possibly some readers have already met B. J. on the comic page of the daily newspapers. For those who have not, a few character references might not come amiss. (Let me here confess that I do not know the little fellow really well . . . yet. Hardly a day goes by that he does not surprise me with a personality facet I did not know existed. And there is one faculty he has which baffles me completely: he can open his mouth and say something funny without taking a moment's thought. It takes me months to dream up the same punch line.)

Brother Juniper is a man of parts. At last count he was:

> *One part Friar Tuck*
> *Two parts Victor Moore*
> *Three parts George Bungle*
> *Four parts Everyman*
> *A pinch of Pogo*
> *A soupcon of Bishop Sheen*

But mostly he's himself: optimistic, bustling (never lets any grass grow under his flagstones), hard-working, helpful, honest (with himself, his fellow man, and his God), genial, mischievous, long on good example if a trifle short on dignity, holy (without ever suspecting it), occasionally wistful, frequently a fall guy, and forever hilarious.

Like Jack Benny, he's a sort of undefeated underdog. If things go well, he's pleased; if they go ill, he's delighted. B. J. is, in a word, "unsinkable"!

For this can we envy him and for this can we honour him, as a lower-case St. Francis from upper Manhattan.

Should you wish to pay him a visit, he's a cinch to find. Always available at the usual intersection, corner of Grace and Main. If you'd like to know him better, I would suggest you approach him as the children do: with a smile. For they are onto his secret. They know he has never ceased to be one of themselves . . . And of such is the kingdom of Heaven.

I should like to take this occasion to thank my publishers for inviting me to do this book, my religious superiors for granting me permission to attempt it, and Brother Juniper for making the whole task a pleasant one.

FATHER MAC
Brookline, Mass.

Author's Note

(From the first edition release of the final Brother Juniper book.)

HE WOULDN'T HURT A SOUL

One day Pope John XXIII went strolling through the Vatican gardens. Suddenly there materialized a crowd of Roman street urchins. Pushing and shoving, they swarmed around the beaming Pontiff, all but crushing him with their delighted homage.

At once the Papal Guards swung into action. Quickly they formed a cordon about the Holy Father and succeeded in driving away the ragamuffin throng. A dismayed Pope John questioned the Captain of the Guards: "Why did you do that?"

"For reasons of security, Your Eminence," was the reply.

Crestfallen, the old Pontiff shook his head. "I wouldn't have hurt them," he murmured.

In the golden tradition of good Pope John comes another humble, well-beloved, ecumenical personage. His name is Brother Juniper. Small of stature yet somehow bigger than life, he has become a magnet to men of good will. Hundreds of thousands read his books. Millions watch his daily comings and goings in the newspapers.

From a pulpy pulpit on the comics page he manages to preach without ever becoming preachy. Interdenominational as laughter, he chirrups his good-humored message to followers of every faith.

By tickling our collective funny bone he gains admittance to our hearts, from where it's only a hop, skip, and jump to reach our souls.

Truly it might be said of Brother Juniper as of good Pope John; "He wouldn't hurt a soul."

F. MCCARTHY

CONTENTS

BROTHER JUNIPER

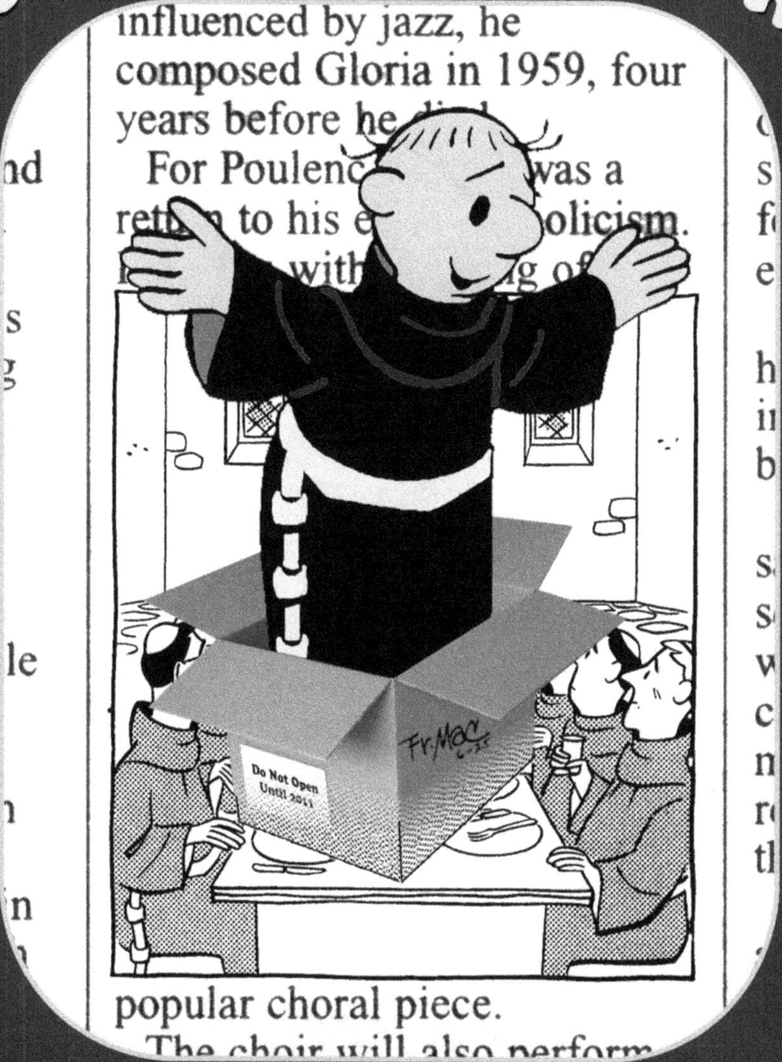

influenced by jazz, he
composed Gloria in 1959, four
popular choral piece.
Do Not Open
Until 2011
Fr. Mac

BY FATHER JUSTIN 'FRED' McCARTHY

Empty-Grave Extended Edition

"...But first, a message from Our Sponsor."

"Hey, Curlie, which way to Capistrano?"

"Look in back of Descartes."

"Just a minute, full fare for him!"

"Oh well, like Durocher says, nice guys finish last!"

"Last year it was cutworms."

"This will keep delinquents off the street corners?"

"Warm up, fellers. You're in the sack race!"

"Say, did we advertise for a printer's devil?"

"Might as well prime the pump."

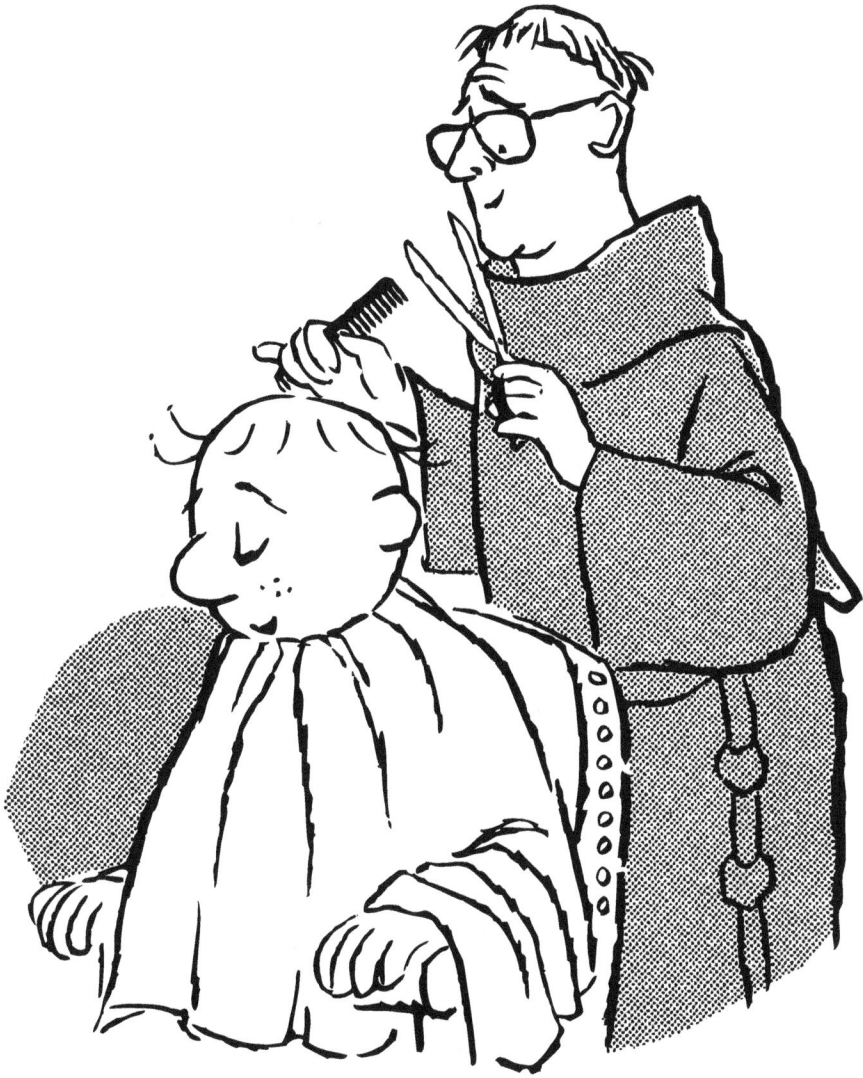

"Give me a Yul Brynner, please."

"Why not do the whole place over in knotty pine?"

"Prithee stop. You're filling the wine barrel!"

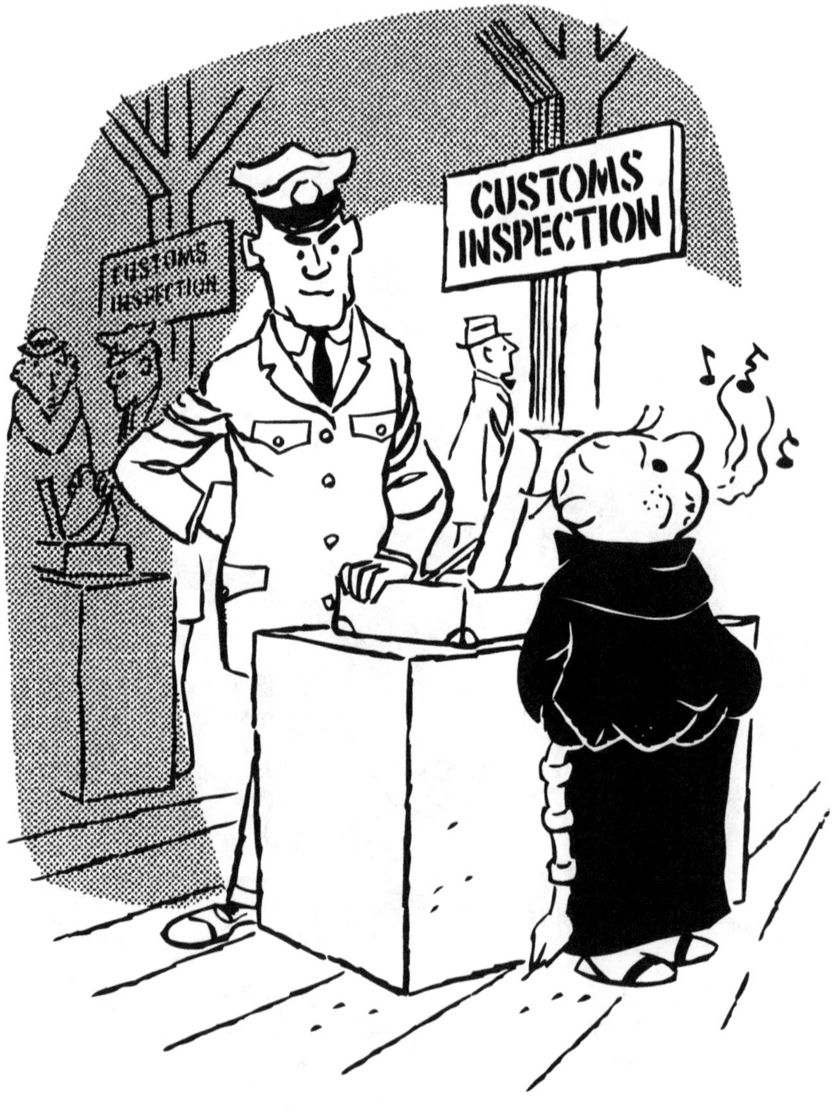
CUSTOMS INSPECTION
CUSTOMS INSPECTION

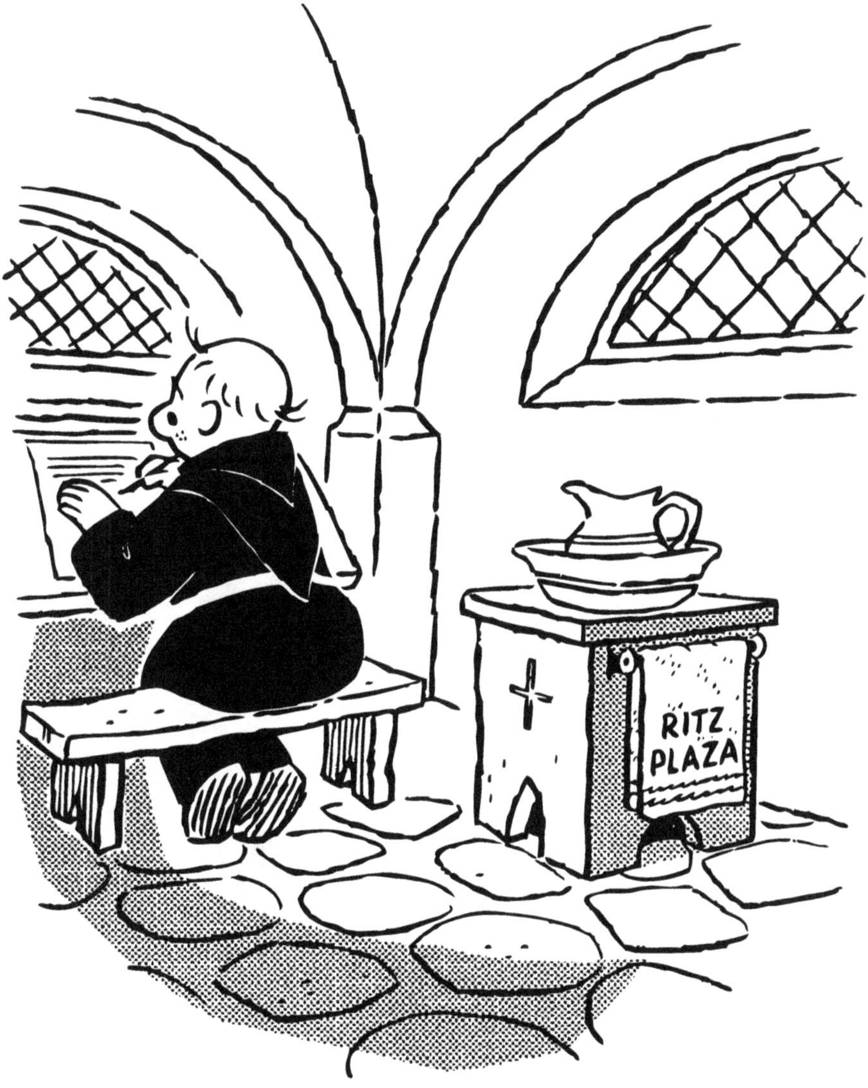
RITZ
PLAZA

"Modern, functional, and it doesn't drip all over you."

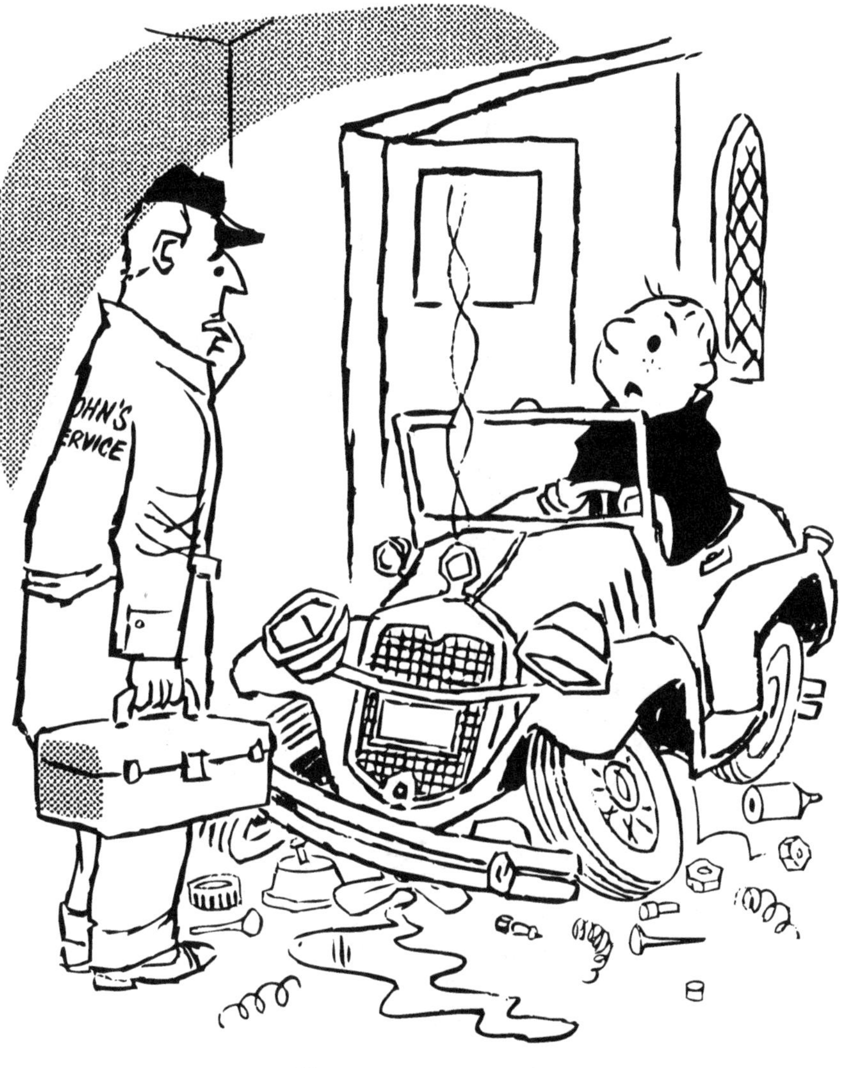
OHN'S
ERVICE

"It won't start"

"Mother knitted it."

"Testing...coal collection...warm hearts
or frigid church...testing."

"I think it's the finest thing you've ever done."

"I favor the overlapping grip."

"**#X!XXX**!"

"Say ah-men."

"Ten for Bishop Sheen; one for GUNSMOKE."

"Good morning, sir or madam, I represent..."

"Can Brother Juniper come out?
We need somethin' to tackle."

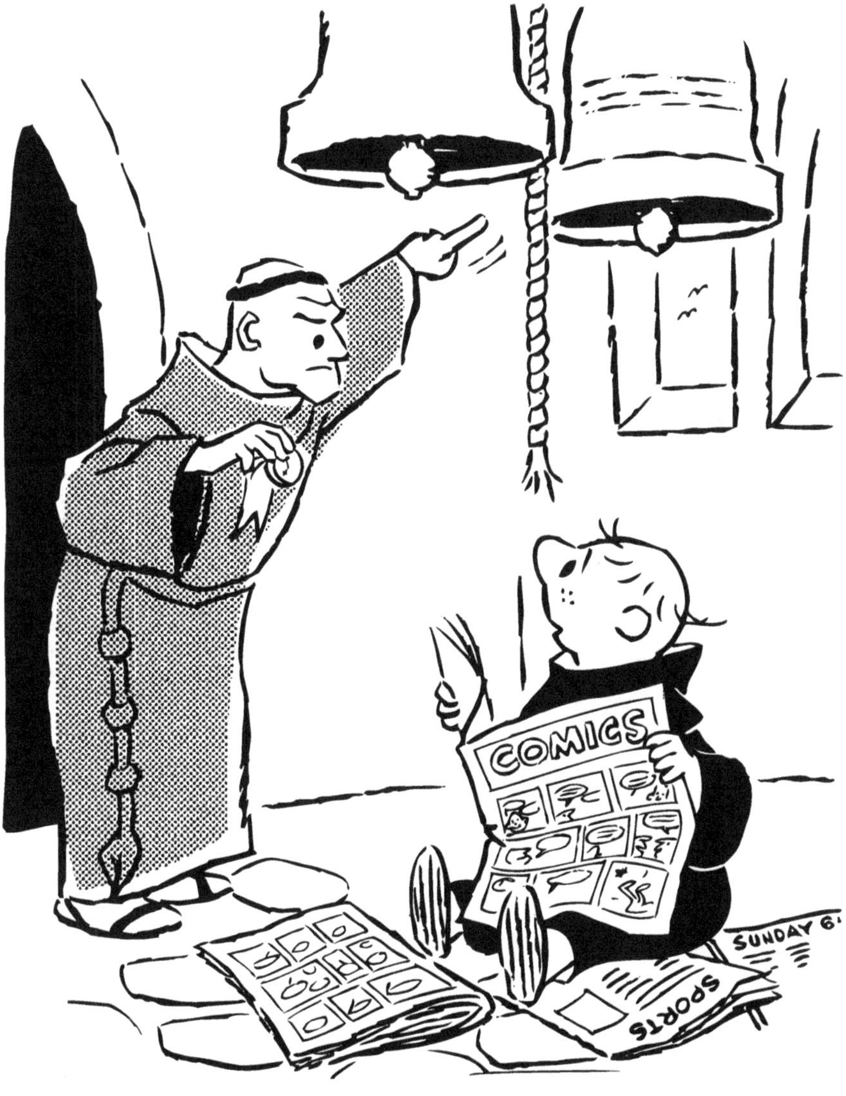
COMICS
SUNDAY 6
SPORTS

"Where does the time go?"

"Up here, hey."

"You do it your way; let me do it my way."

"How old is your third baseman?"

"Who's your tailor?"

"First will come the blinding flash, then the detonation. Throw yourselves on the ground and wait. Try to avoid atomic fall-out. I'll be around to help you as soon as I can."

"My sister's boy."

ST. THOMAS AQUINAS

THINK

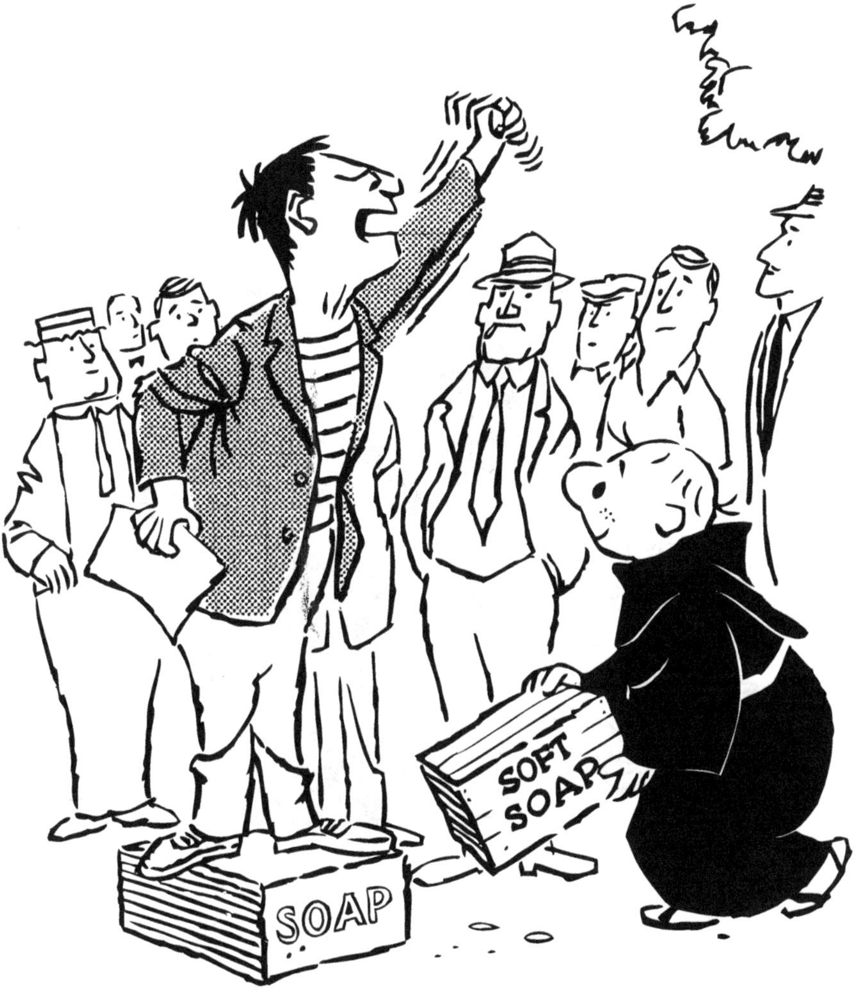
SOAP
SOFT SOAP

"He went thataway, seems as if."

"I see you beat Brother Pacificus again."

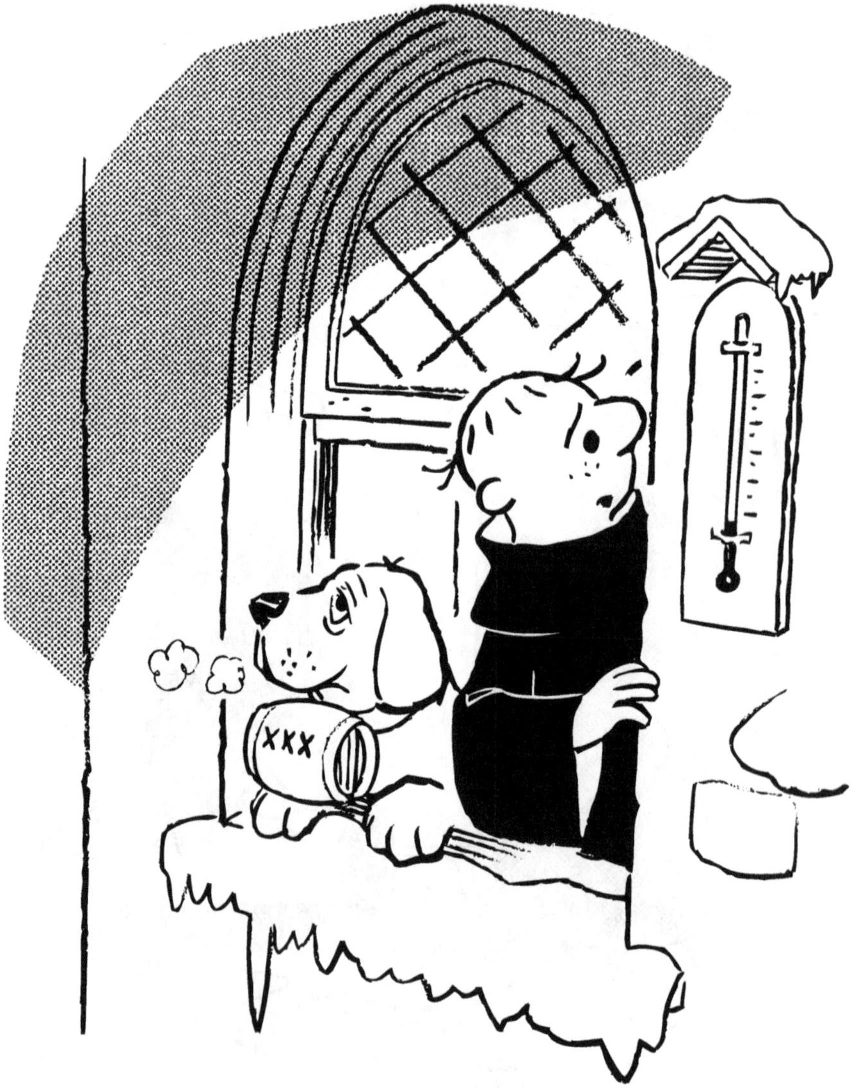
XXX

"Wow, XXX below."

"How are your winters up here?"

"Pour le sport?"

"Talk about separation of church and state!"

"It's His rain, but it's our picnic!"

"R-A-G-G M-O-P-P...I said rag mop...
dah-de-ah-dee-ah-dah..."

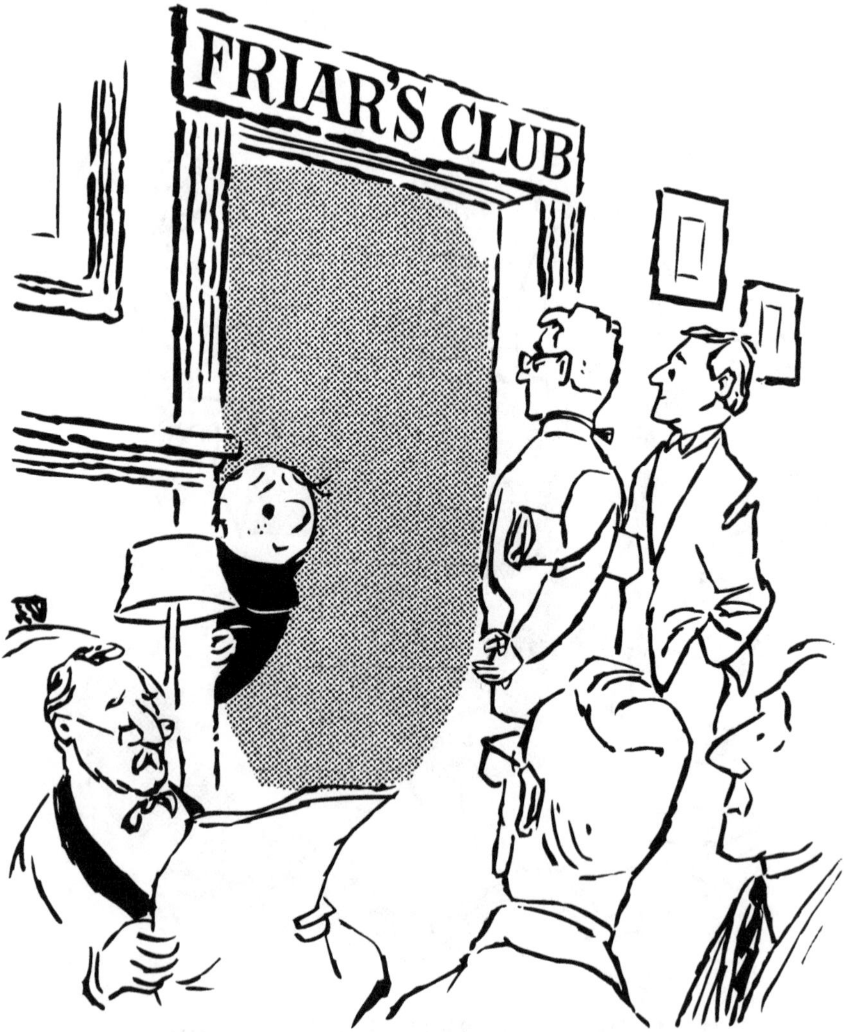
FRIAR'S CLUB

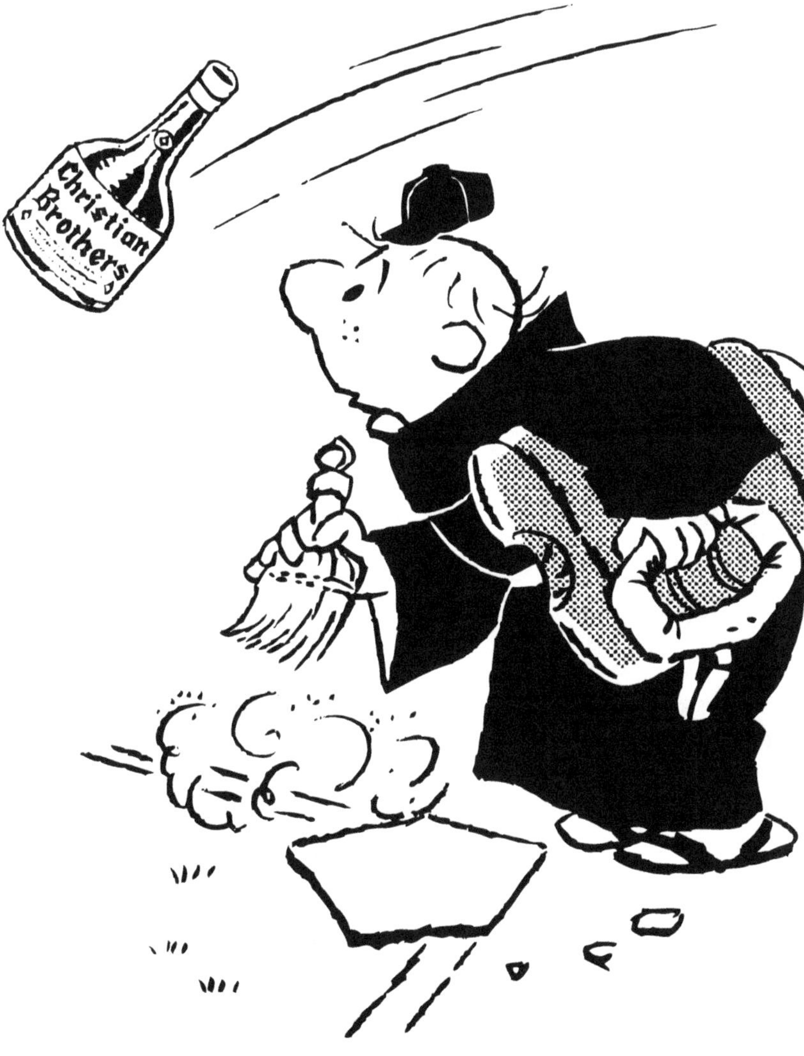
Christian
Brothers

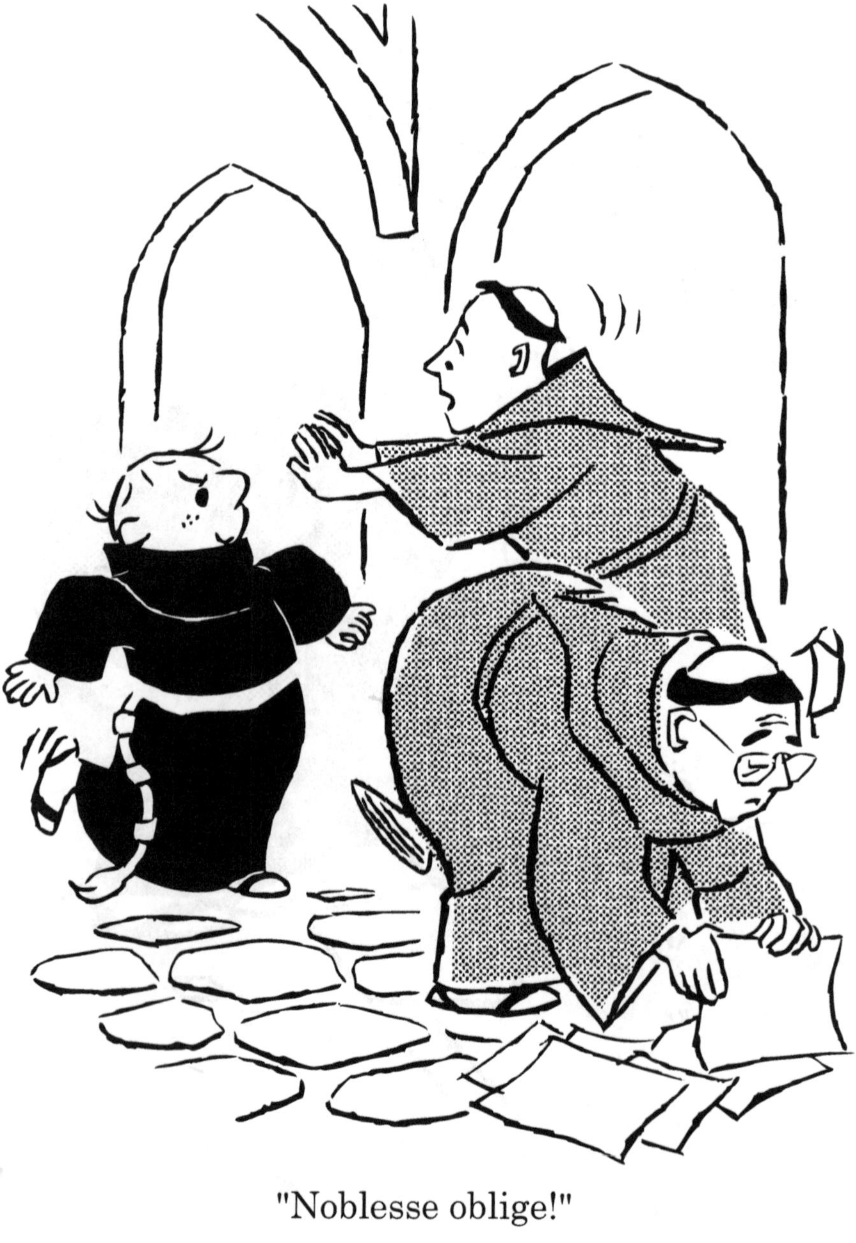

"Noblesse oblige!"

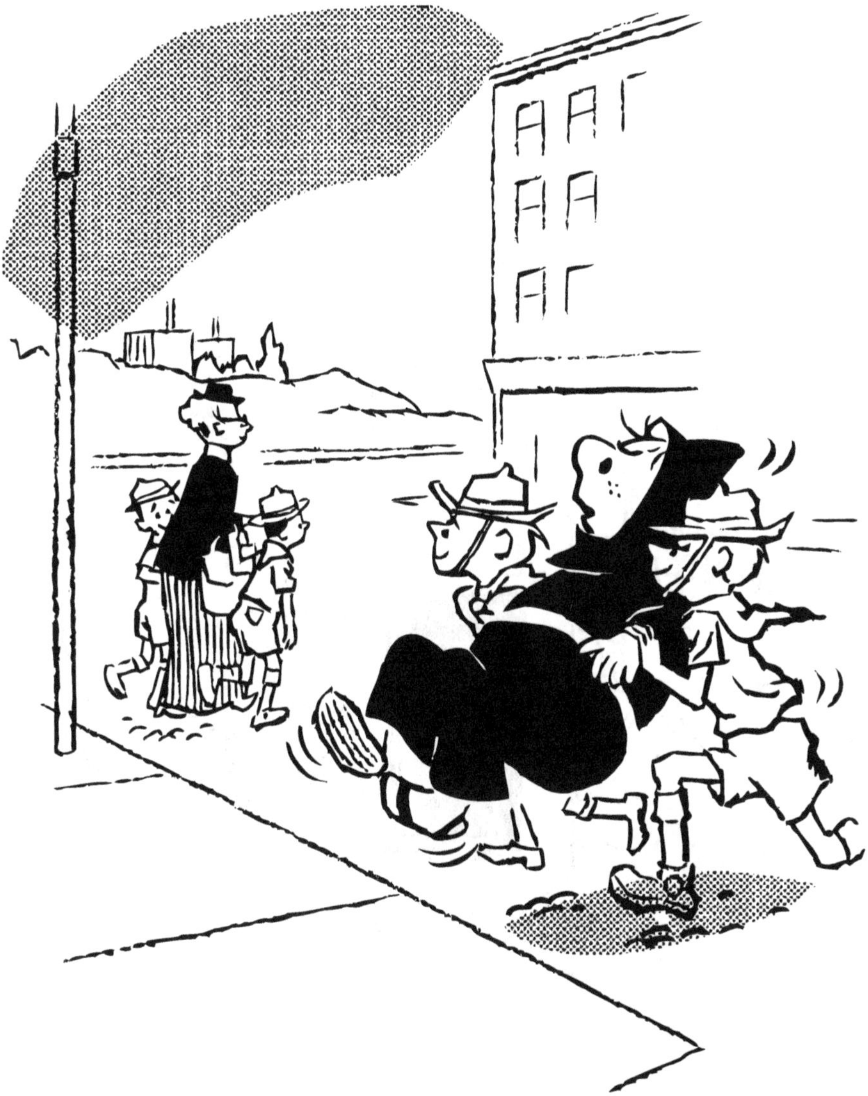

"Wait a minute!!"

"Is there any chance for advancement?"

"Balk!"

"Ninety-eight cents this week. Not bad!"

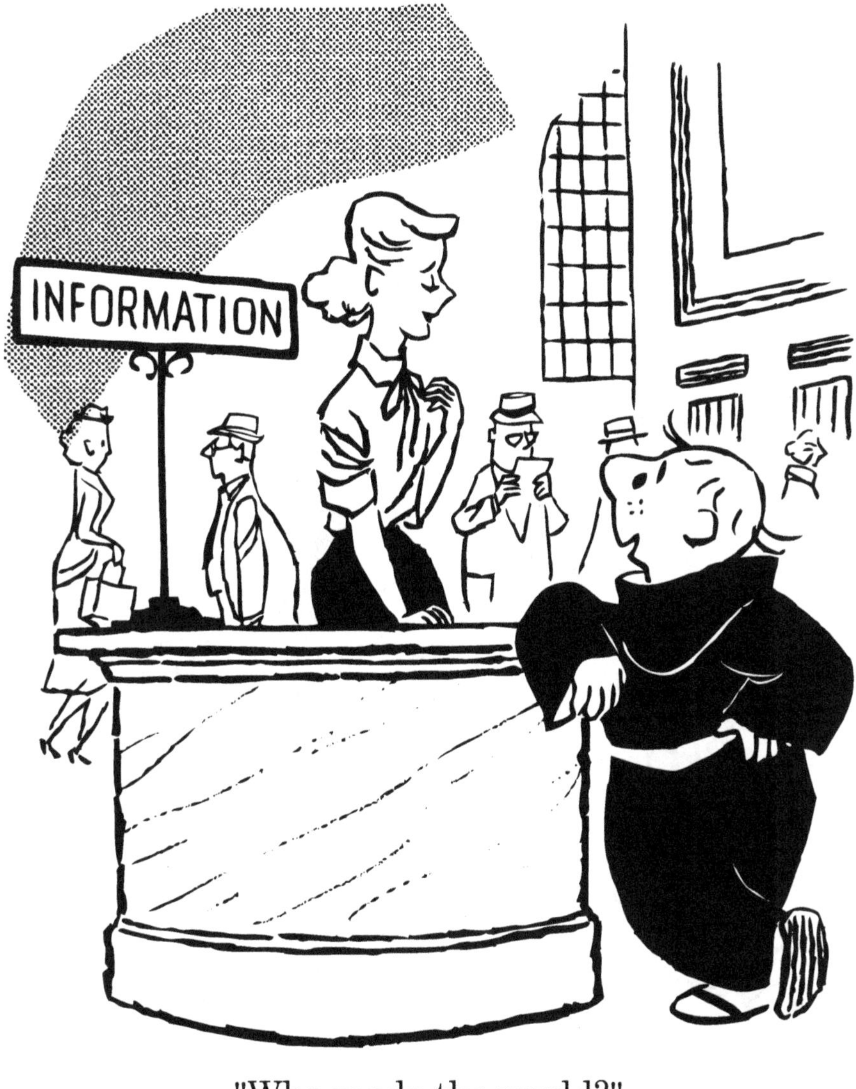
INFORMATION

"Who made the world?"

"Gotta keep after those weeds."

"Mineself, I don't see how they can
blame it all on Terry Brennan."

"You are going on a long fast."

"Hey, O'Sullivan, are mine ready yet?"

"How long can he keep up this terrific pace?"

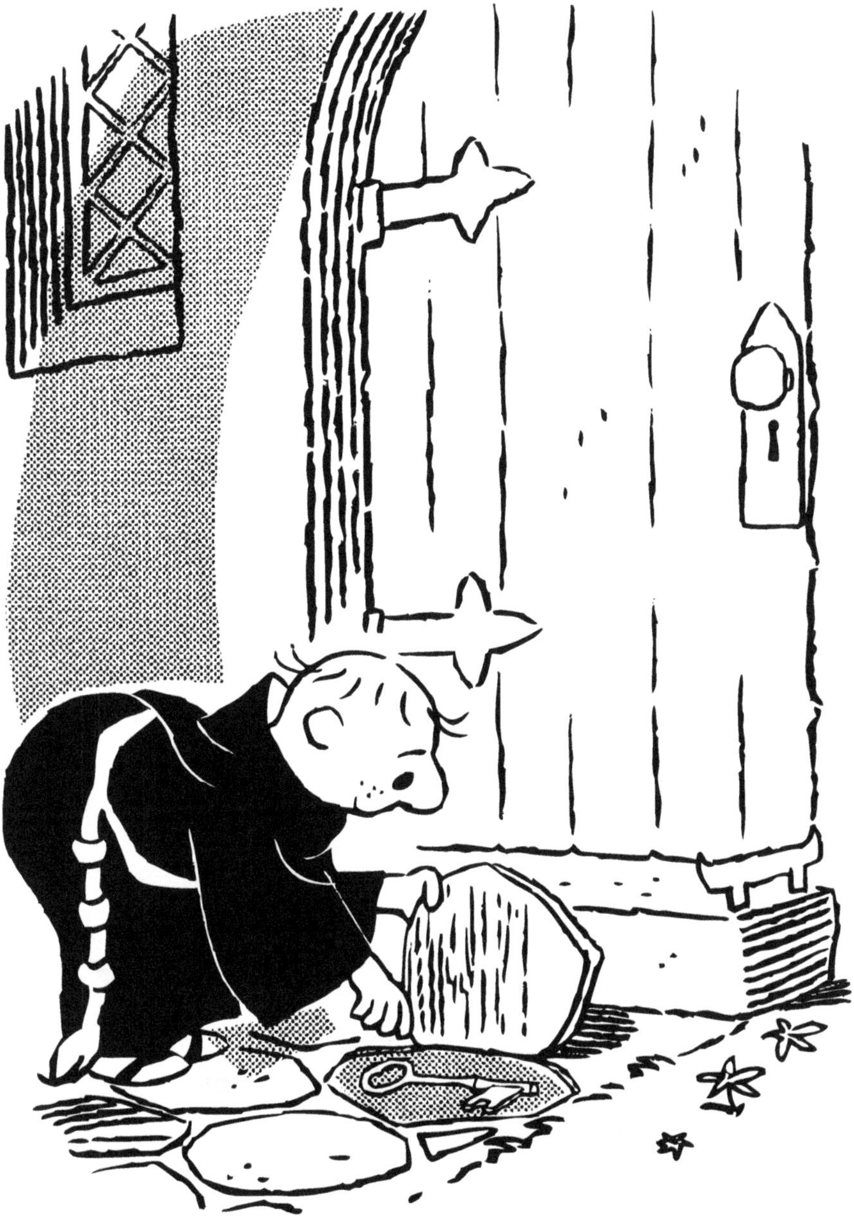

"Whatever will be, will be..."

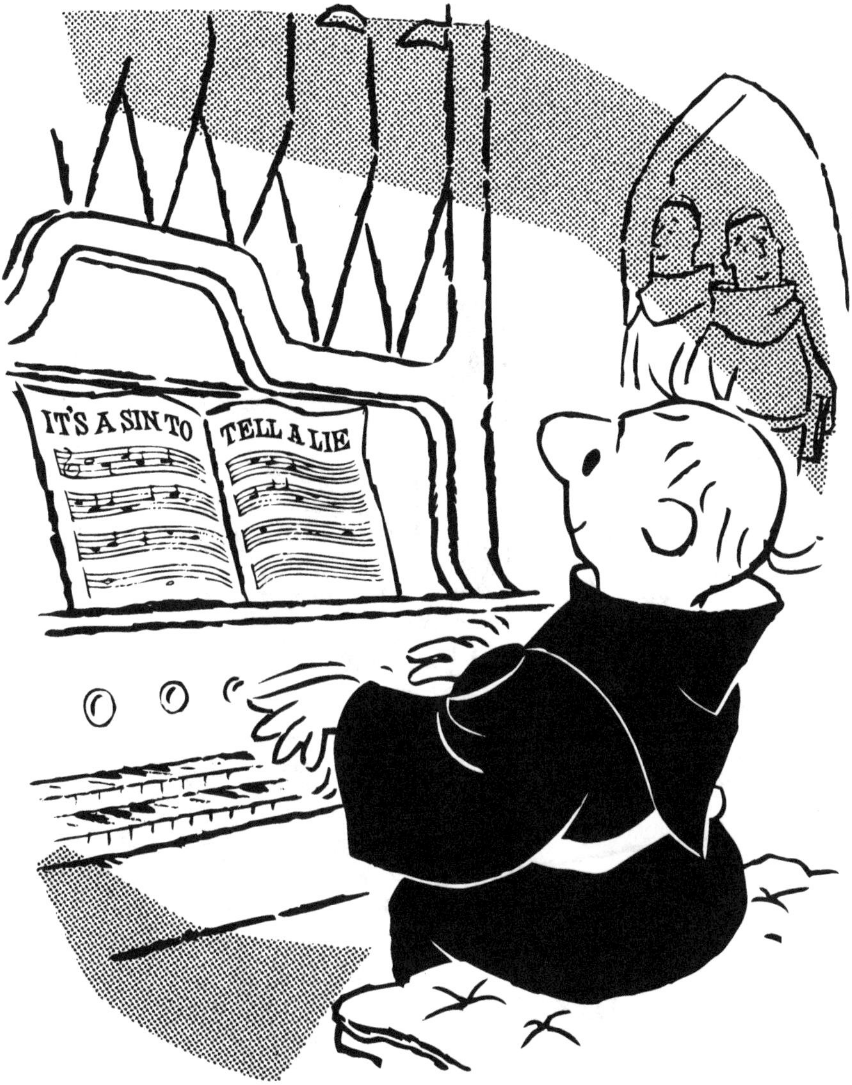
IT'S A SIN TO
TELL A LIE

"Is that the one we're supposed to be as poor as?"

"It can't compare with the Book."

"You certainly can't tell a book by its cover!"

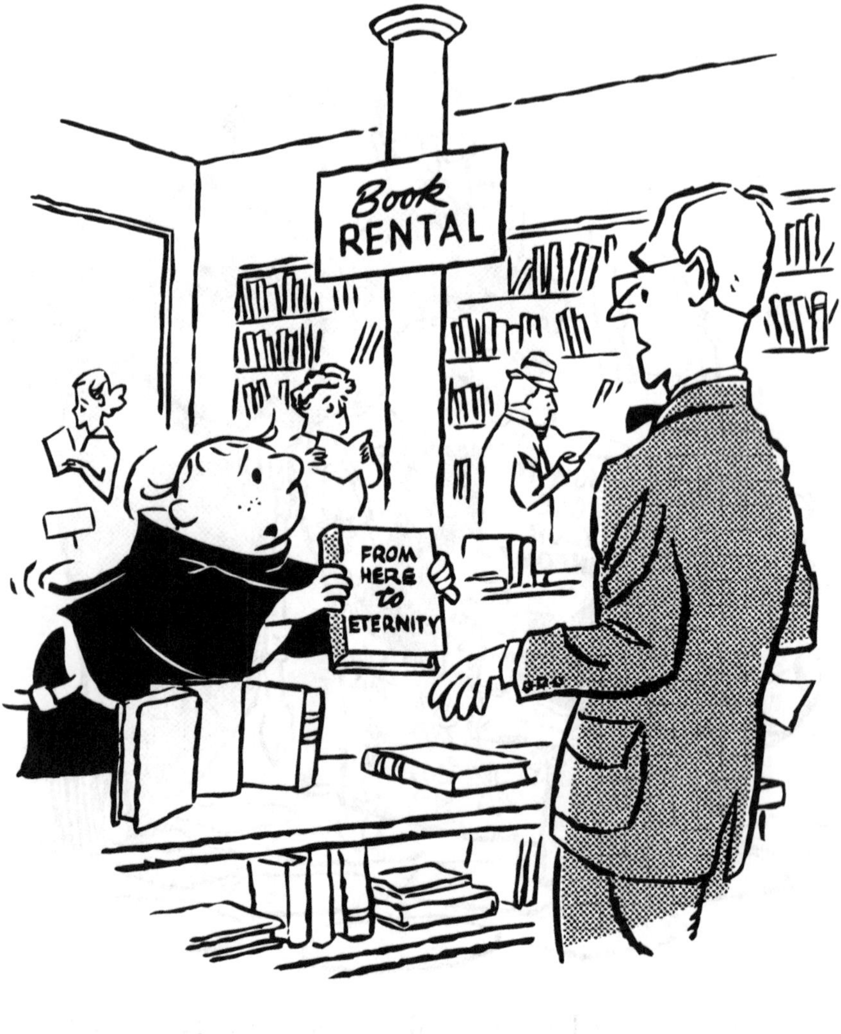
Book
RENTAL
FROM
HERE
to
ETERNITY

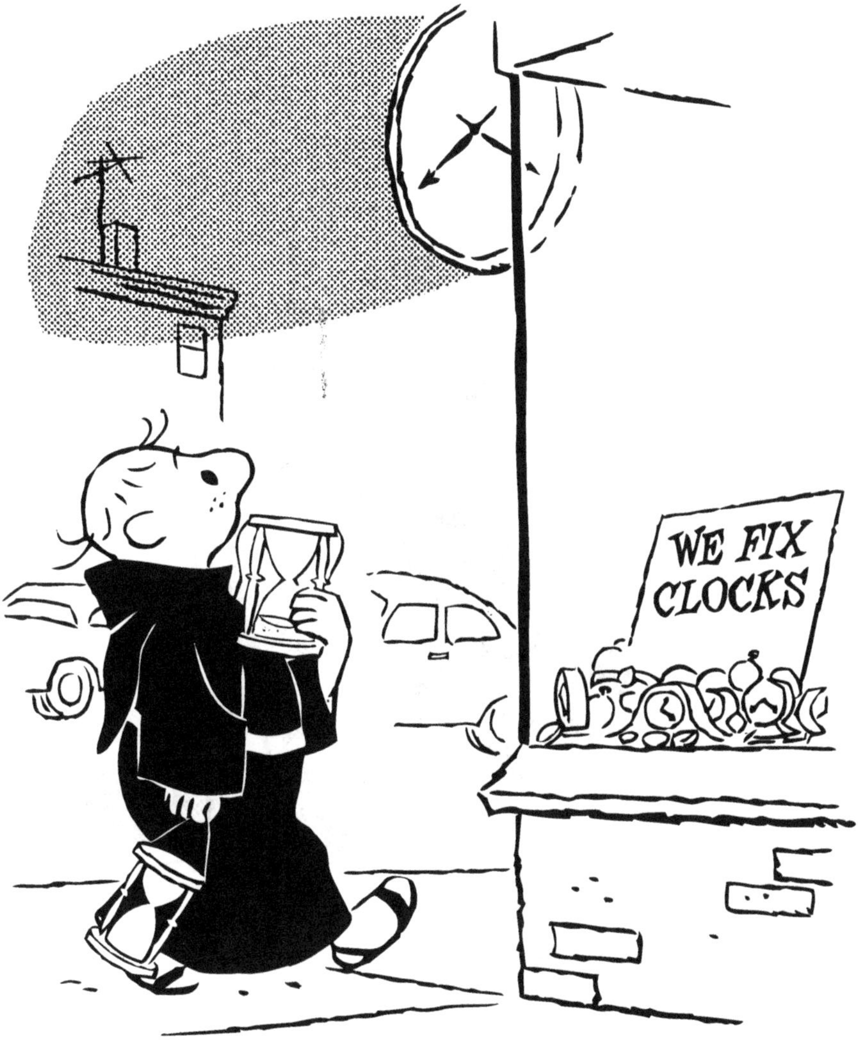
WE FIX
CLOCKS

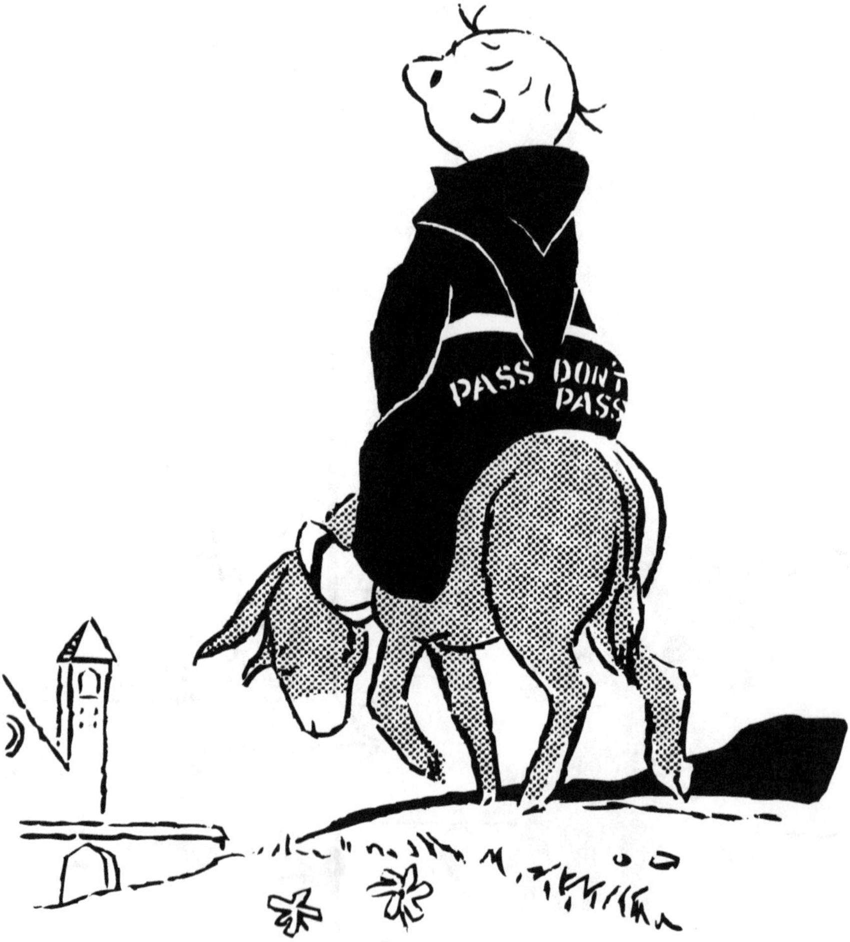
PASS
DON'T PASS

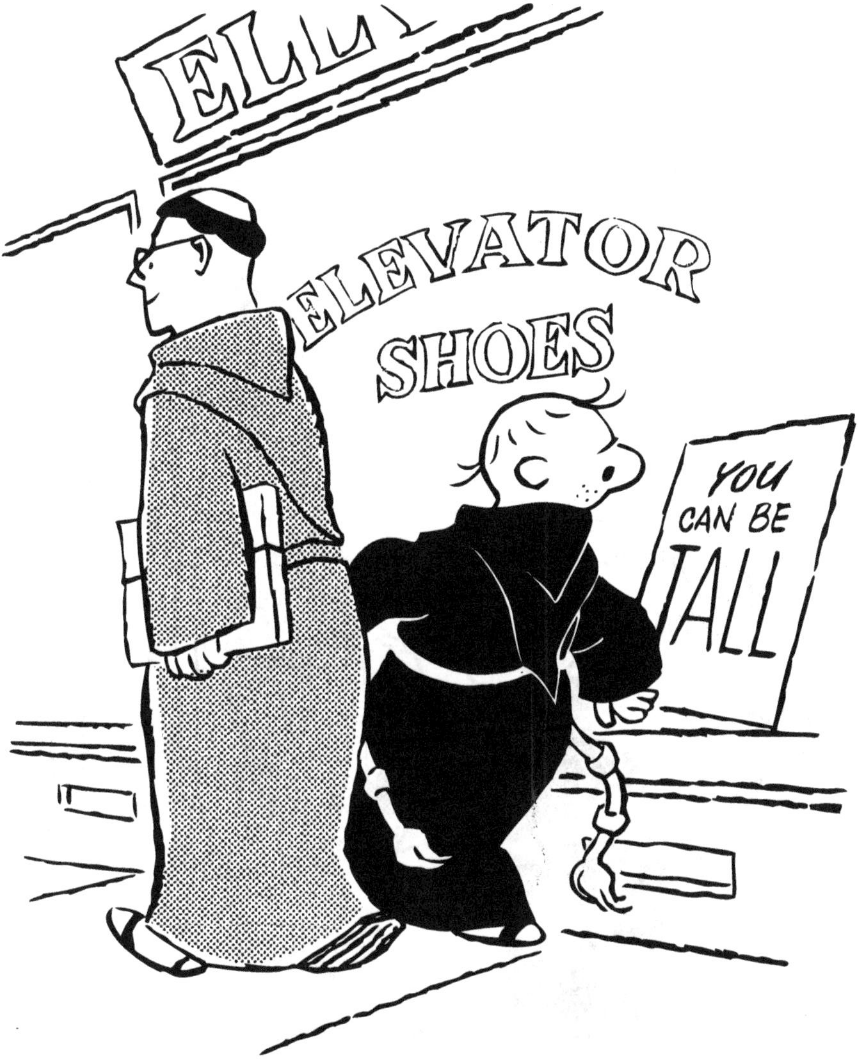
ELEVATOR
SHOES
YOU
CAN BE
TALL

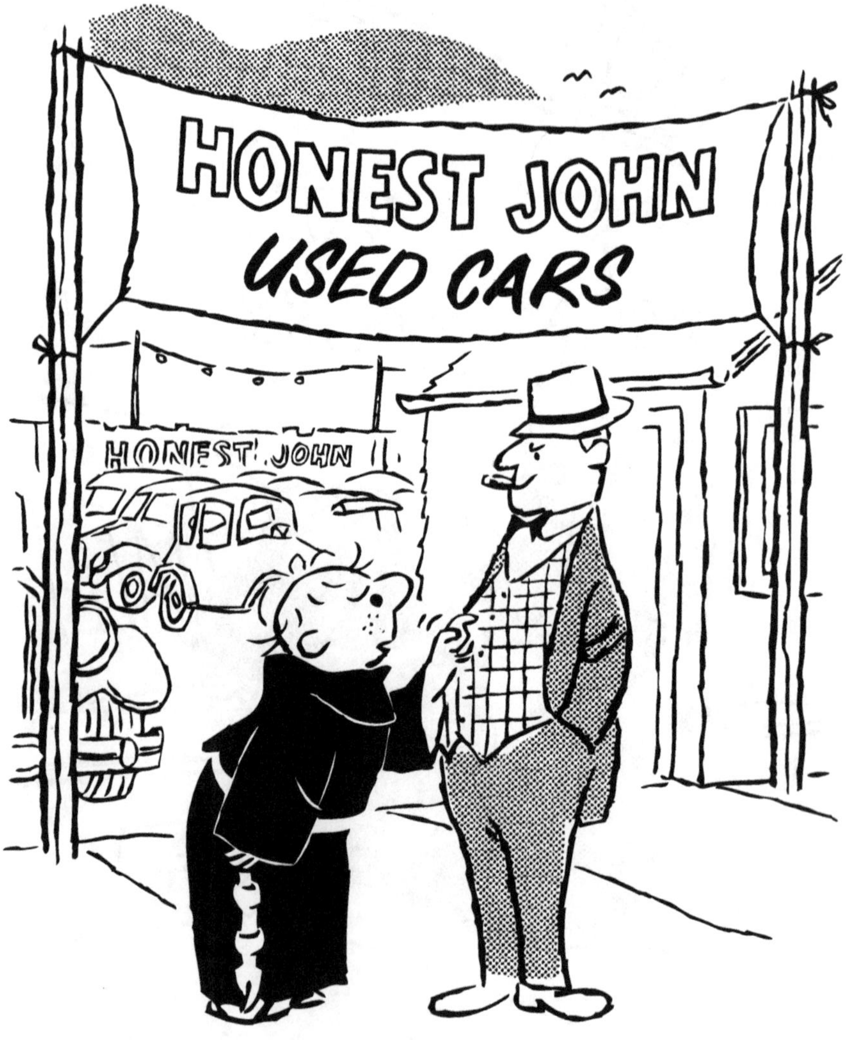
HONEST JOHN
USED CARS
HONEST JOHN

"Cross your heart?"

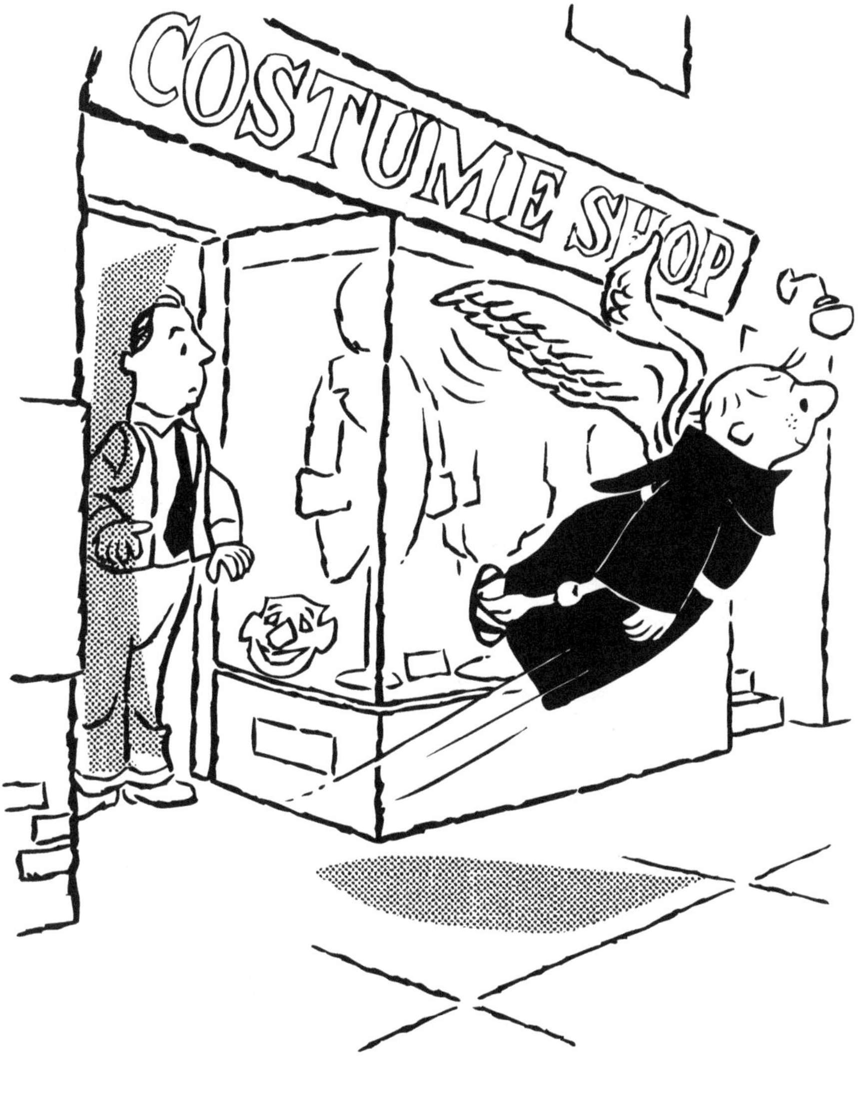
COSTUME SHOP

"That your idea of shorthand?"

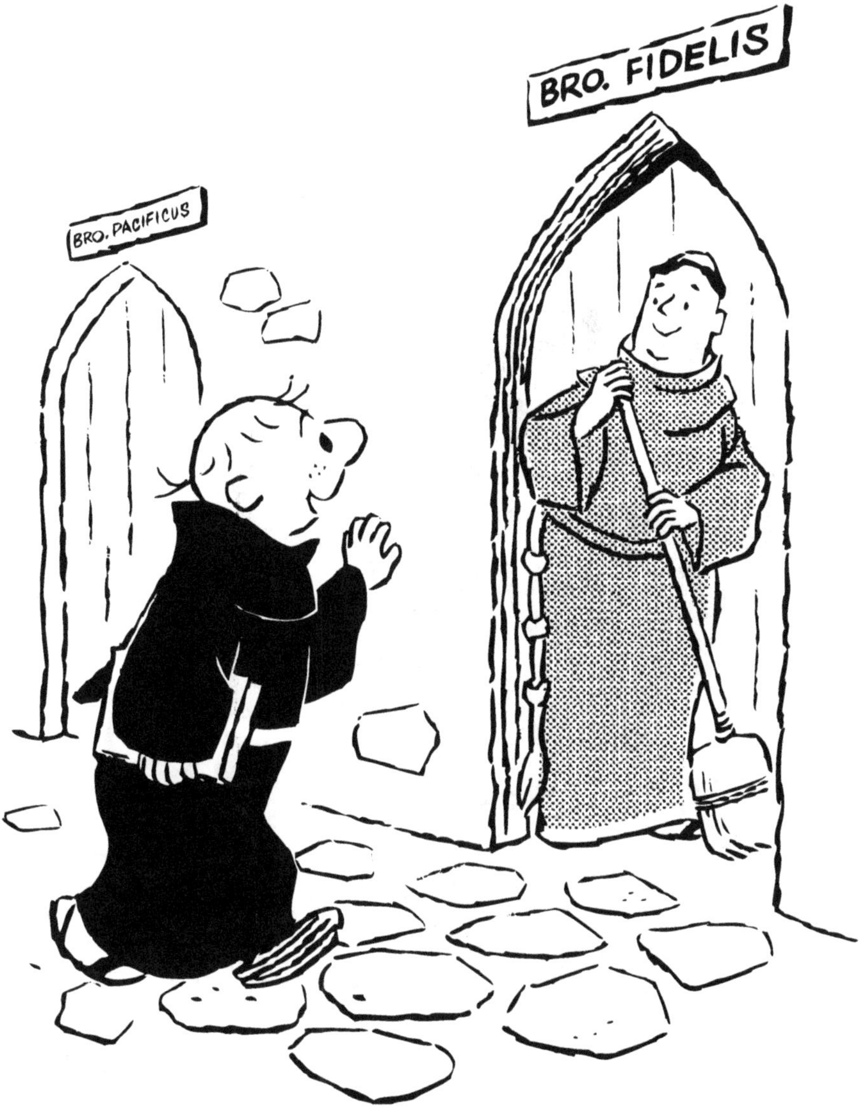
BRO. PACIFICUS
BRO. FIDELIS

"Hi Fi!"

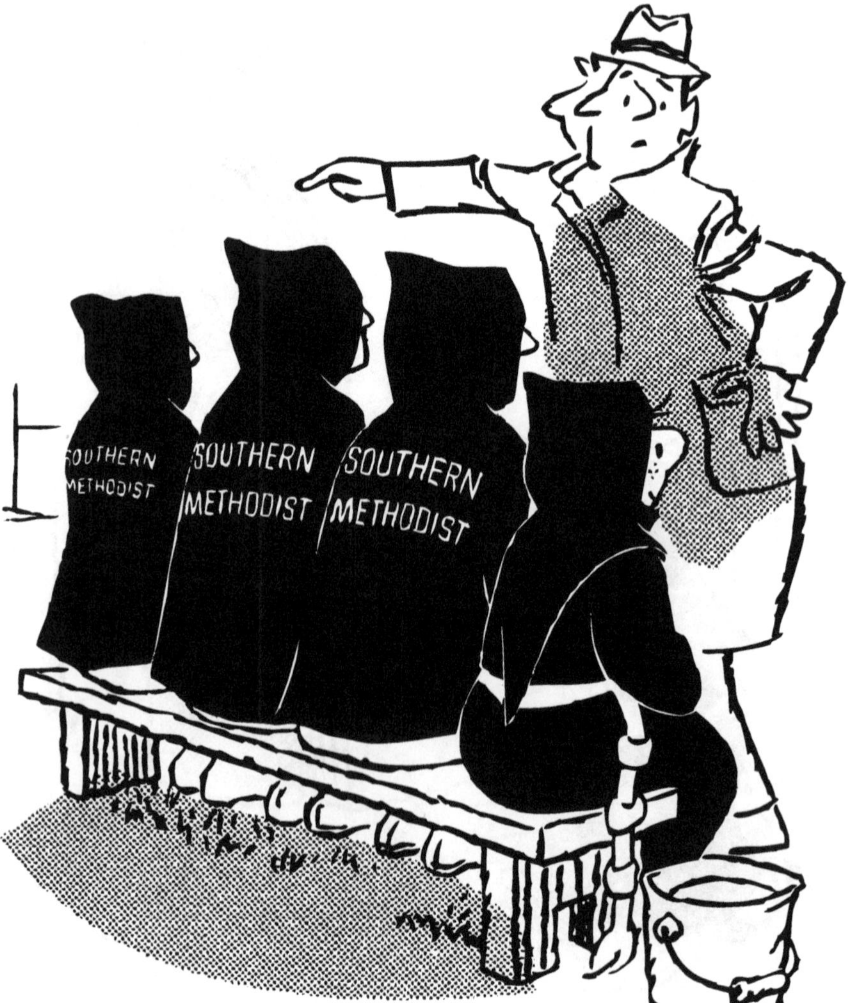
SOUTHERN
METHODIST
SOUTHERN
METHODIST
SOUTHERN
METHODIST

"Over where you are, will be the rumpus room."

"Hereafter, if there's something you don't like around here, tell me; don't write your congressman!"

"Read any good books lately?"

"Architecturally, we're a combination of
late hospital and early prison."

"You can't sit a do-gooder next
to a don't-give-a-darner!"

"You rang, sir?"

"I don't like to go over the Abbot's head,
but if, just this once, You could..."

"Brother Juniper said we could
keep our bats in your belfry."

"Why don't you go back and
tell him about Saint Francis?"

"Fox! What fox?"

"Possibly, I have enough material
to make you a new robe."

"If you don't stop following me around, I won't take
any more thorns out of your feet!"

"Do you have 'The Darnation of Faust'?"

"Aw, fellers, not in the madrilene!"

"Brother Juniper dipped my cord in the inkwell!"

"It gives me great pleasure to present our honored
guest, who has flown in at great expense..."

"Man, dig that crazy drape!"

"It's in excellent condition, sir.
It belonged to an atheist."

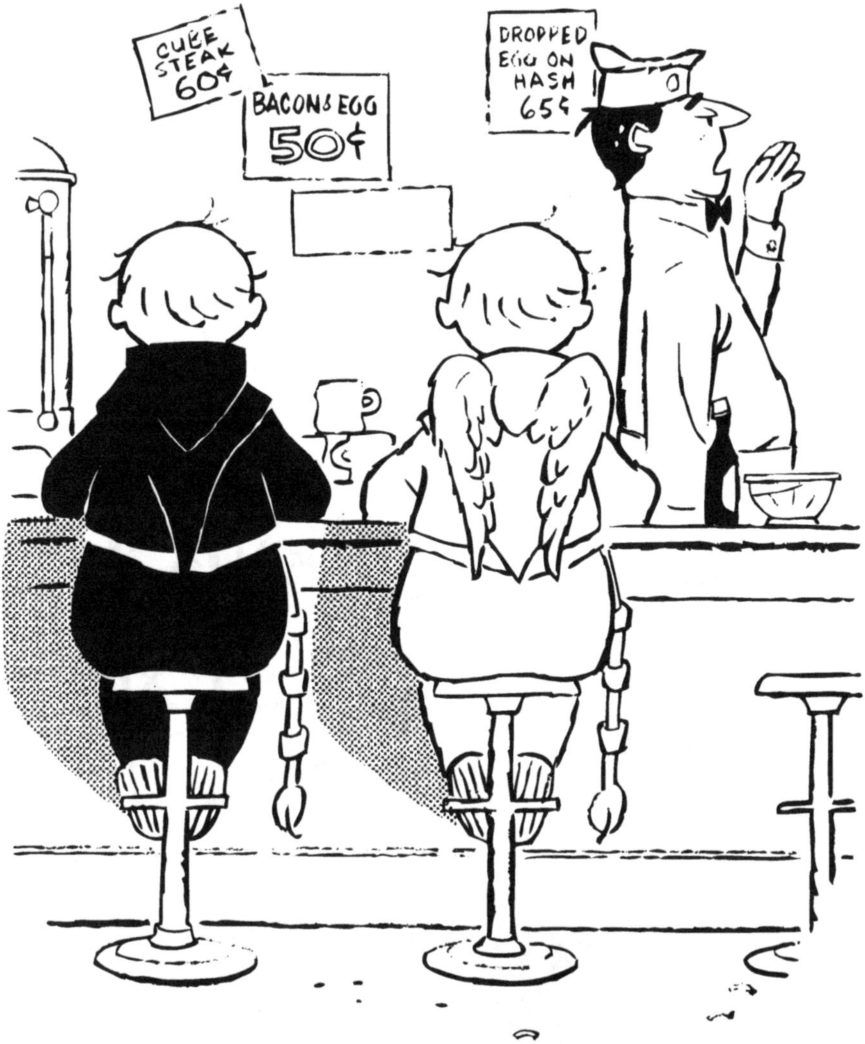
CUBE STEAK 60¢
BACON & EGG 50¢
DROPPED EGG ON HASH 65¢

"Two franks, one to go."

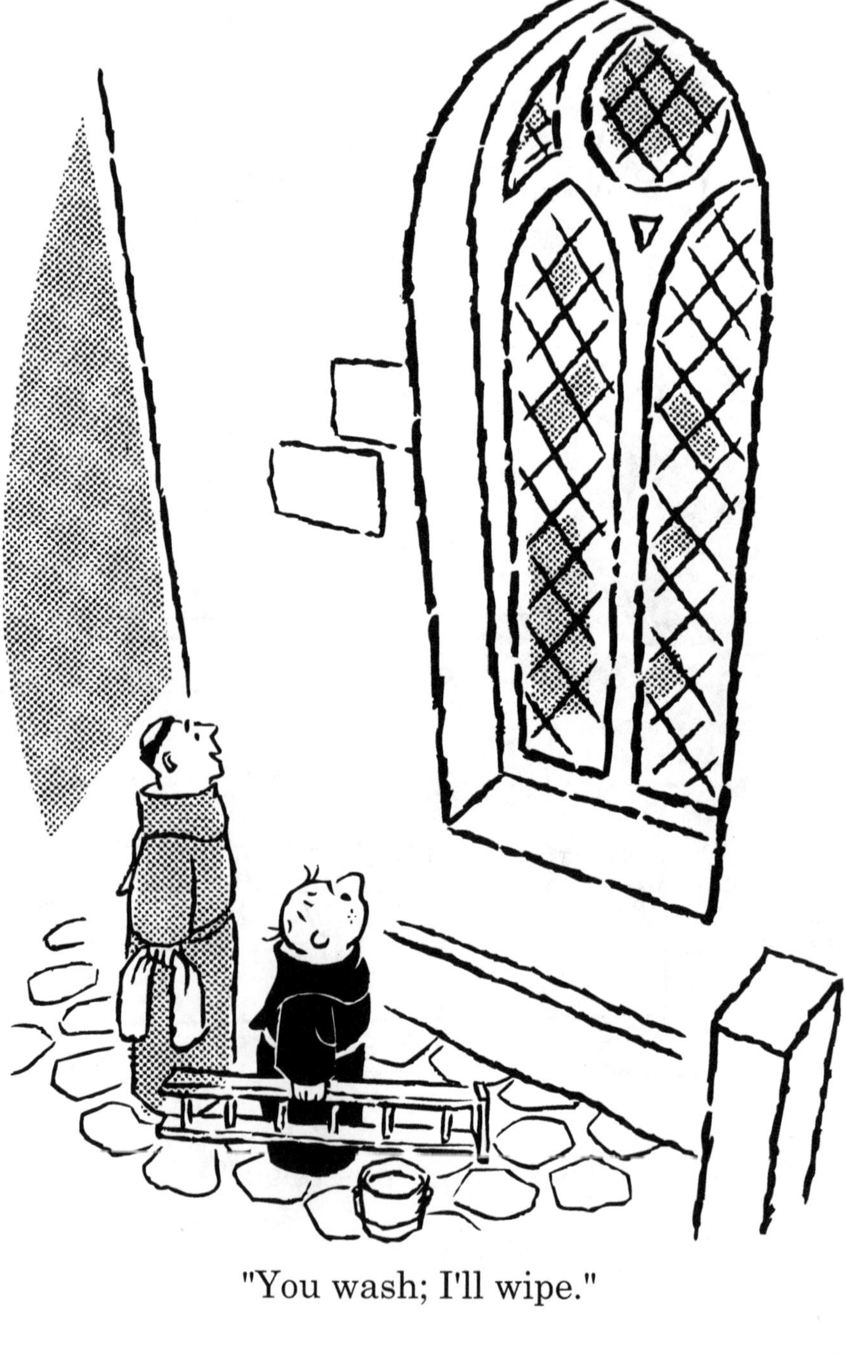

"You wash; I'll wipe."

"Hi, fellers! What's the good word?"

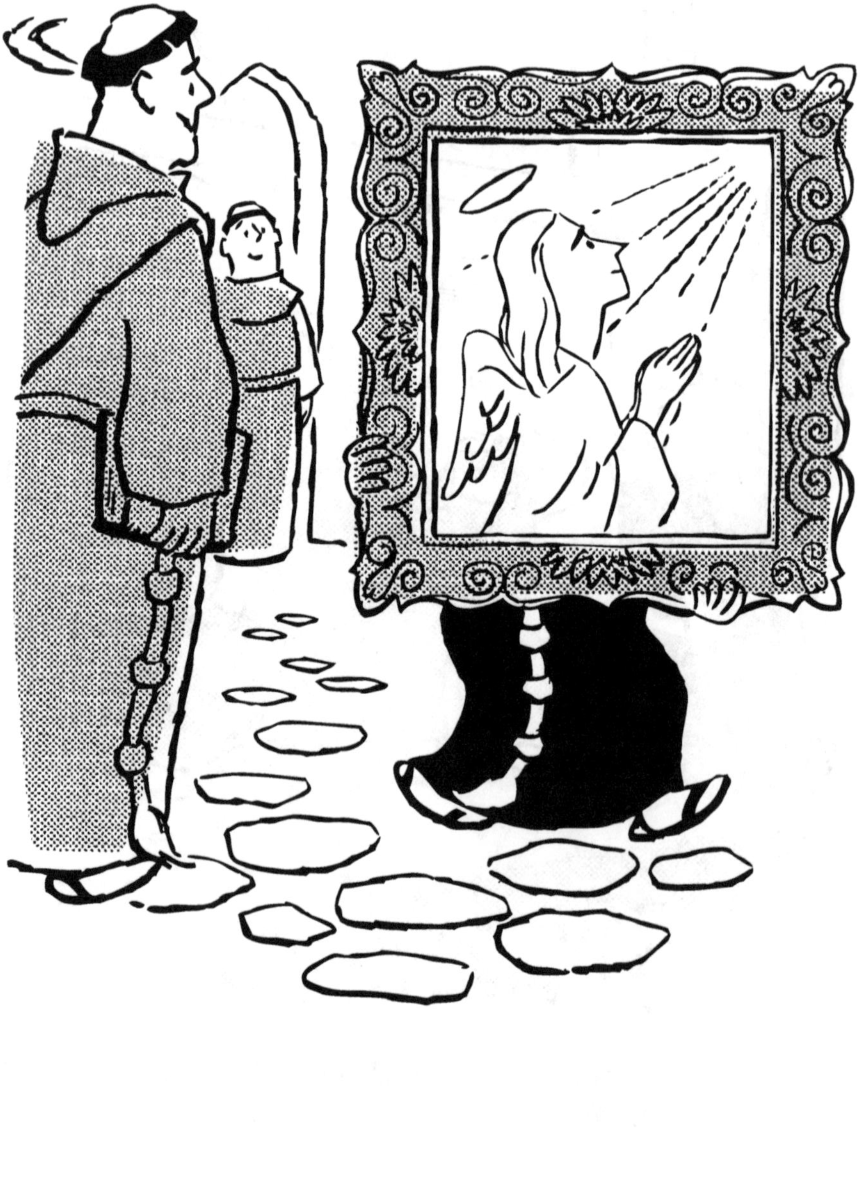

"A punt and a prayer are not enough!"

"I wasn't cut out for this copy-copy-copy stuff; I should be in some executive job."

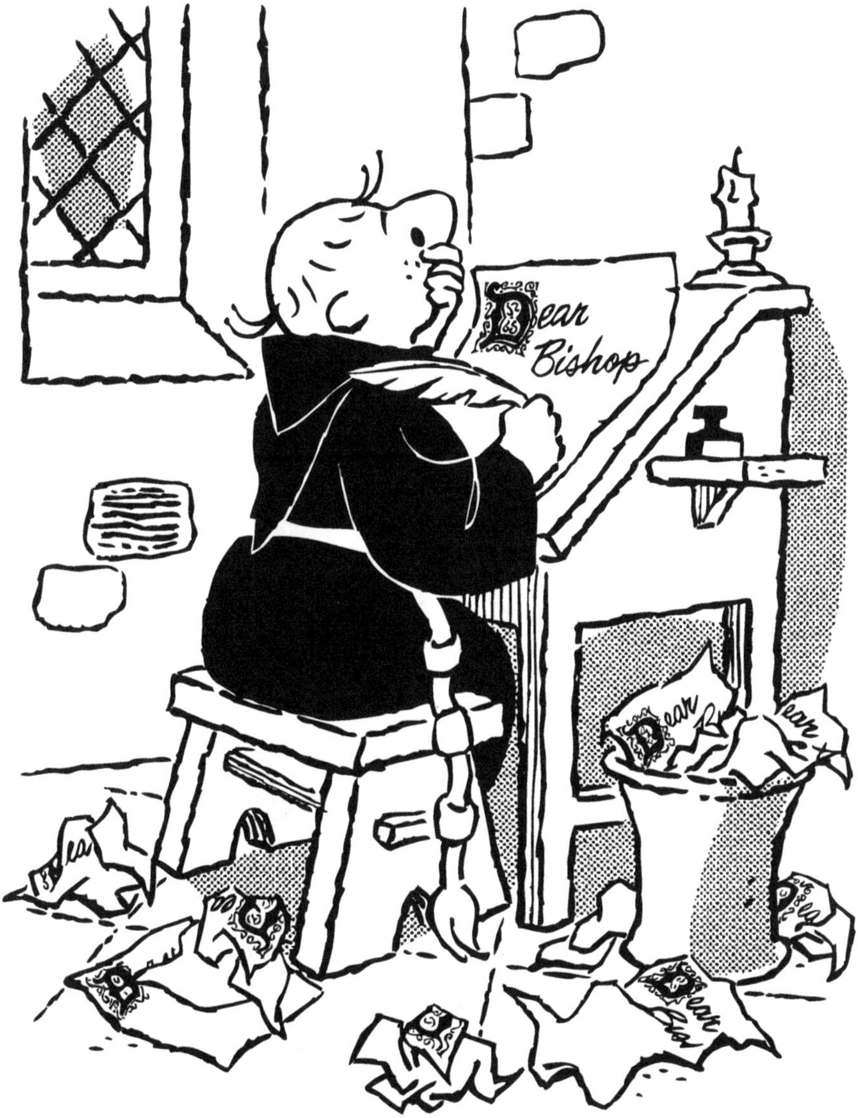
Dear
Bishop

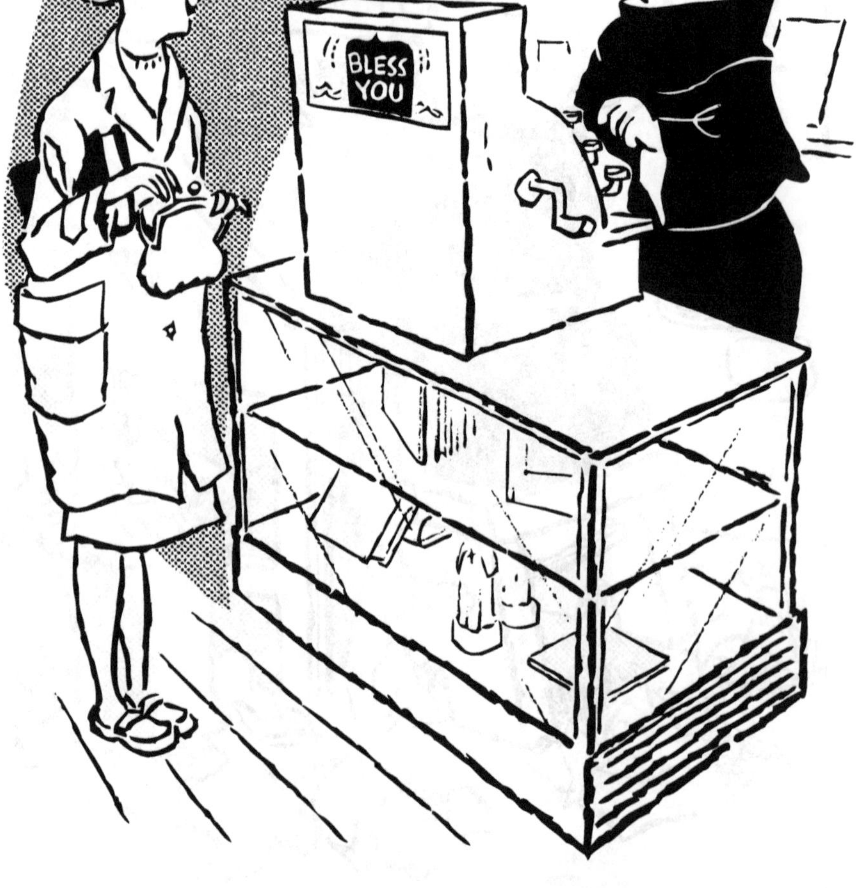
BLESS YOU

"Hello, Apex Laundry? Take it easy on the starch!"

"After all, his days are spent surrounded by lanolin."

"Happy Hanukkah, Mrs. Goldberg!"

"Do something pious with action in it."

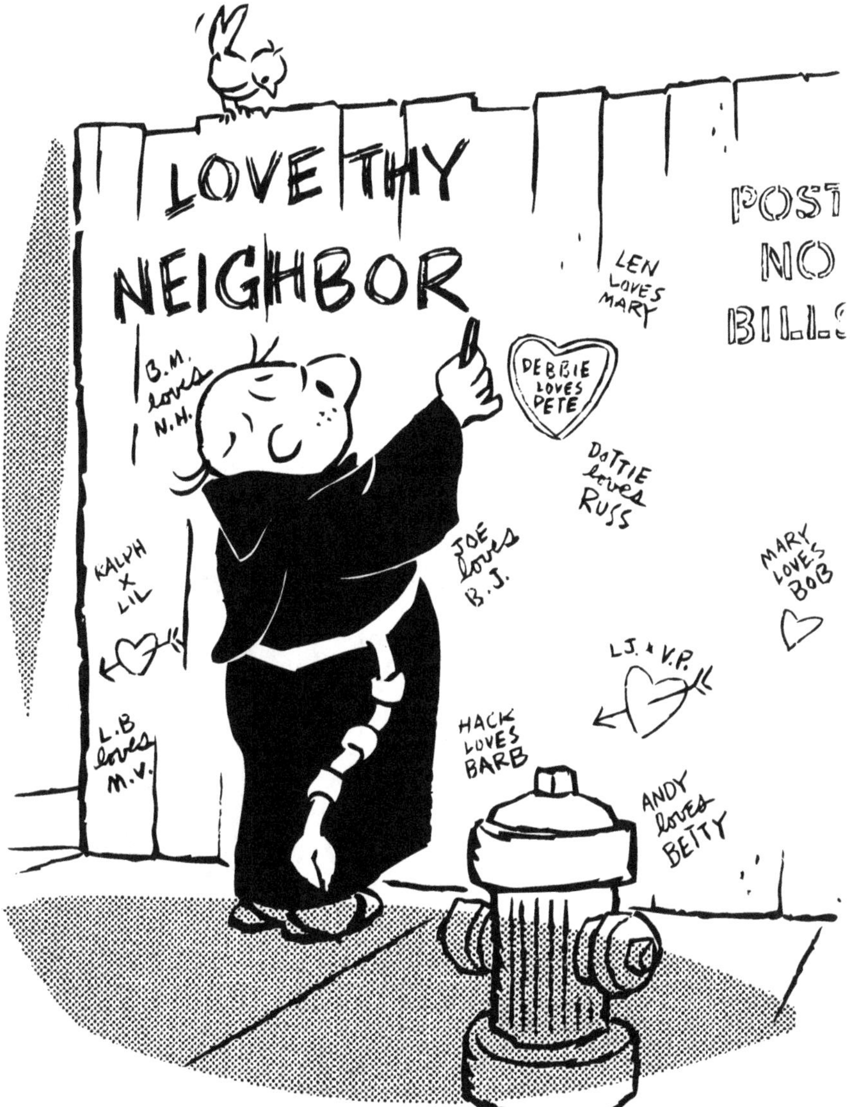
LOVE THY
NEIGHBOR
POST
NO
BILLS
LEN LOVES MARY
B.M. loves N.H.
DEBBIE LOVES PETE
DOTTIE loves RUSS
RALPH X LIL
JOE loves B.J.
MARY LOVES BOB
L.J. + V.P.
L.B loves M.V.
HACK LOVES BARB
ANDY loves BETTY

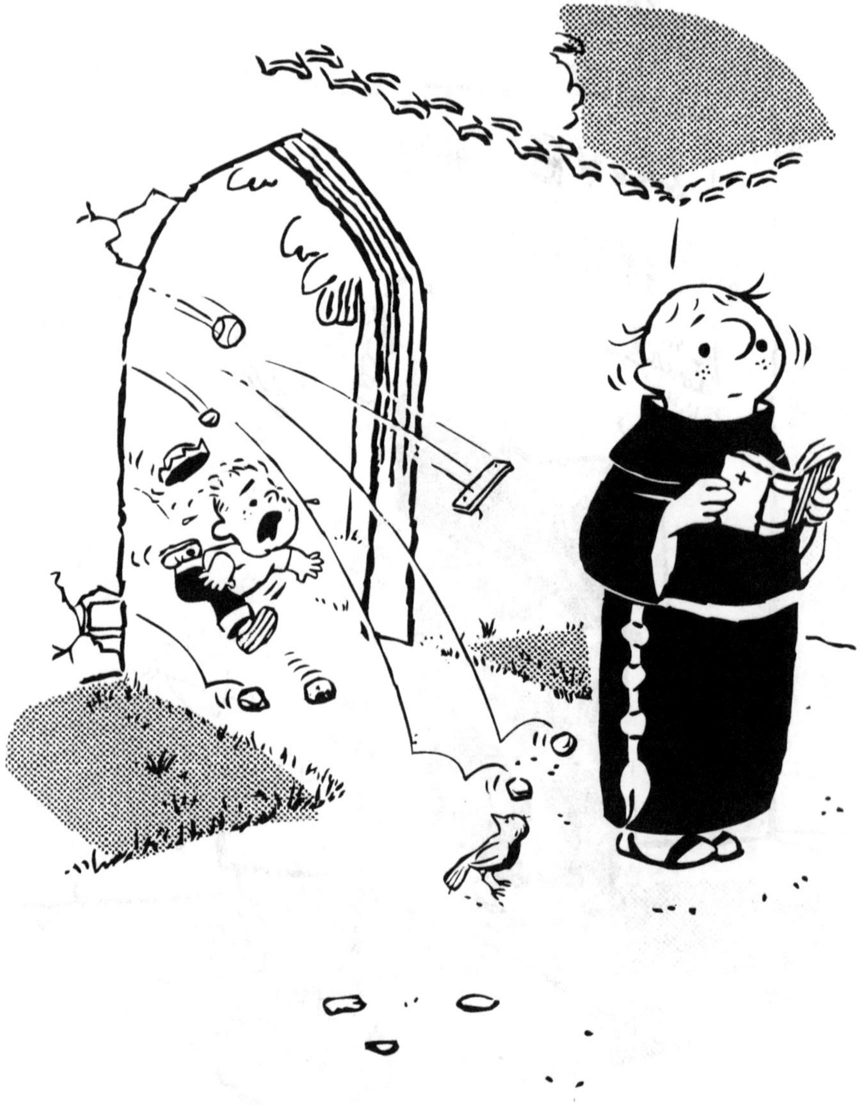

"Sanctuary!"

"Lord, what a day this has been!"

"I have III o'clock, but I may be a particle fast."

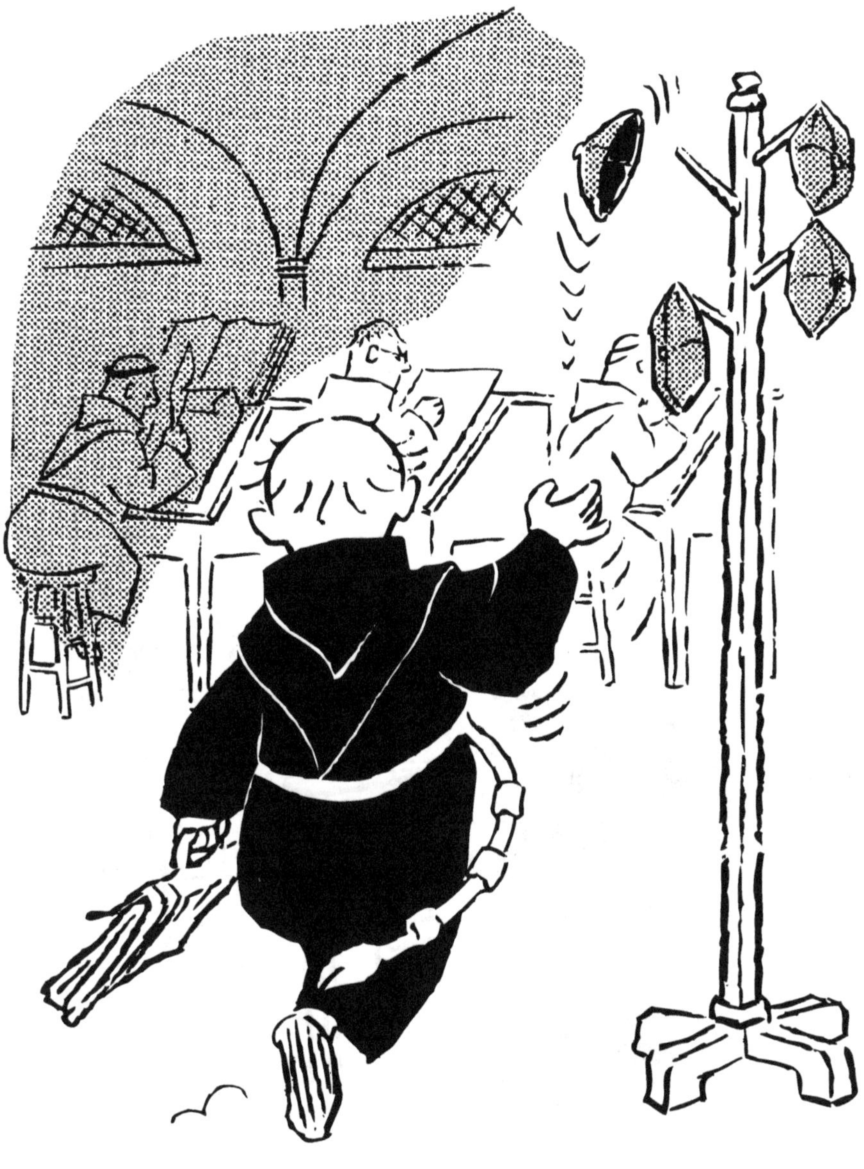

"You want the truth?"

"The switch is on, boys. We're
going in for pocket books."

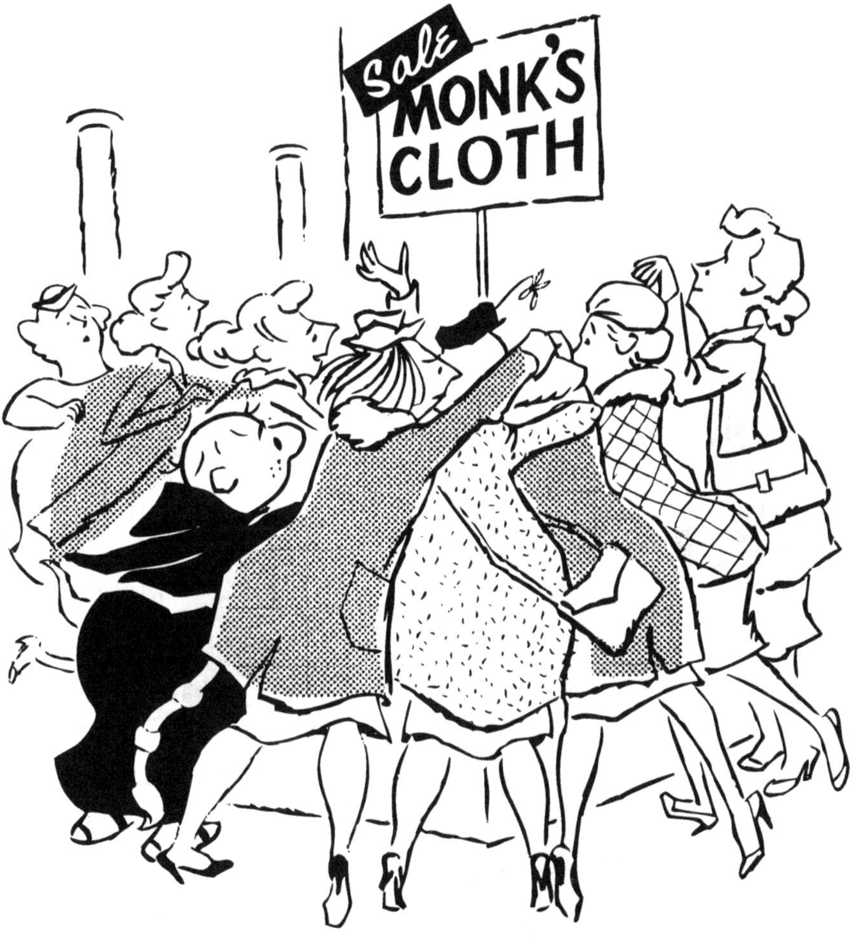
Sale
MONK'S
CLOTH

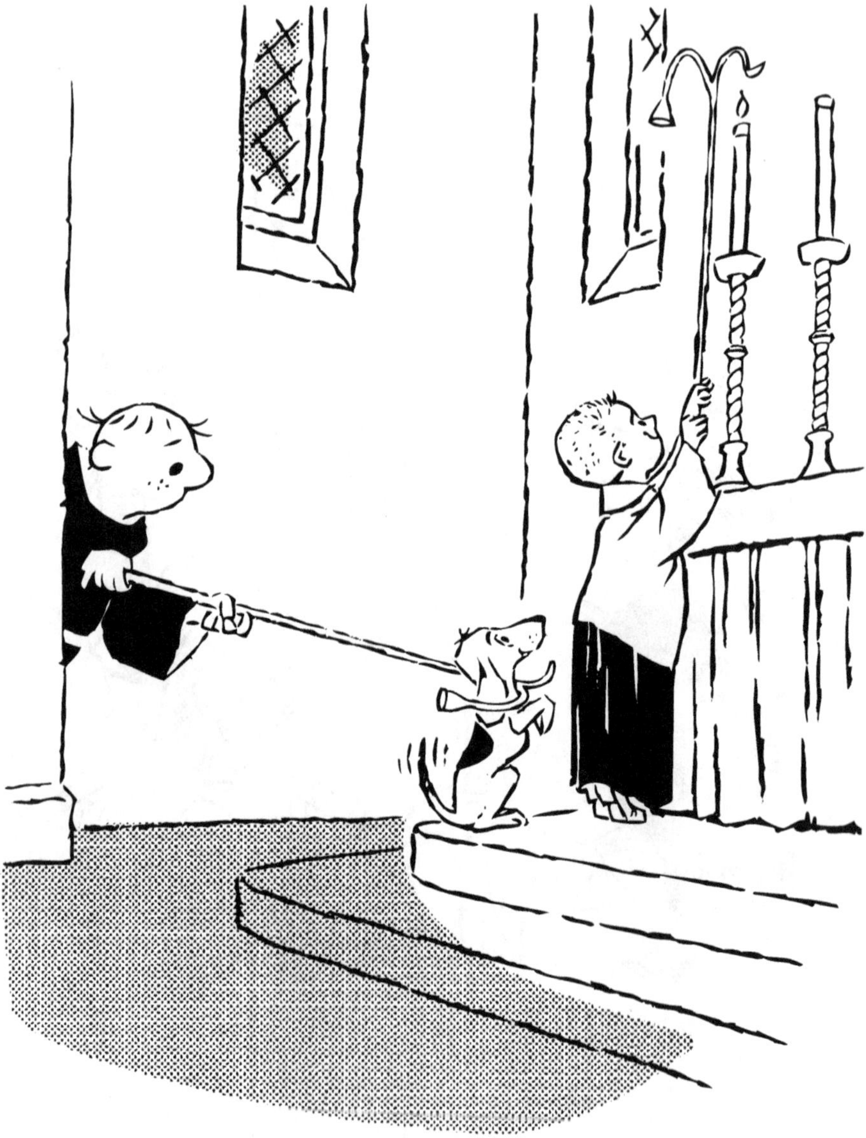

"But you gotta admit it was a terrific ending!"

BROTHER JUNIPER AT WORK AND PLAY

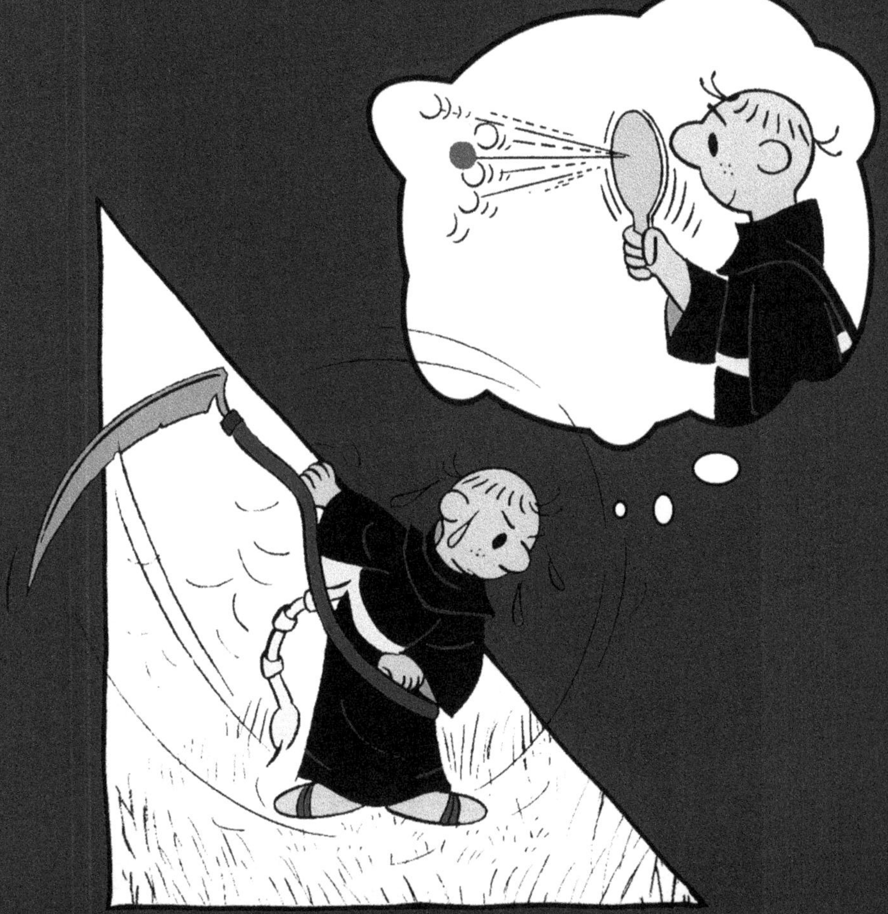

BY FATHER JUSTIN 'FRED' McCARTHY

Empty-Grave Extended Edition

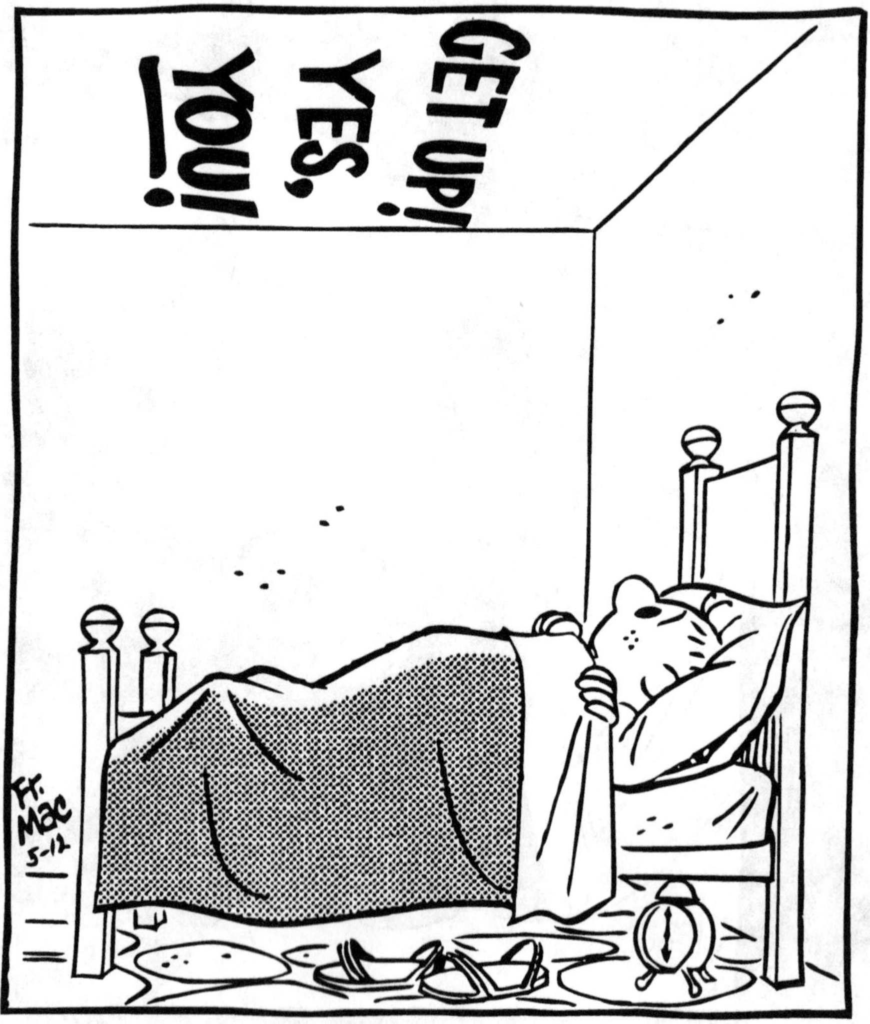
GET UP!
YES,
YOU!
Fr. Mac 5-12

"Hi Jack, Hi Bill, Hi Tom, Hi Charlie!"

"Watch out for Ben Hur on the next lap around!"

"Please DO NOT refer to the collection as 'payola.'"

"...and on a REAL clear day, you can see heaven—
just the outskirts, of course!"

"Would you believe it, I didn't hear the alarm!"

"Do you have a church mouse? Ours died."

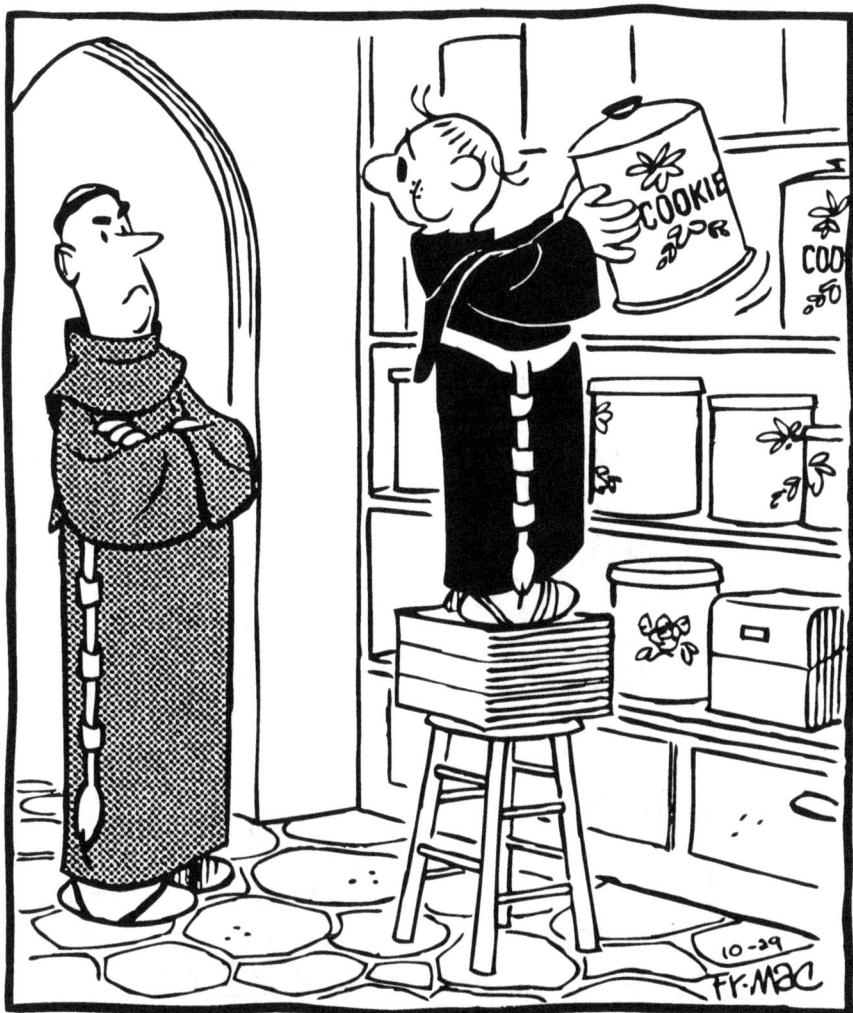

"Well, I guess it takes one to catch one!"

"No, no. Not ding ding; ding DONG!"

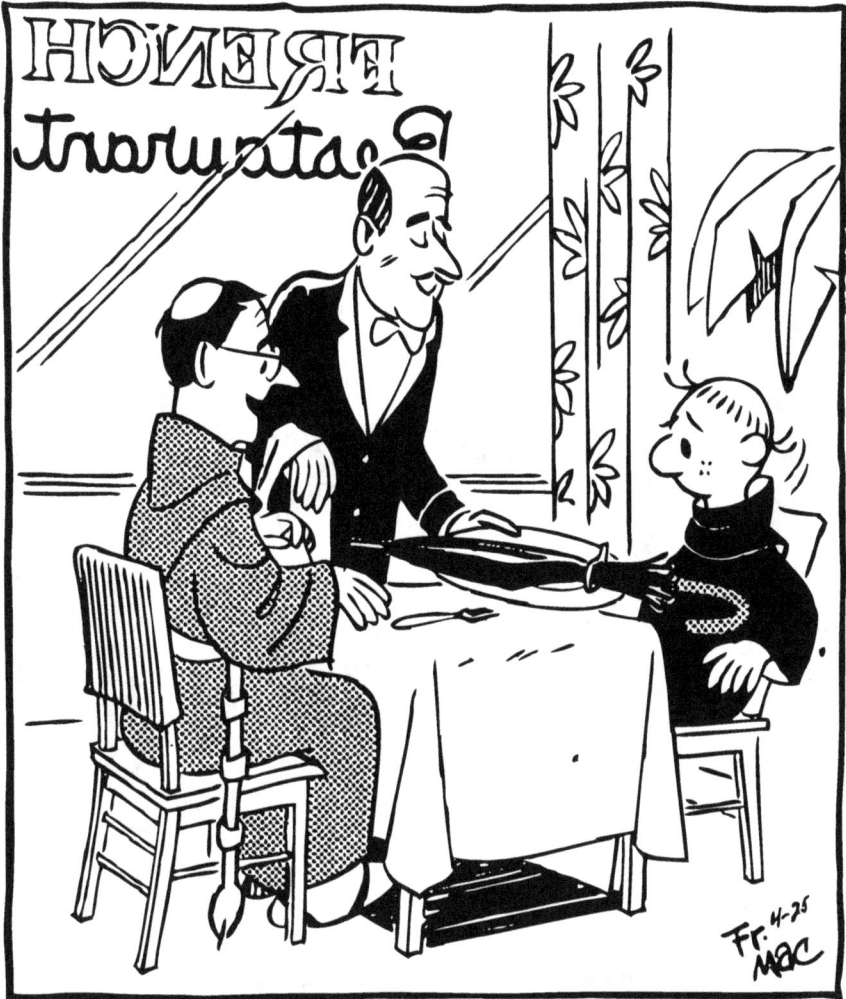

"I thought you knew how to order in French."

"Just put in regular. High
test always makes it nervous."

"Take your time, sir. I can stall as long as you can."

"Tell PANCHO VILLA to come to lunch."

"What do you charge for office visits?"

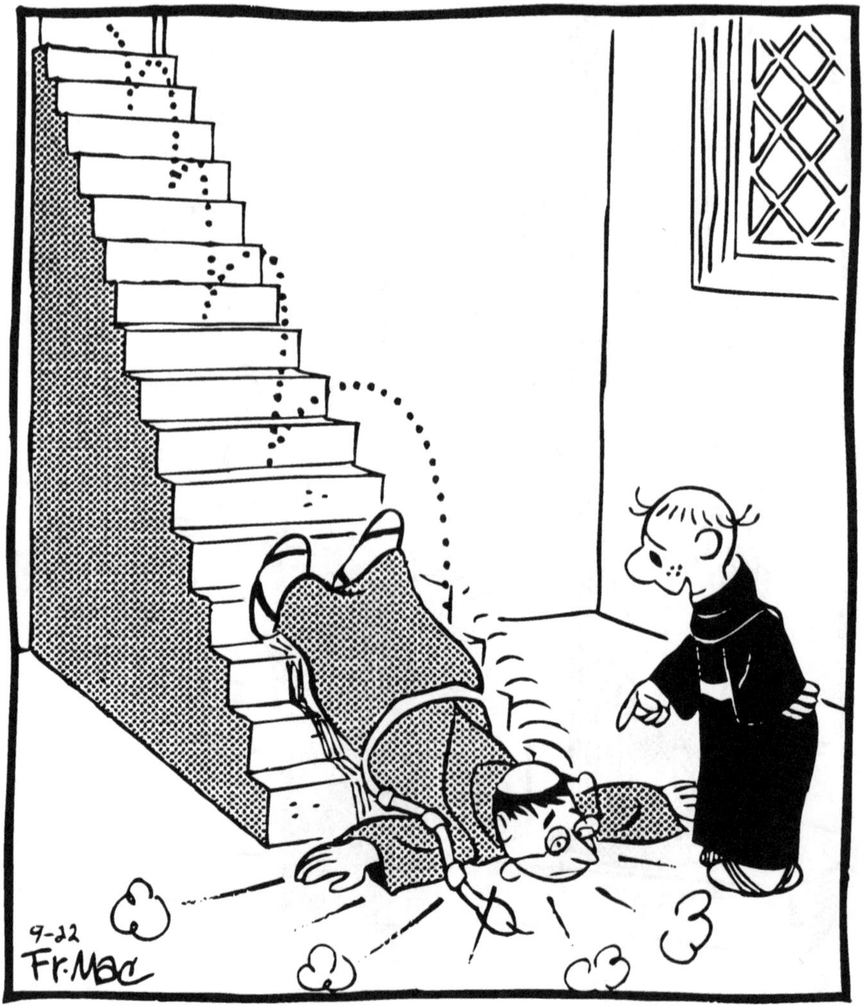
9-22
Fr. Mac

"Bifocals, right?"

"What's so great about hitting the moon?
We hit HEAVEN every day."

"I can see you; can you see me?"

"I can never tell whether he's meditating
or just staring into space."

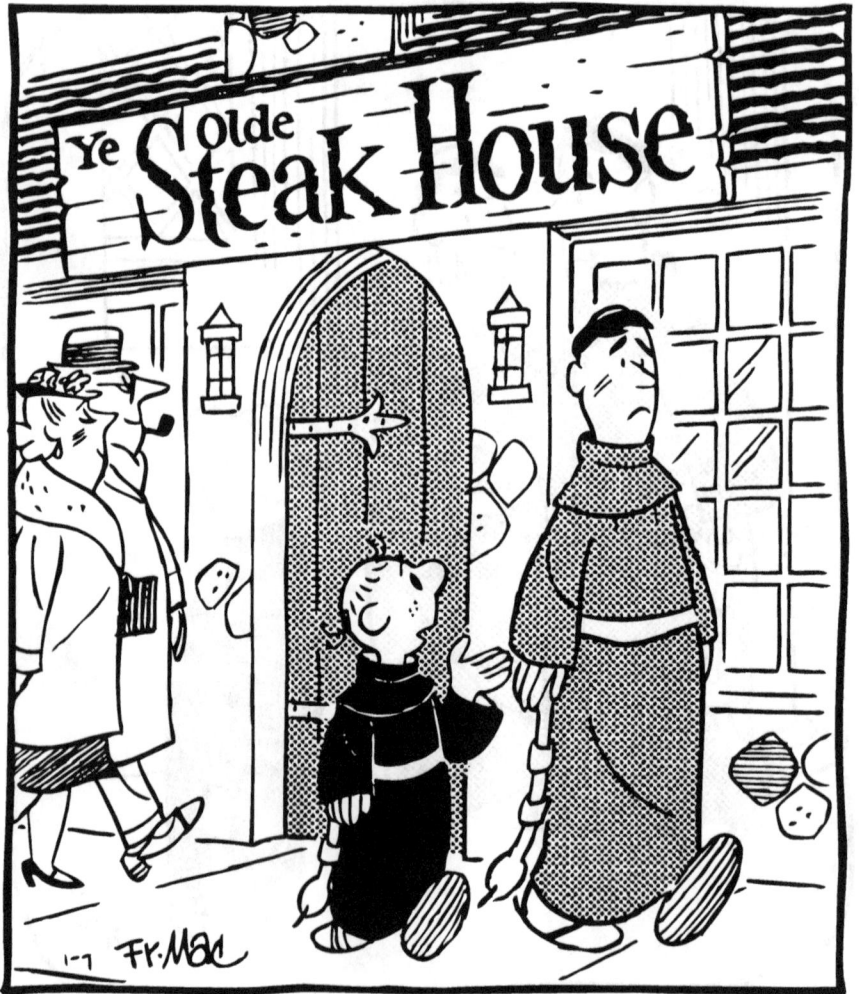

"Not only was ye steak olde, it was also toughe."

"This seems almost TOO good to be true!"

"Great little competitor!"

"In my opinion, his coffee is the greatest threat to the church in OUR generation."

"For fifty years of service, we
present this timepiece..."

"Well, SOMEBODY hasn't been living right."

"I've discovered the trouble.
You're riding the clutch!"

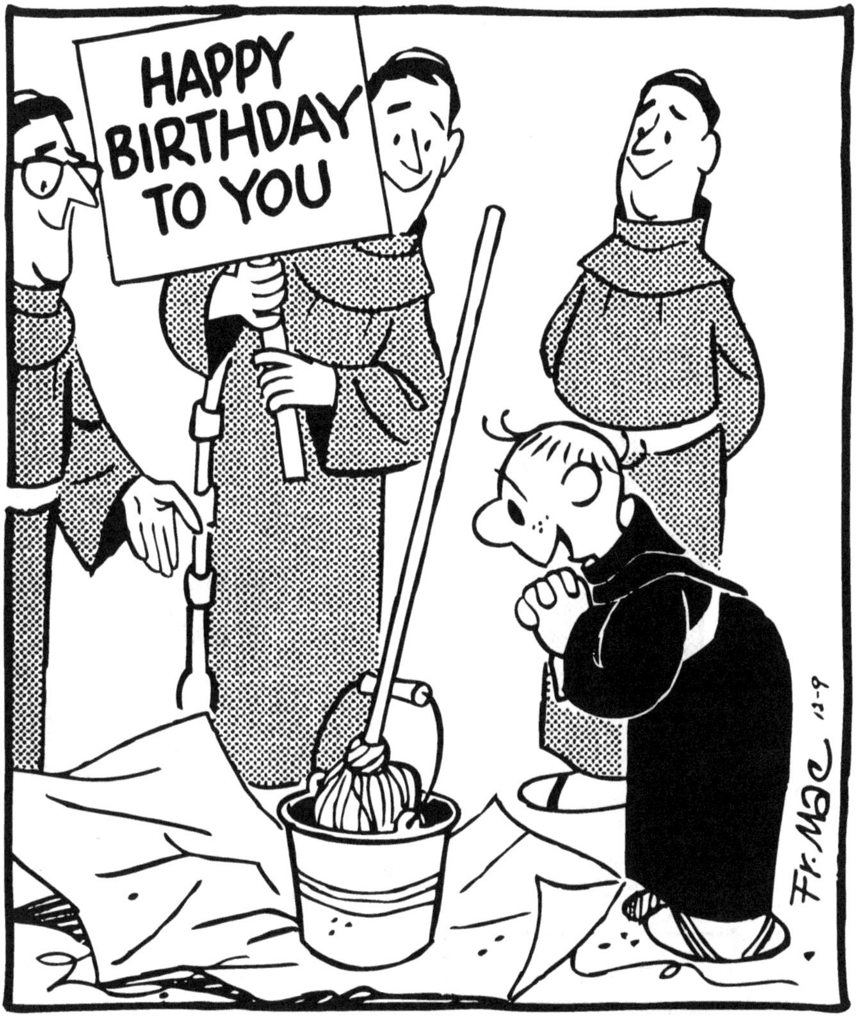
HAPPY
BIRTHDAY
TO YOU
Fr. Mac

"Oh, you SHOULDN'T have!"

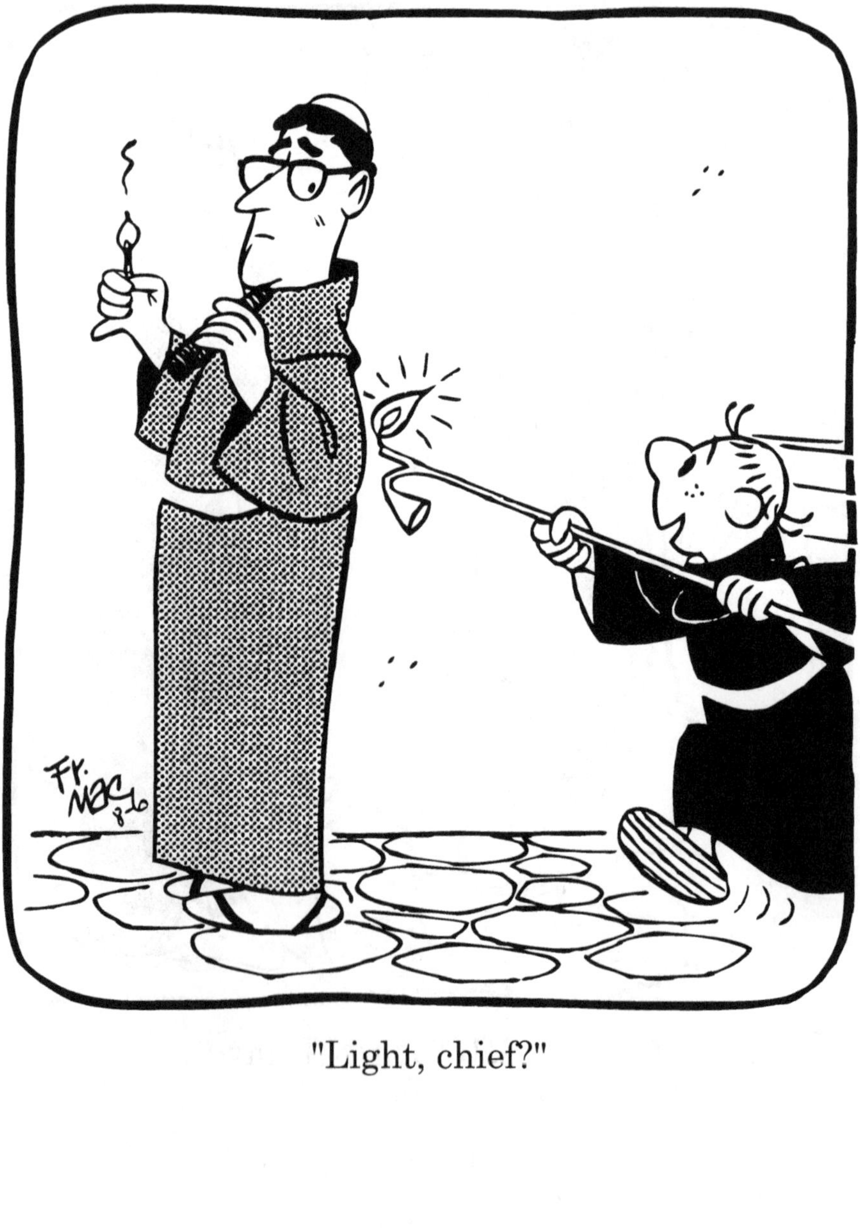
Fr. Mac 8-16

"Light, chief?"

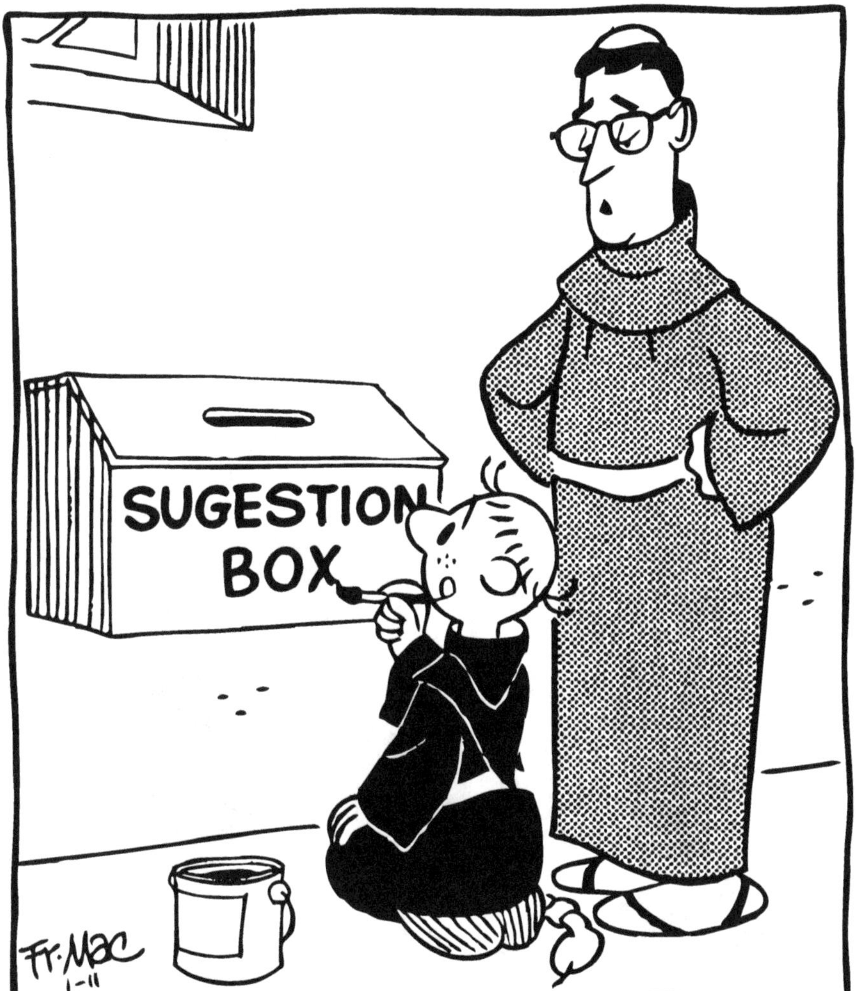
SUGESTION
BOX
Fr. Mac
1-11

"Mind a suggestion?"

"Yours must have TIRED AIR, Brother Juniper."

"Your soup's pretty good, but
it suffers in translation."

"My arthritis can outpredict him
any day in the week."

"I'm glad I don't like mushrooms, because if I liked
'em, I'd eat 'em, and I HATE 'EM!"

"...and this time, try not to get carried away!"

"I don't know who he is. He says
he's on an unscheduled flight."

"That's the trouble with these superhighways: you miss your turn-off, and you've had it!"

"It's their answer to the small-car trend."

"That was March coming in like a you-know-what!"

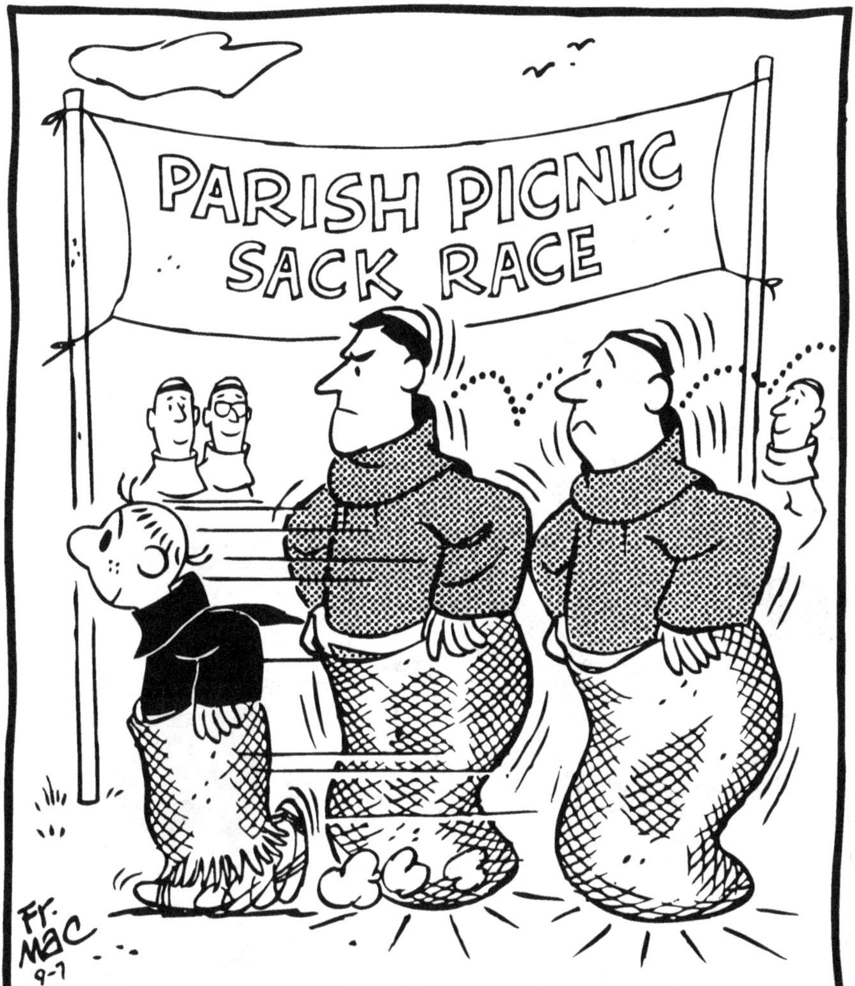
PARISH PICNIC
SACK RACE
Fr. Mac
9-7

"One reason you've improved so much is because
you were pretty terrible to start with."

"I took a carefree 37 on that hole."

"I will now attempt to render
'The Angry Janitor Blues.'"

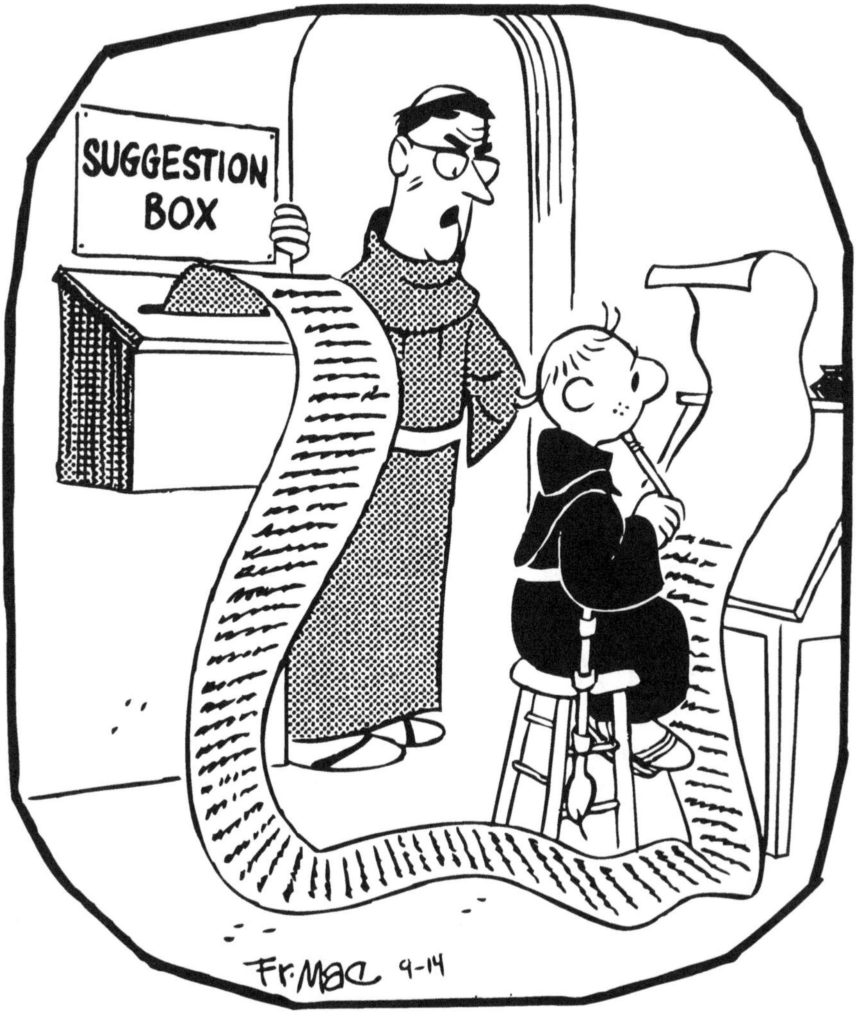
SUGGESTION BOX
Fr. Mac 9-14

"Aren't you happy here?"

"It gives me 30 miles to a gallon,
if I could only get it to start."

"Will I tell him or will you tell him?"

"Head down...keep that arm straight...
now follow through. THAT'S IT.
You have a beautiful natural swing."

"Why don't we ever have any old-fashioned
winters—like they have in Bermuda?"

"Gotta protect my Achilles heel."

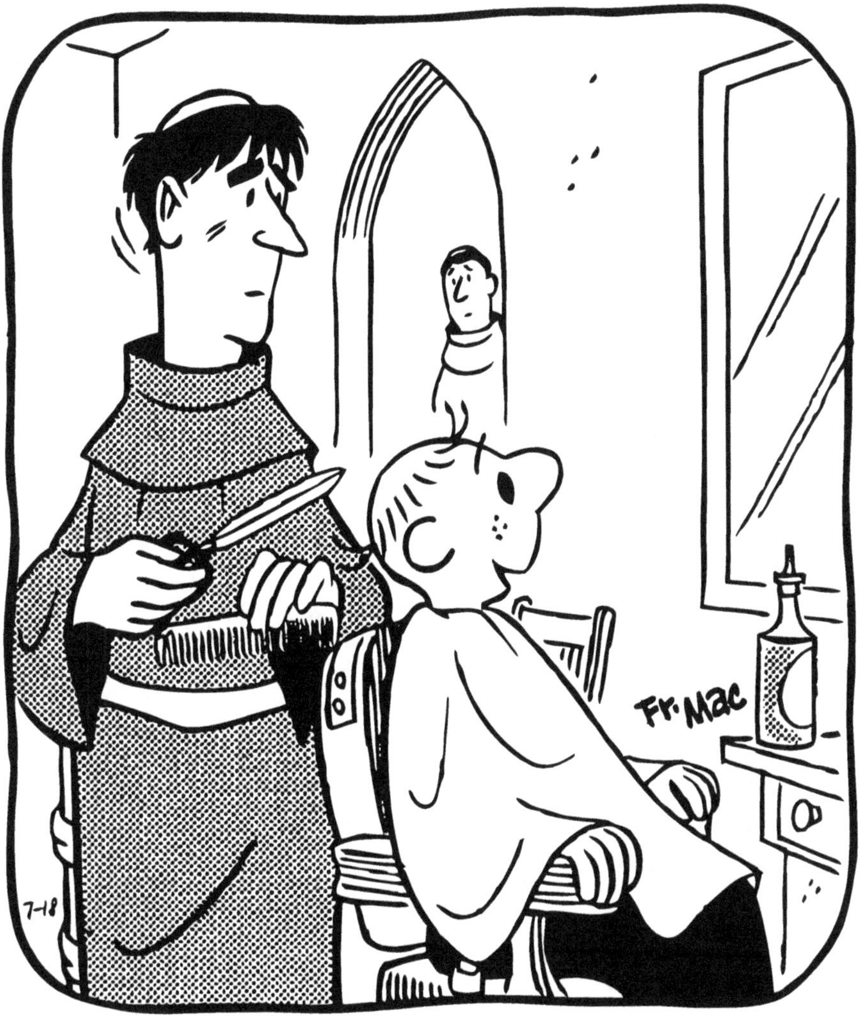
7-18
Fr. Mac

"Give me one like yours."

"You'd better see an eye doctor. That's the fifth
gasoline pump you've said hello to today!"

"...Oh, we have our good days and our bad days."

"Where were you people last winter—
when I NEEDED you?"

"You have a choice today.
You can take it, or leave it."

"All I said was, what are you selling...
and the next thing I know—!"

"I just crave ATMOSPHERE!"

"Of COURSE, I washed the organ with soap.
Doesn't everyone?"

"...but you should hear how
good I sing in the SHOWER!"

"Somebody up there must love me."

"Forgetting the failures in math and spelling,
you did very well - if you don't count your marks
in science, civics, and history."

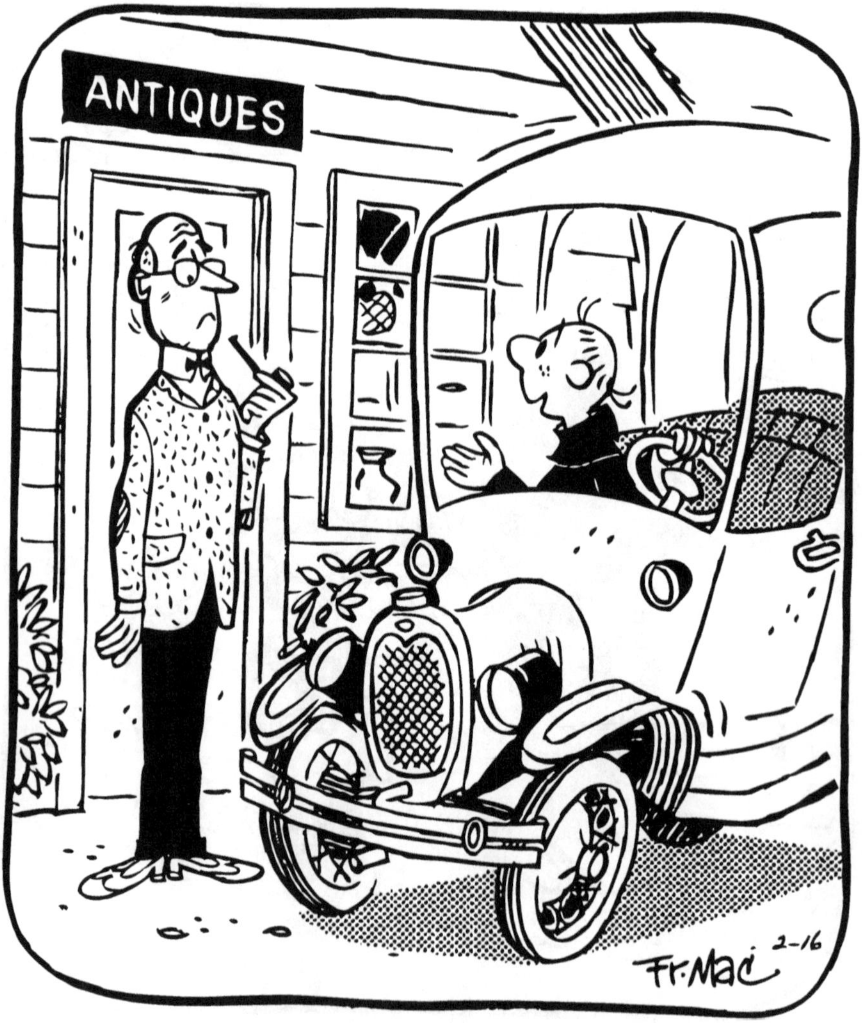
ANTIQUES
Fr. Mac 2-16

"Make me an offer!"

"Thought I'd just tidy up a bit before they get here."

"I didn't see any money change hands, but those Indians MUST have been paid to take a dive."

"Hit it again, lad; you have the wind with you."

"You know, I'm convinced
half my patients are quacks."

"I can't bear to part with the ol' crate.
I'm thinking of having it STUFFED!"

"My ambitions are to play the harp and get to heaven - but not necessarily in that order!"

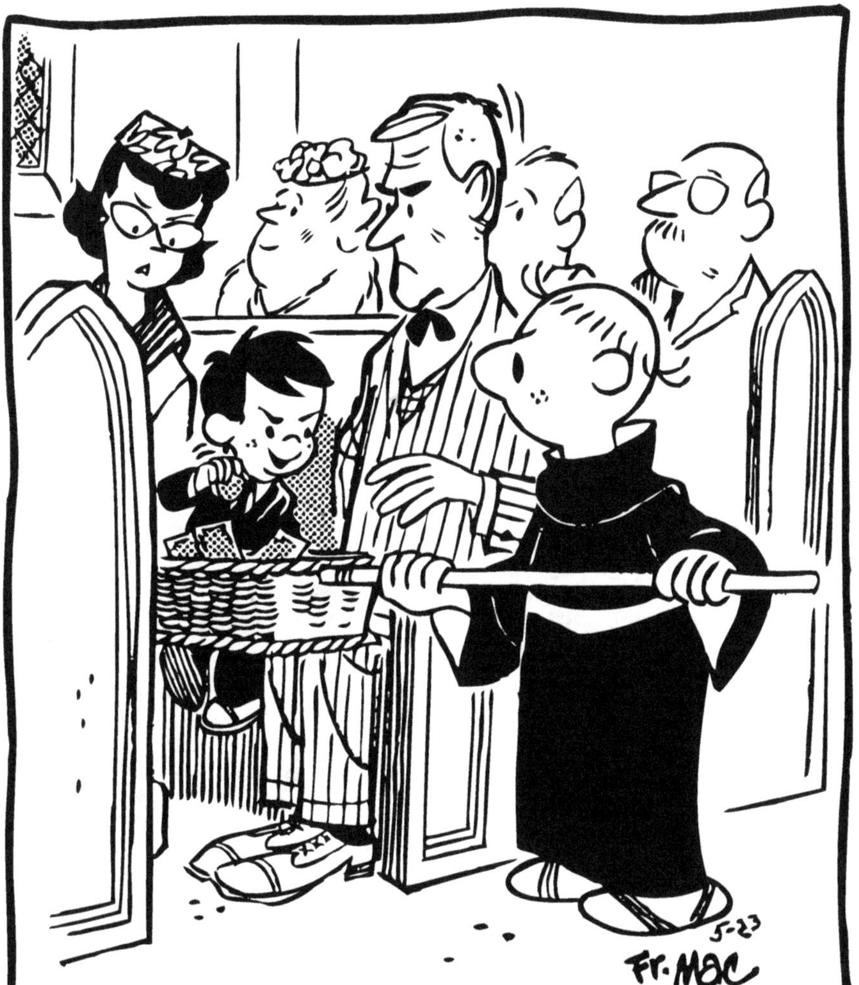
5-23
Fr. MAC

"Say 'PLEASE!'"

"Some big Republican, I guess."

"It says: '125 pounds; no fortune!'"

"Are you a right-handed cow or a left-handed cow?"

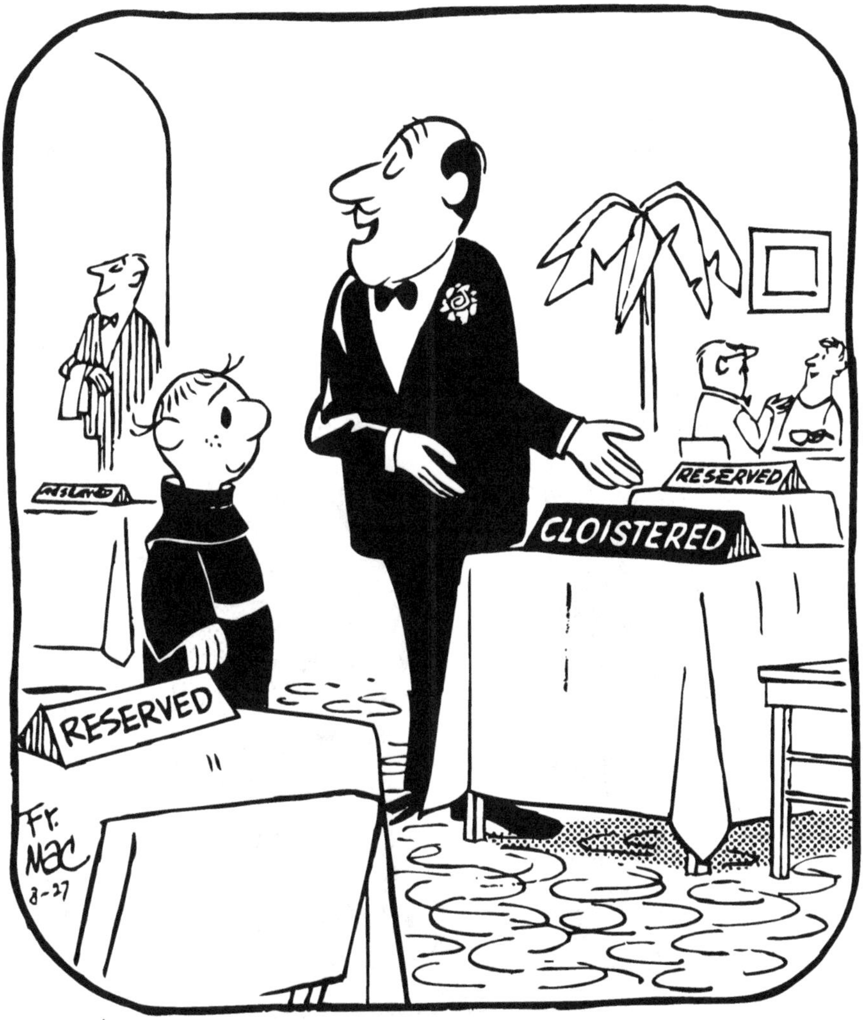
CLOISTERED
RESERVED
RESERVED
Fr. MAC
8-27

"YOUR table, sir!"

"As you can see, Grandfather was rather short."

"Hey, you fellers were right. Those things were TOADSTOOLS, not mushrooms!"

"When she misses, she misses by a mile!"

"Doc, you wouldn't repeat anything I might say in a moment of stress...would you, Doc?"

"WHO said we couldn't lose 'em all?"

"Will the owner of car number X275311..."

"What I really need is one with a
WRAP-AROUND BUMPER!"

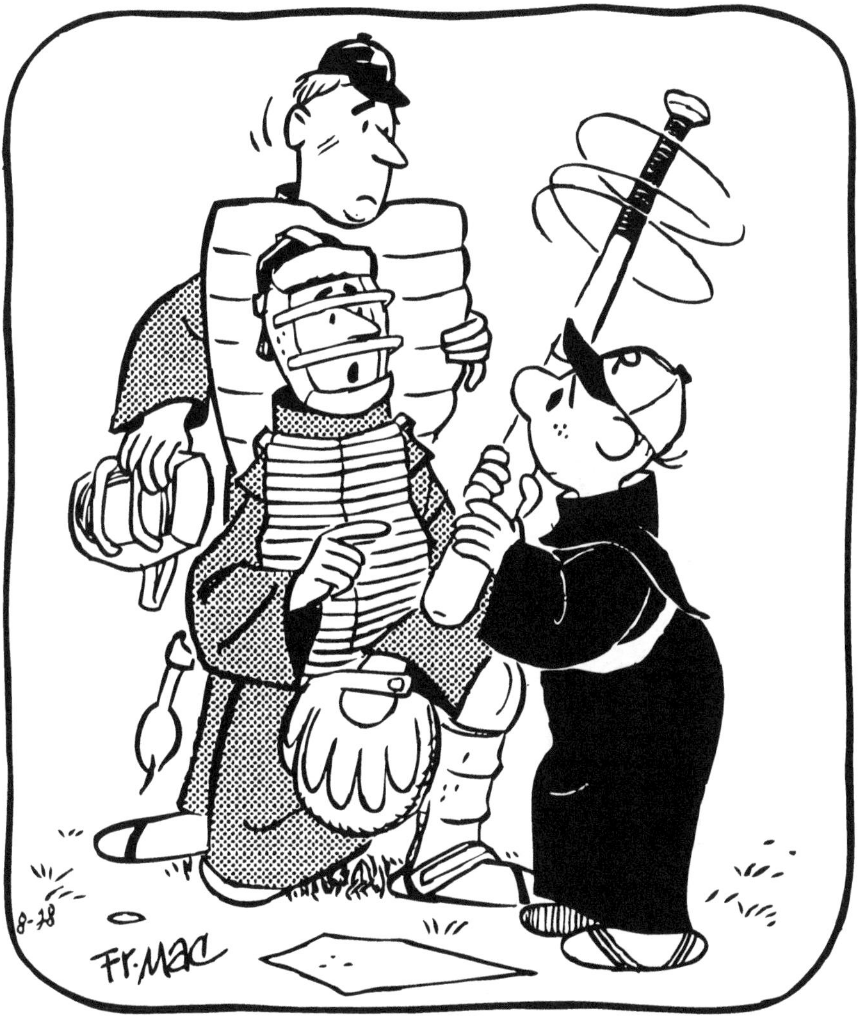
8-28
Fr·Mac

"Mind a suggestion?"

"Just a little background music - it was my idea!"

"But you cannot order zat, m'sieu.
ZAT is the assistant chef!"

"Don't worry, miss, I'm SURE
the groom will show up."

"What a tough break. His PRAYING knee, too."

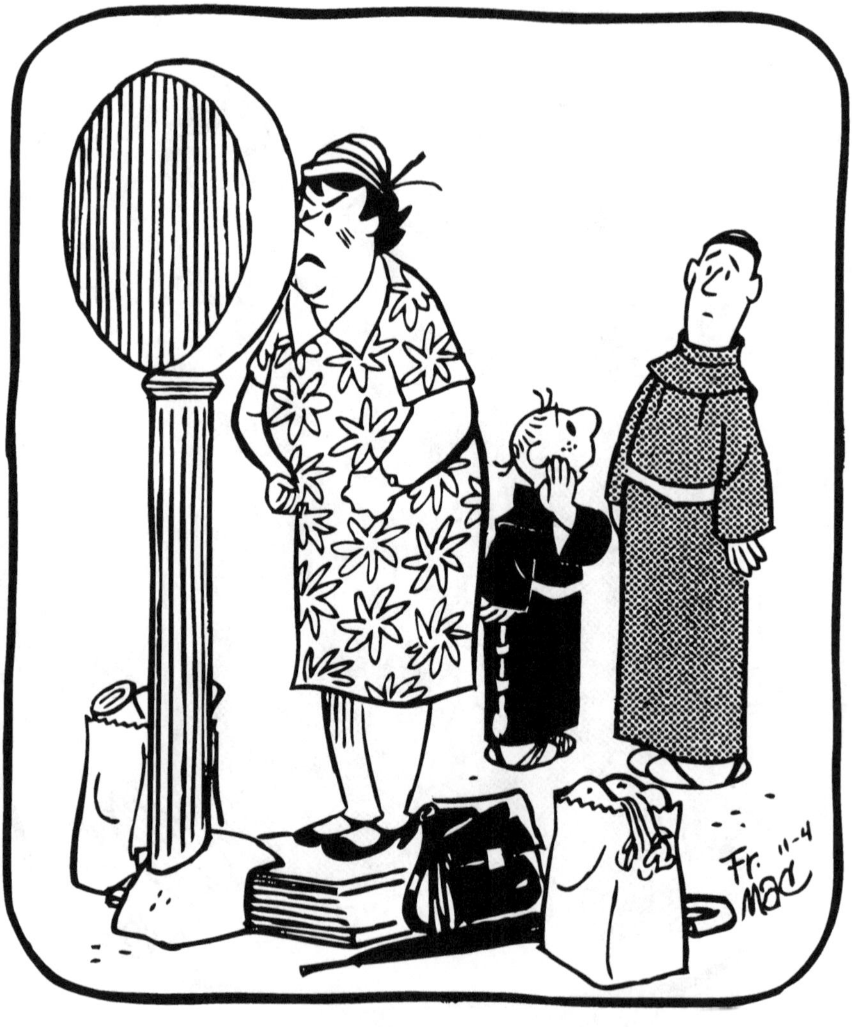
Fr. Mac 11-4

"Boy, is she a poor loser!"

"Just try to put yourself in my place."

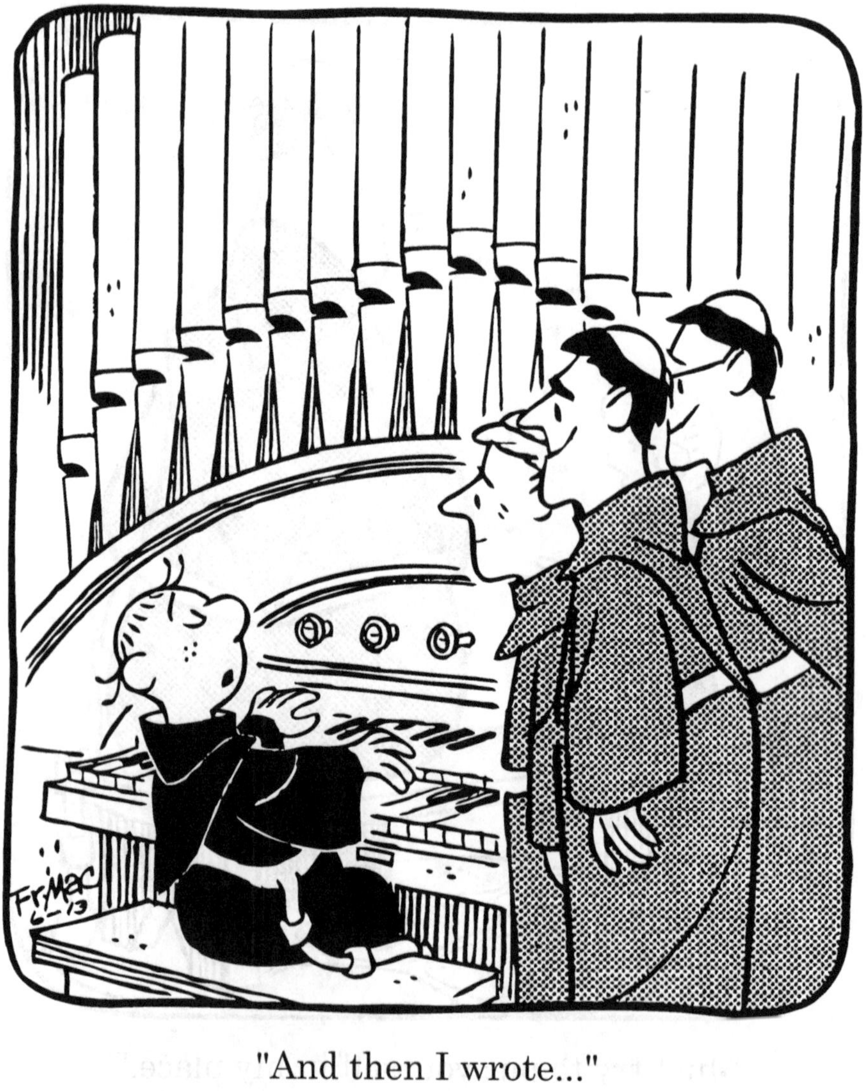
Fr.Mac
6—13

"And then I wrote..."

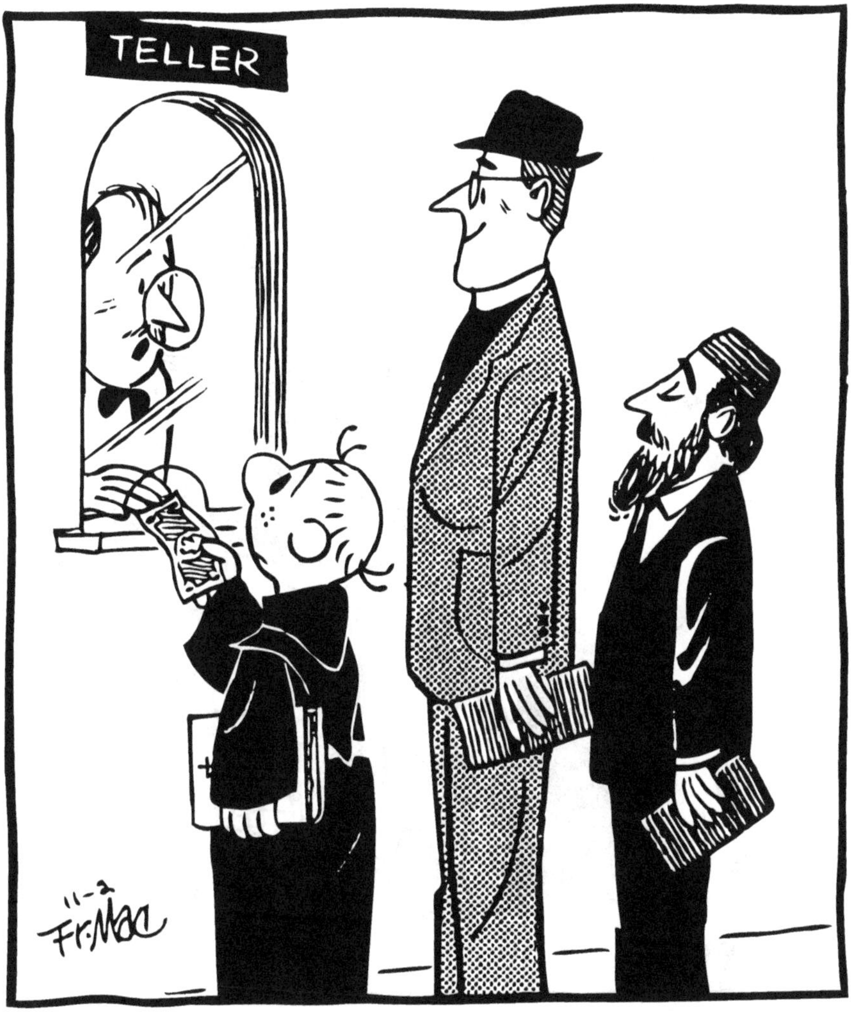
TELLER
11-2
Fr. Mac
"What denomination?"

"You're in trouble. It's the supermarket manager!"

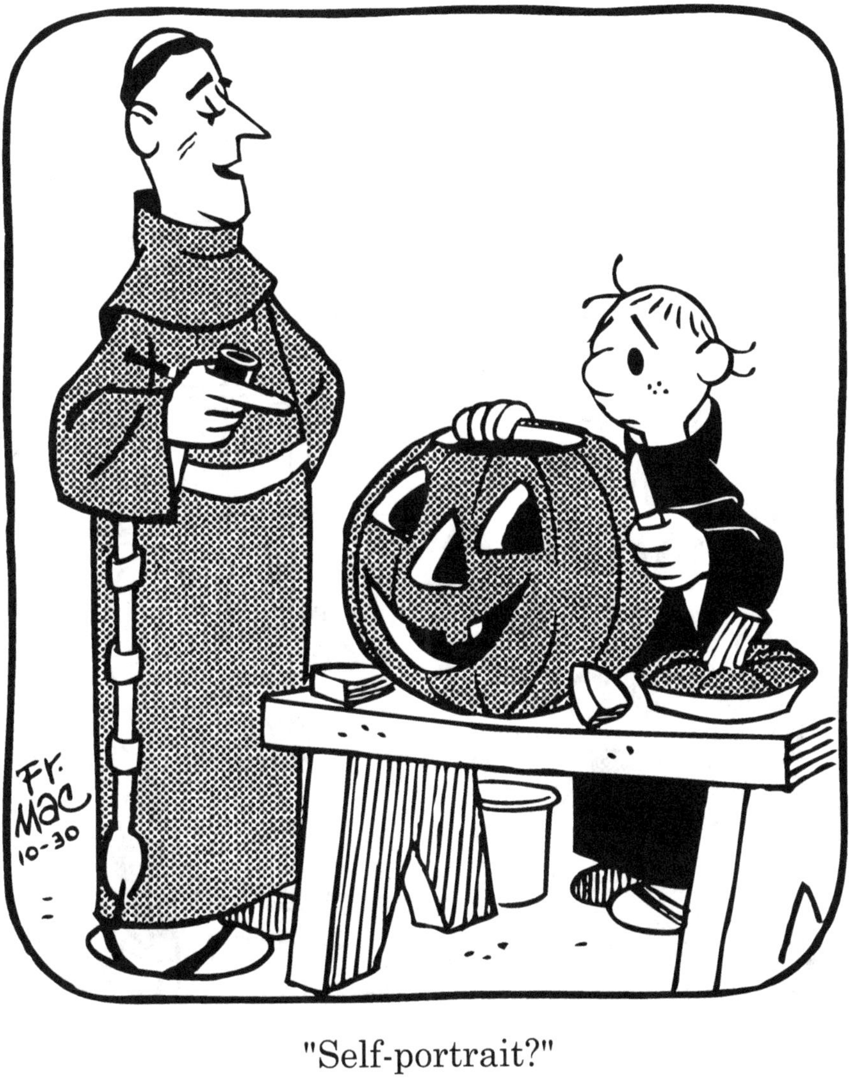
Fr.
Mac
10-30

"Self-portrait?"

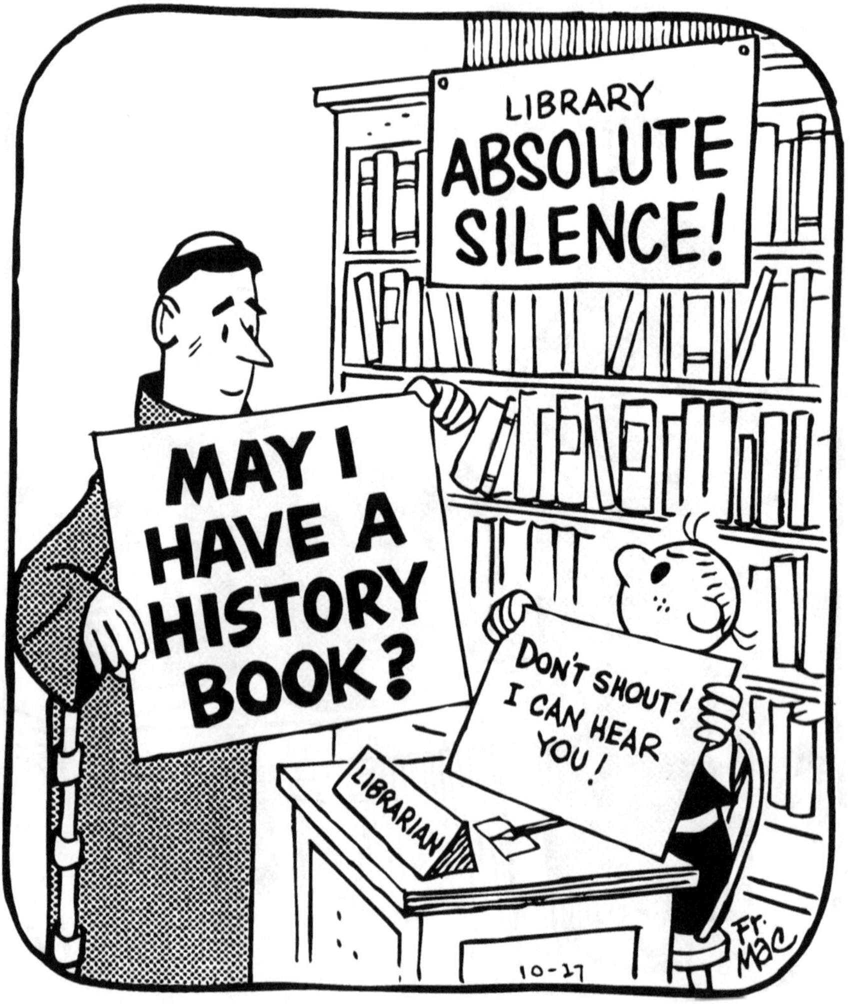
LIBRARY
ABSOLUTE SILENCE!
MAY I HAVE A HISTORY BOOK?
DON'T SHOUT! I CAN HEAR YOU!
LIBRARIAN
10-27
Fr. Mac

"The name is Gladstone, NOT Rhinestone!"

"No need to worry. We'll soon
have him 100 proof again."

"Is the commercial your idea?"

"You really HAVE arrived!
Wall-to-wall flagstones!"

"You're in luck. There's one left."

"Are you SURE you have the right address?"

"I wouldn't mind so much,
but they happen to be MY cigars!"

"Well, it was only a suggestion."

"Congratulations, Spike. This makes nineteen straight years you've had PERFECT attendance."

"They revoked his license."

"I'm practicing patience...what are you practicing?"

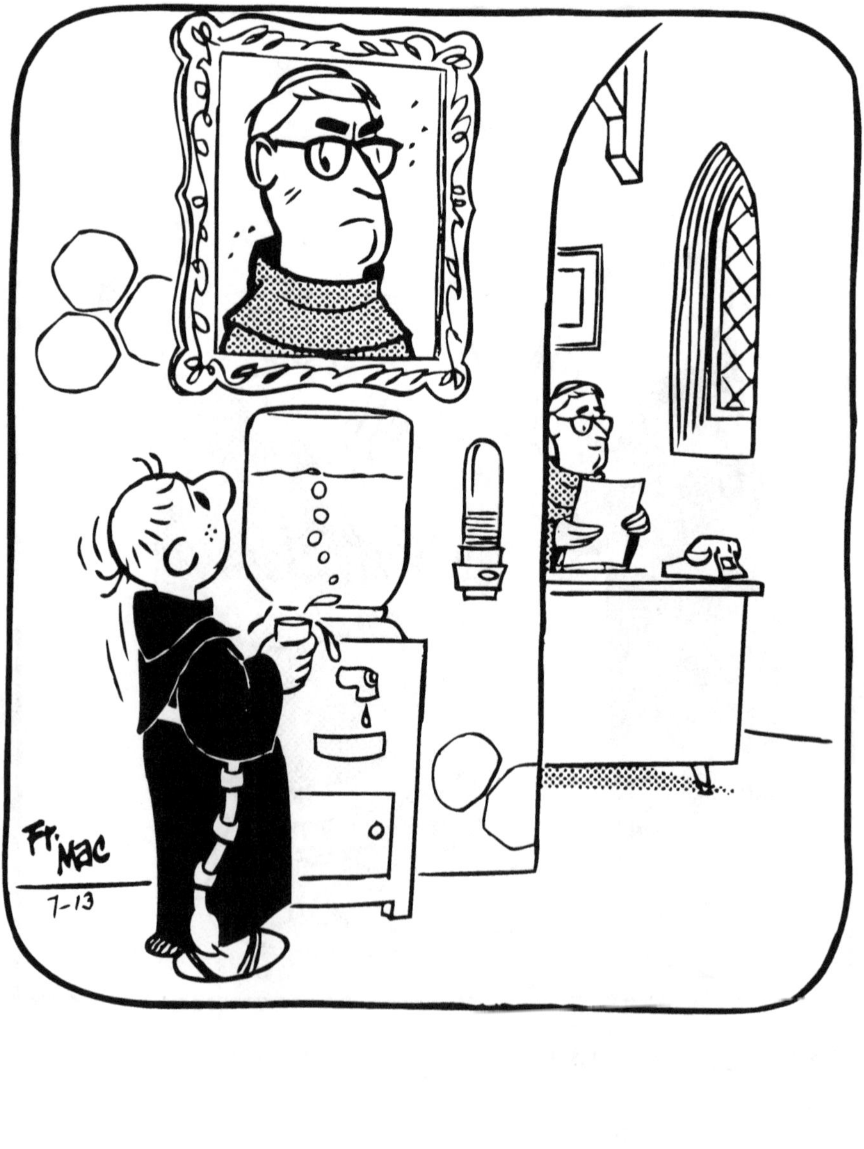
Fr. Mac
7-13

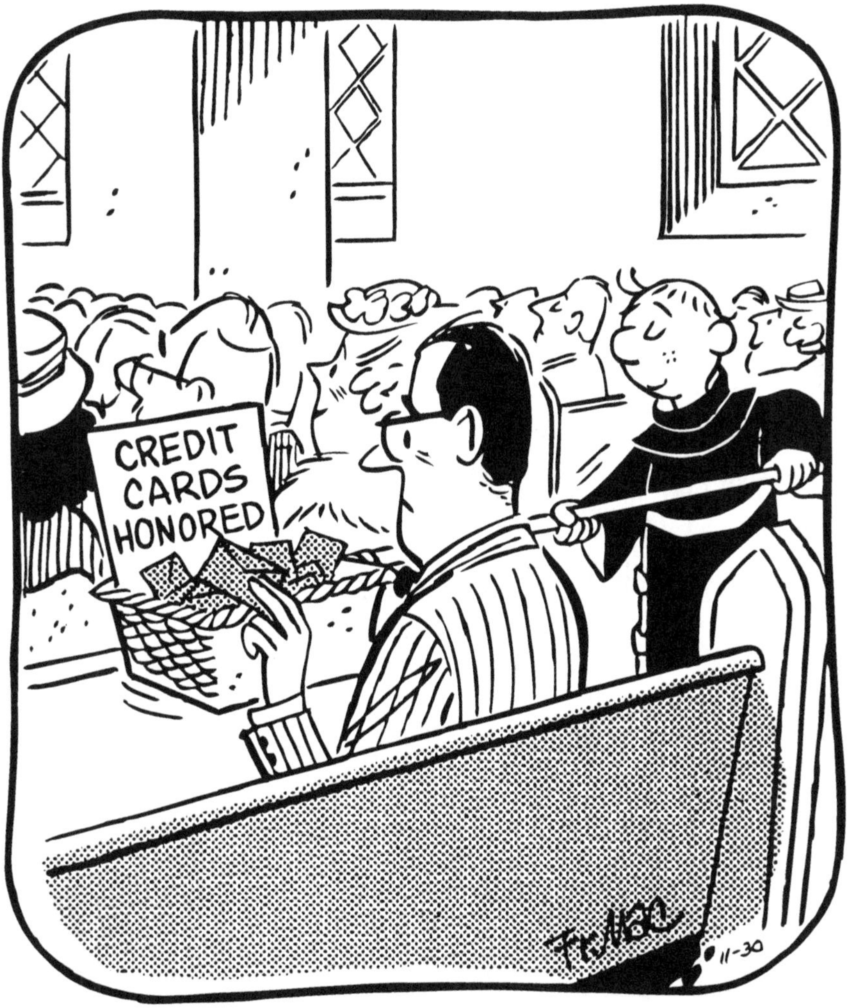
CREDIT
CARDS
HONORED

"Please limit your call to three minutes."

"This is the job I dread...putting up SCREENS!"

"You say you've bowled before?"

"Care to step outside and pray in them?"

"Read your own breakfast cereal!"

"Don't come crying to me when your
sinuses are kicking up tomorrow!"

"Every time I wash mine, it rains."

"On you, living color looks good!"

"I got so nervous, I voted for EVERYBODY!"

"Boy, look at that: wall-to-wall music!"

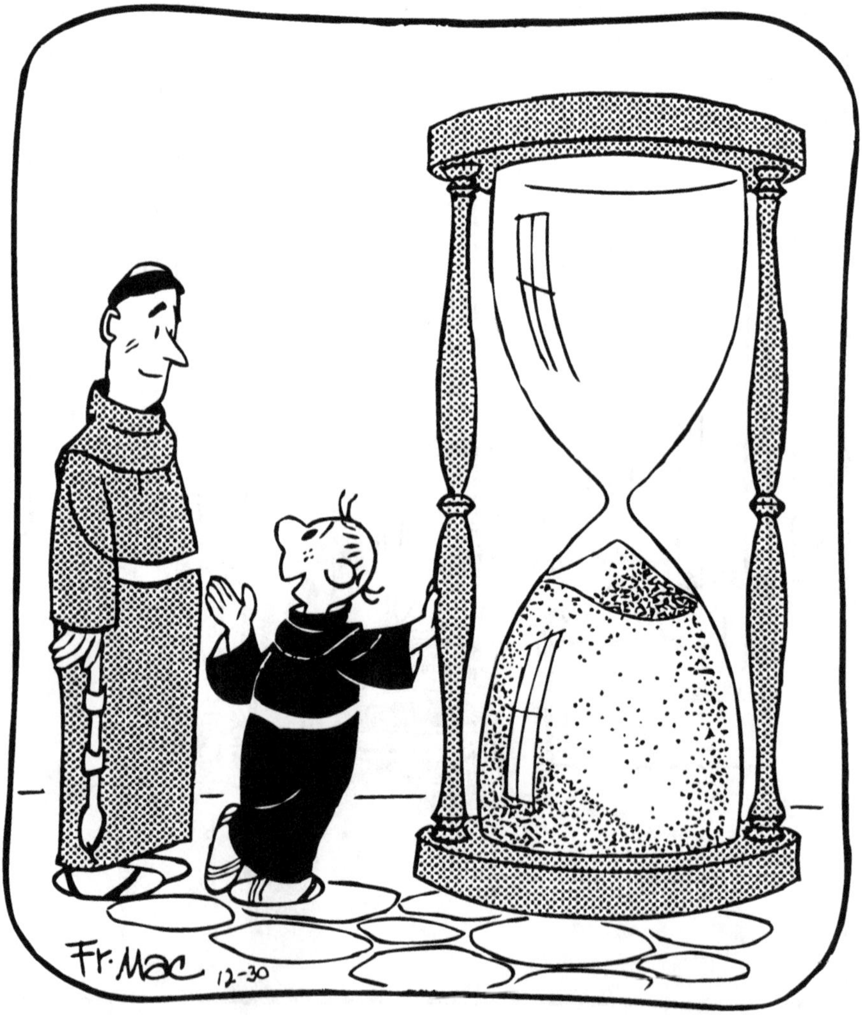
Fr. Mac
12-30

"Where DID the year go?"

FR. MAC
10-17

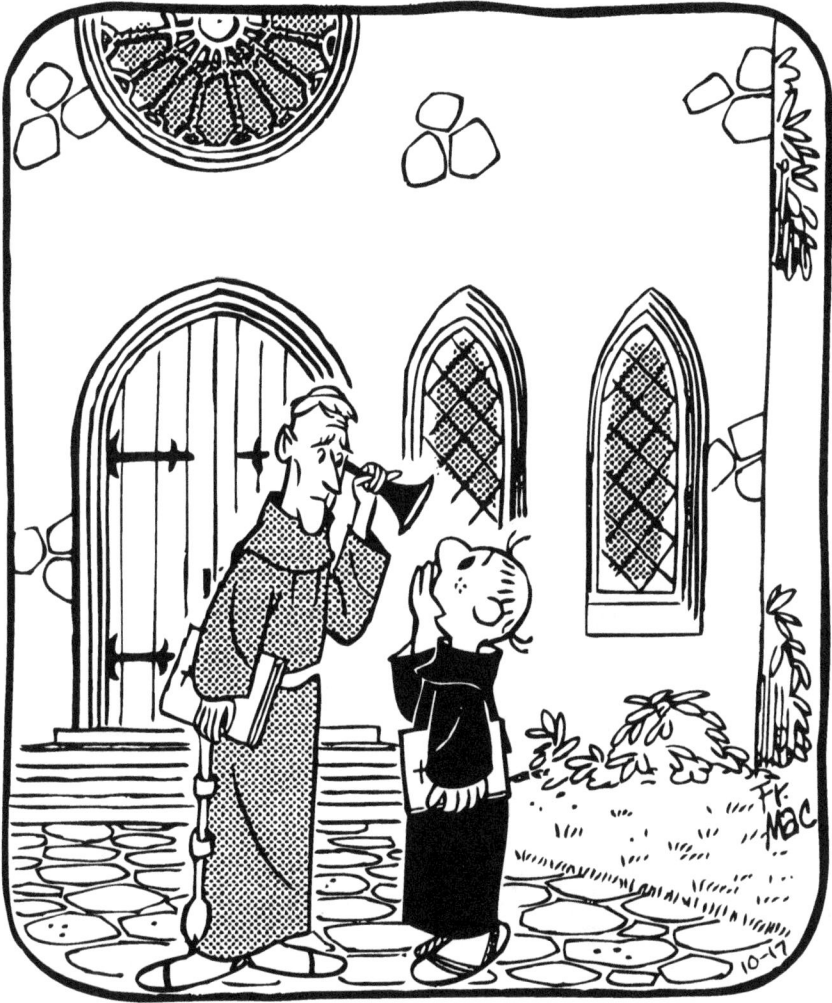

"I SAID: 'See you in church.'"

HEALTH BAR
MILK SHAKES
FRUIT JUICE
EGG SHAKES
Fr. MAC 3-3

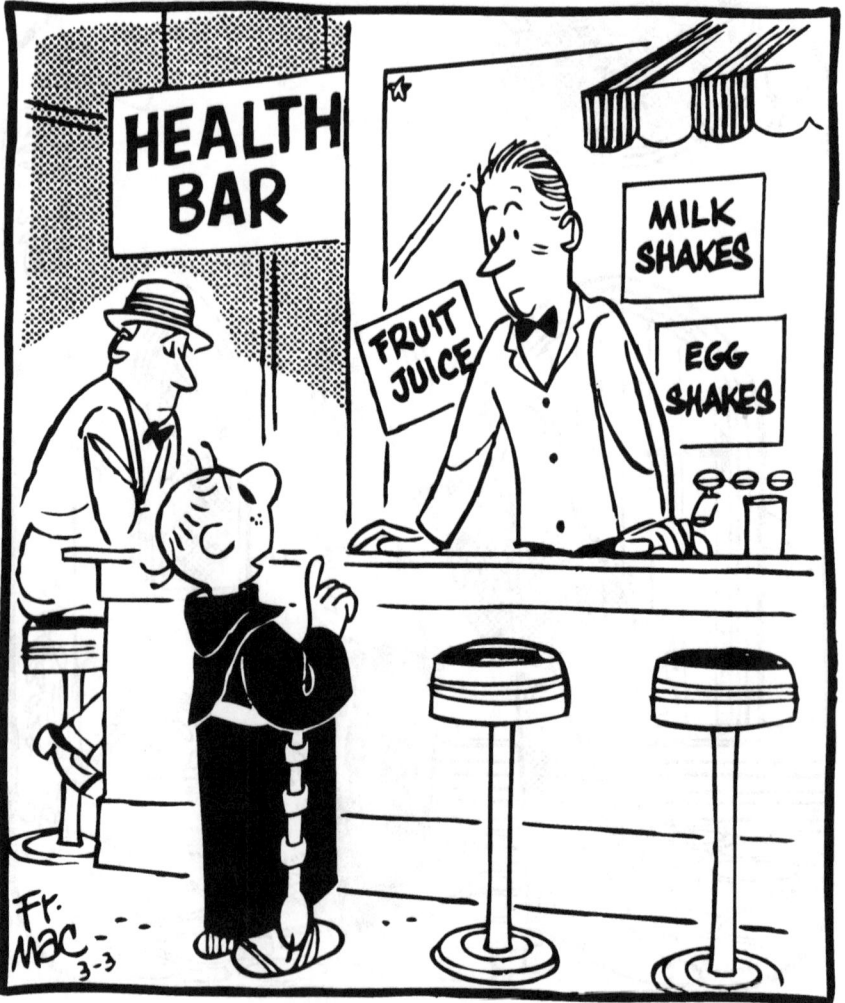

"I'd like one for the road."

"You always have to have the last word!"

"Don't push ma'am. I'm waiting as fast as I can."

BROTHER JUNIPER
STRIKES AGAIN

BY FATHER JUSTIN
'FRED' MCCARTHY

Empty-Grave Extended Edition

"Stop me if you've heard this one..."

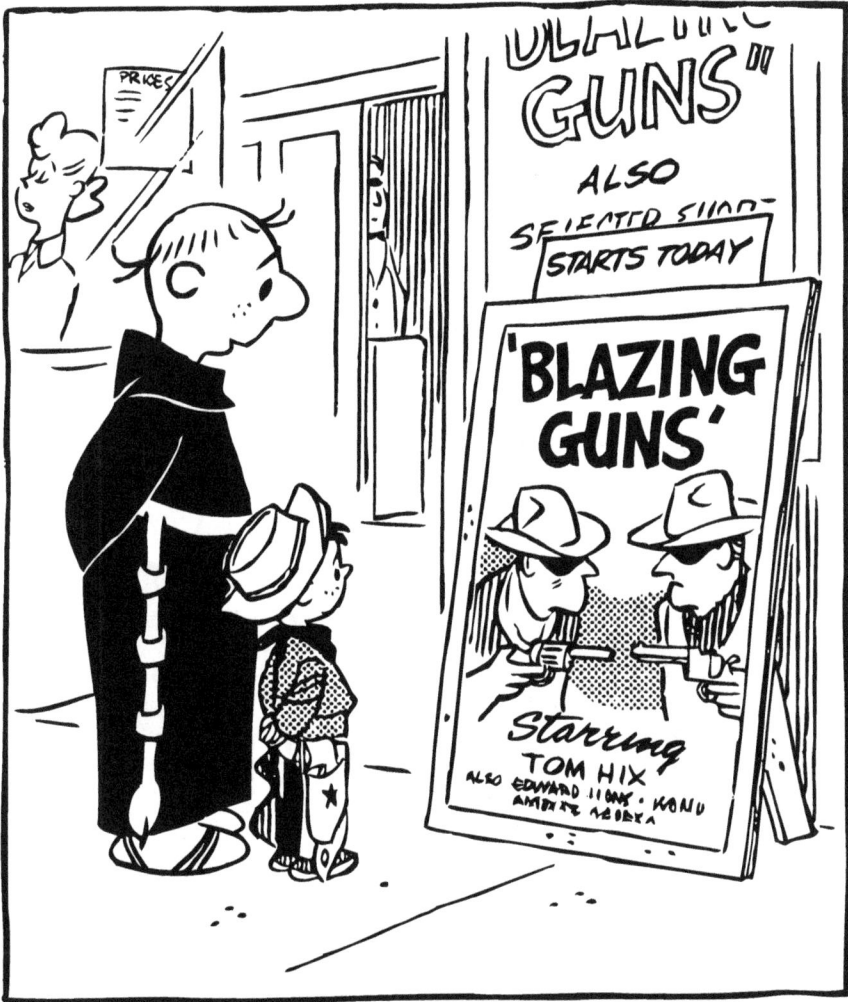

"It's hard to tell if they have honest faces
when they wear masks."

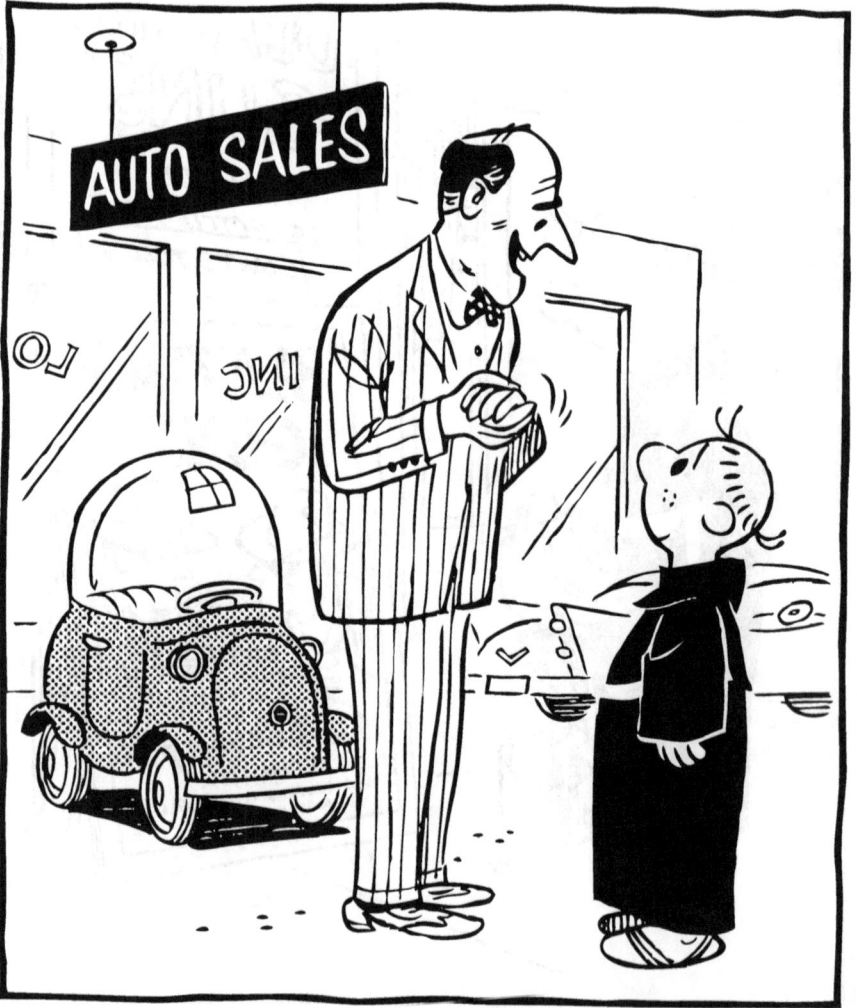

"Yessir, Brother, I think I have something
right up your alley."

"Stop whistling? Who, me?"

"What kind of a PLATE do I want? Oh, anything good - how about Wedgwood?"

"Chief, he says he'll buy a ticket to the Policeman's
Ball if you'll buy one to the Parish Picnic."

"I said, do you have 'Silent Night'?"

"Looks like a bad case of housemaid's knee.
Do much kneeling?"

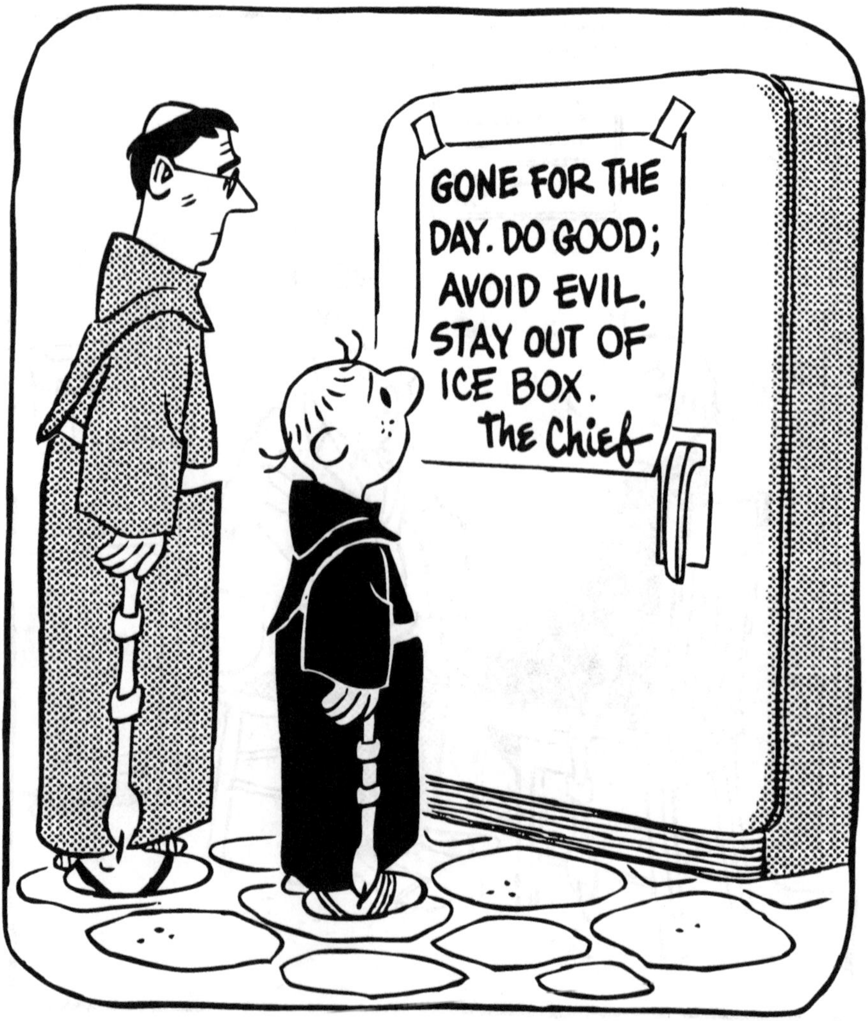
GONE FOR THE
DAY. DO GOOD;
AVOID EVIL.
STAY OUT OF
ICE BOX.
The Chief

"Just answer me one question.
Was it done in SELF-DEFENSE?"

"That's not the speed limit, that's the route number!"

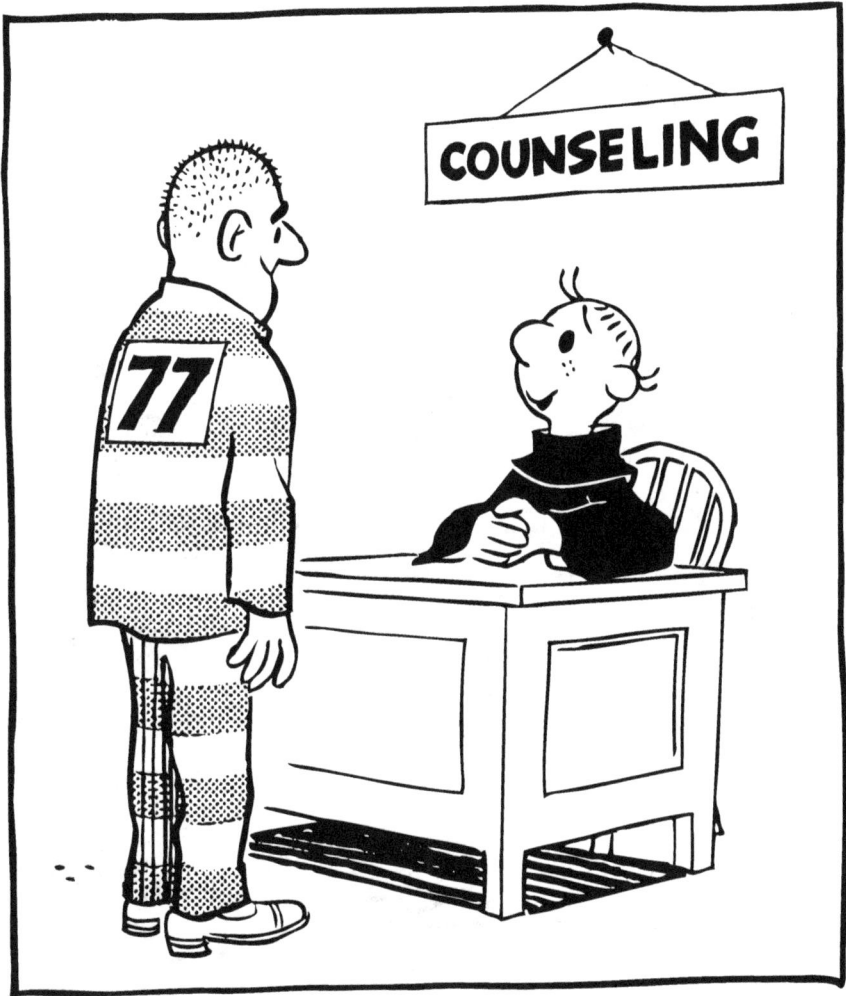

"I have wonderful news, Spike. They plan to retire your number when you graduate."

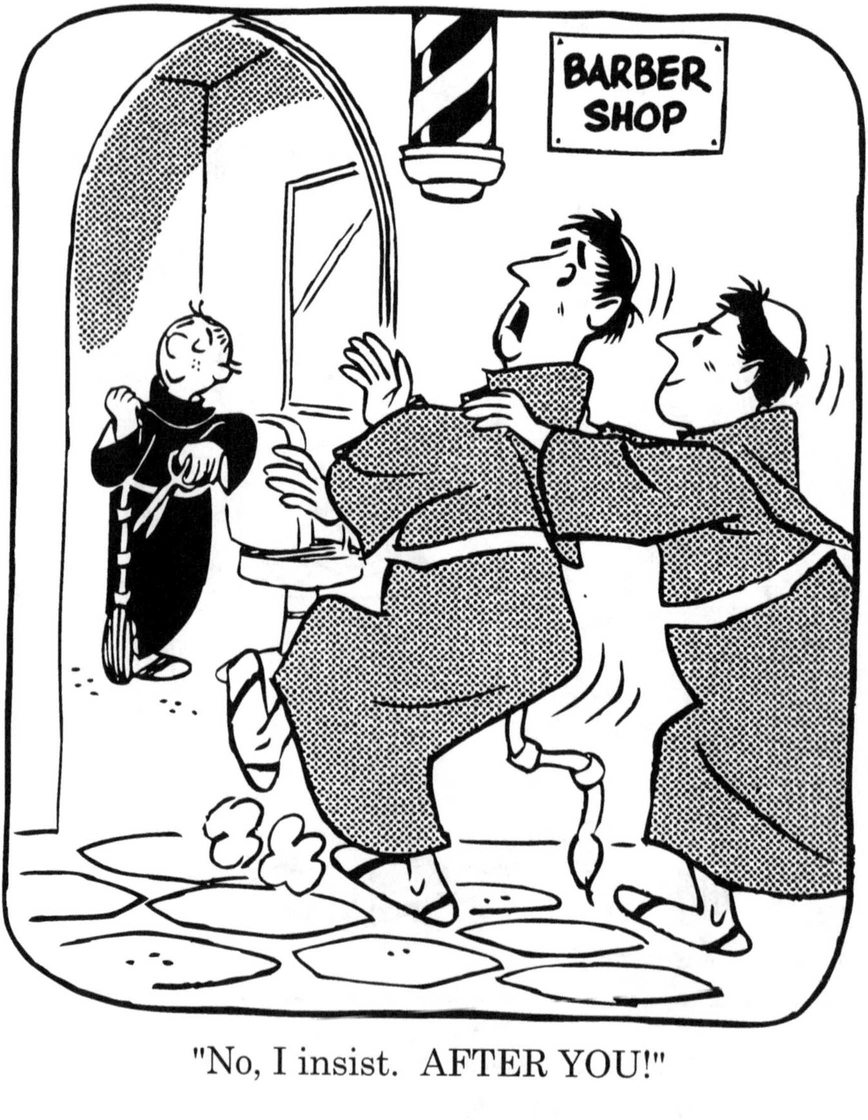
BARBER
SHOP

"No, I insist. AFTER YOU!"

"Psst...We're on!"

"What did I do wrong?"

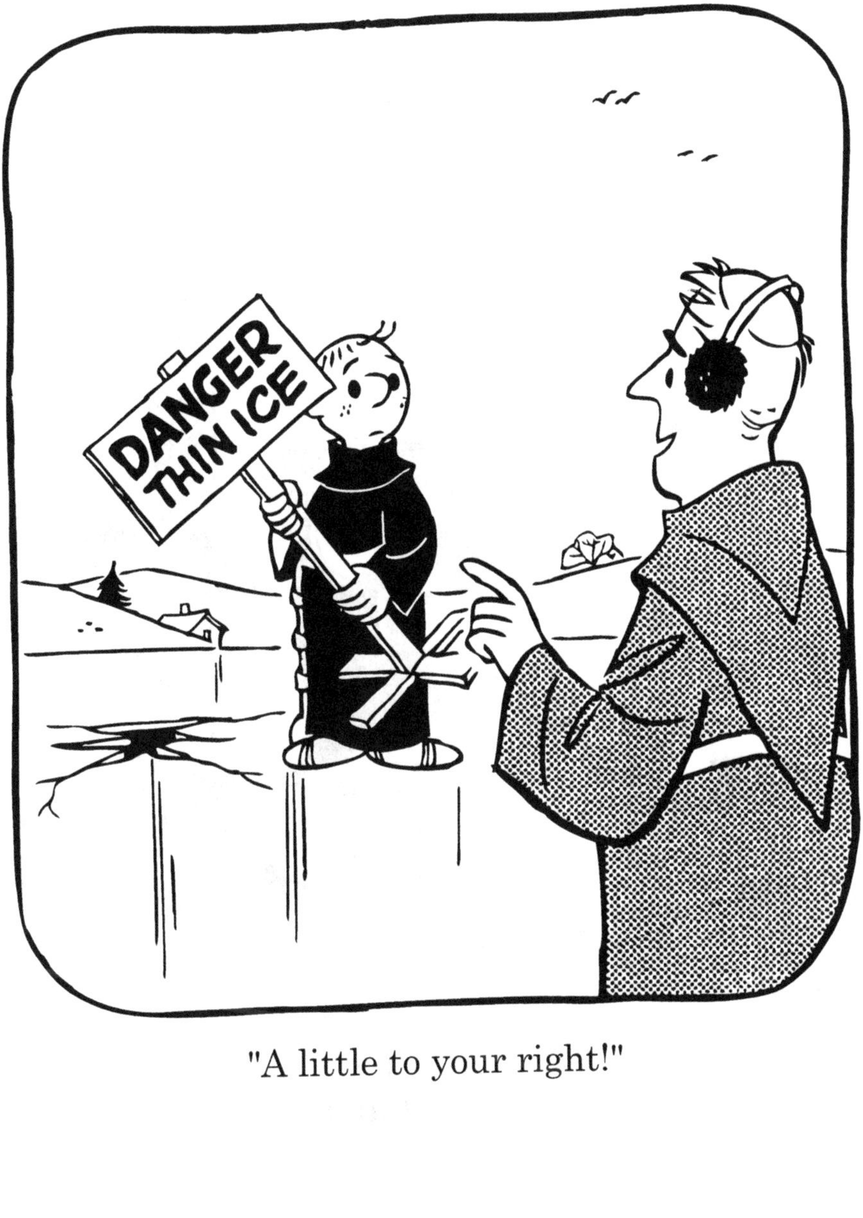
DANGER
THIN ICE

"A little to your right!"

"These cold mornings I like to
serve them toast and coffee."

"Give me two quarts of your fortified milk."

"Well, there's another pressure cooker
you've put in orbit!"

"Both feet planted firmly in midair as usual."

"This oyster stew IS pretty gamey!"

"Mind a suggestion, Junior?"

"Ah...uh...oh, give me a closed Sunday, please."

"Be sure and write when you reach Miami."

"Just as I suspected...TERMITES!"

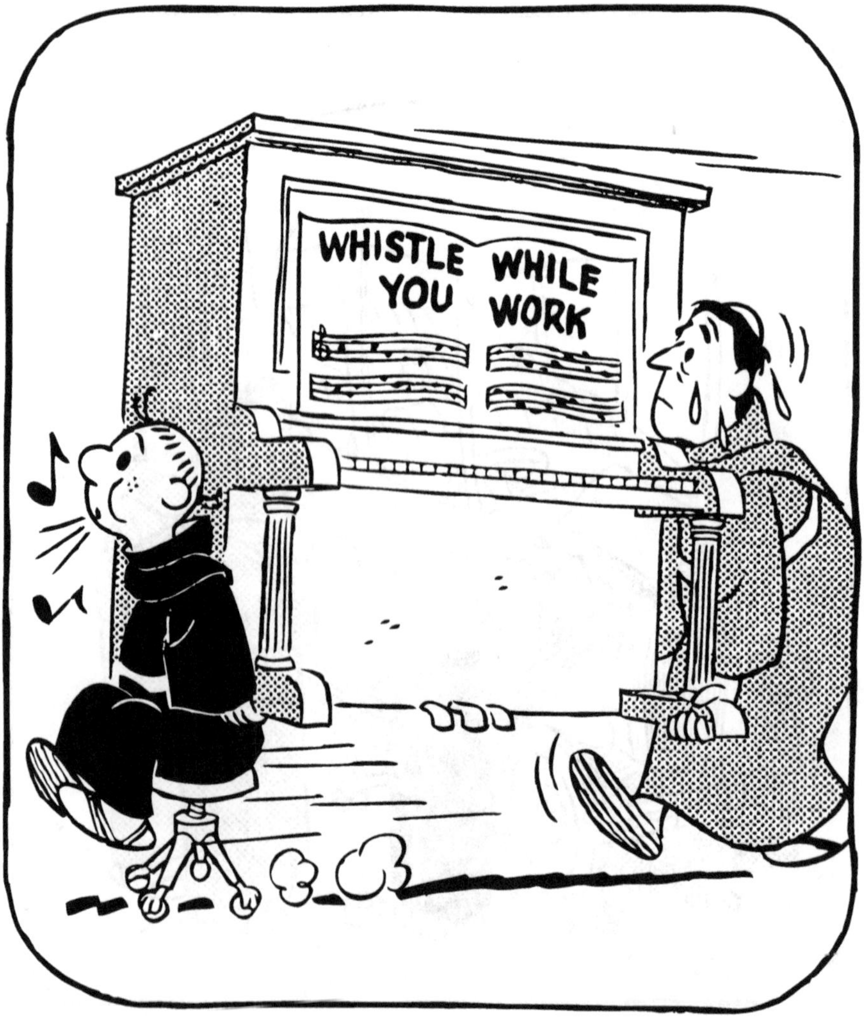
WHISTLE WHILE
YOU WORK

"Matter of fact, sir, my name IS Daniel."

"Hey, only one swing to a pitch!"

"Like they say, cleanliness is next to Godliness."

"I'll be all right in a minute. High prices
always make me dizzy."

"There but for the grace of God go I!"

"Yours just have no character whatsoever!"

"Weddings always make me cry, too, ma'am!"

"It's easy! First you shoot the arrow, then
you just take your paint brush and ..."

"Did you ever TRY going straight?"

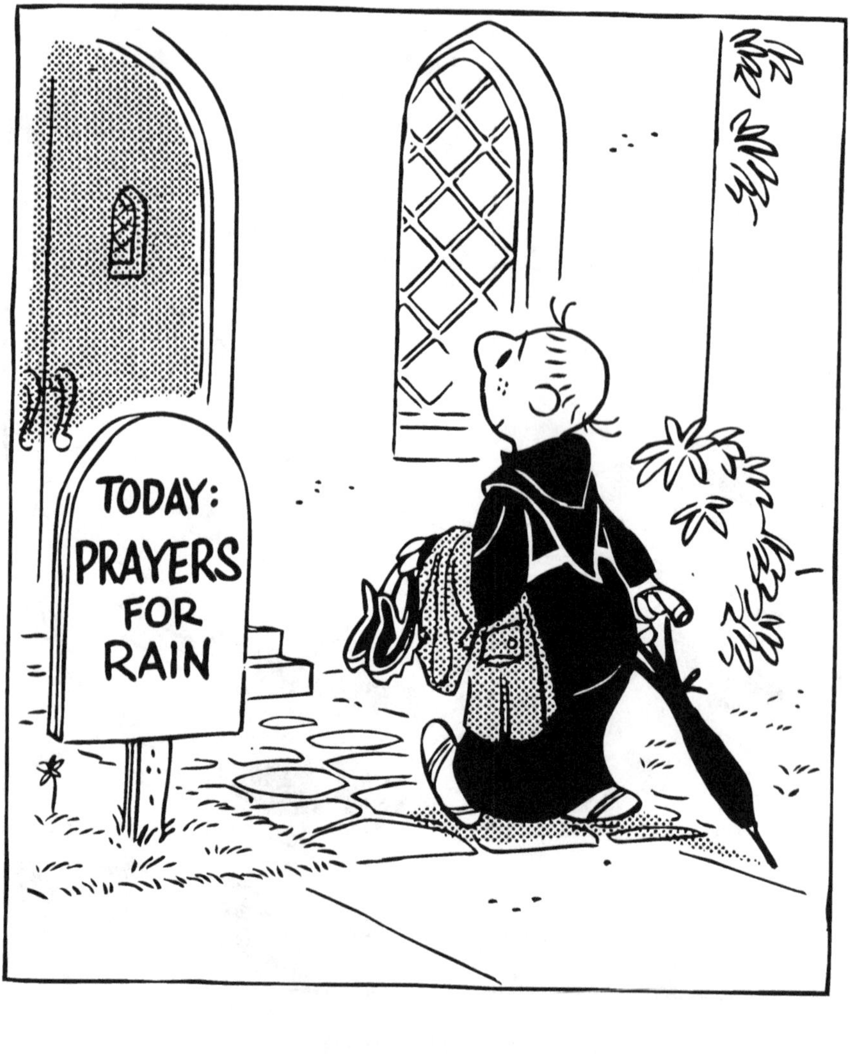
TODAY:
PRAYERS
FOR
RAIN

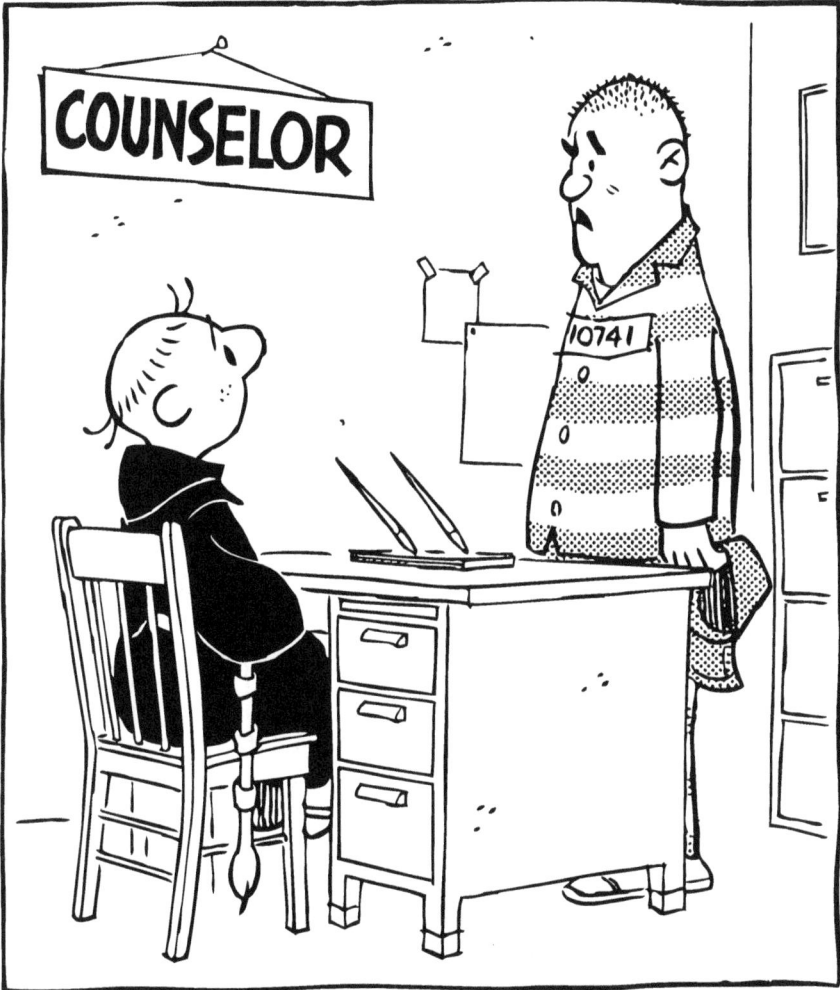

"You see, sir, I just don't feel that I belong."

"Better light only ONE candle tonight ...
Supper's pretty bad if I do say so myself!"

"Try this hole for size, kiddo."

"Now watch! This is a rabbit with a
big nose who needs a haircut."

"I'll drive, you bail."

"I'd appreciate it if you'd wipe your big cubic feet
before walking on my nice clean cellar floor."

"He can do a better job on himself
than anybody I know."

293

"When I bring home a stray cat I don't fool around."

"...And for double yolks you get time and a half!"

"I have a new job. I've been kicked upstairs."

"His insurance must be all paid up!"

"Just act supernatural."

"It's a very poor day for drying."

"The new chaplain is a friendly chap.
Always calls me by my first number."

"Please, no self-portraits in the shrubbery!"

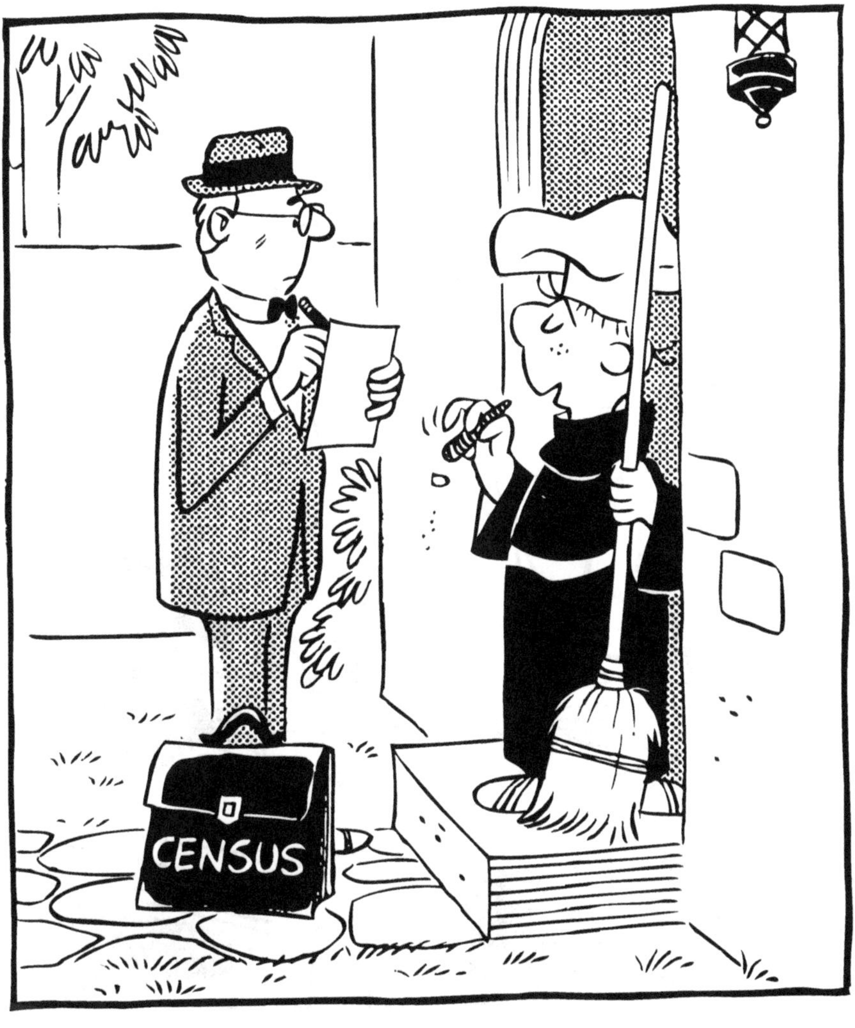
CENSUS

"Oh, just say: Homemaker."

"He's too small for the poultry contest. Why not
enter him in the songbird competition?"

"Sure, I get its meaning. It keeps telling
me I haven't eaten since breakfast."

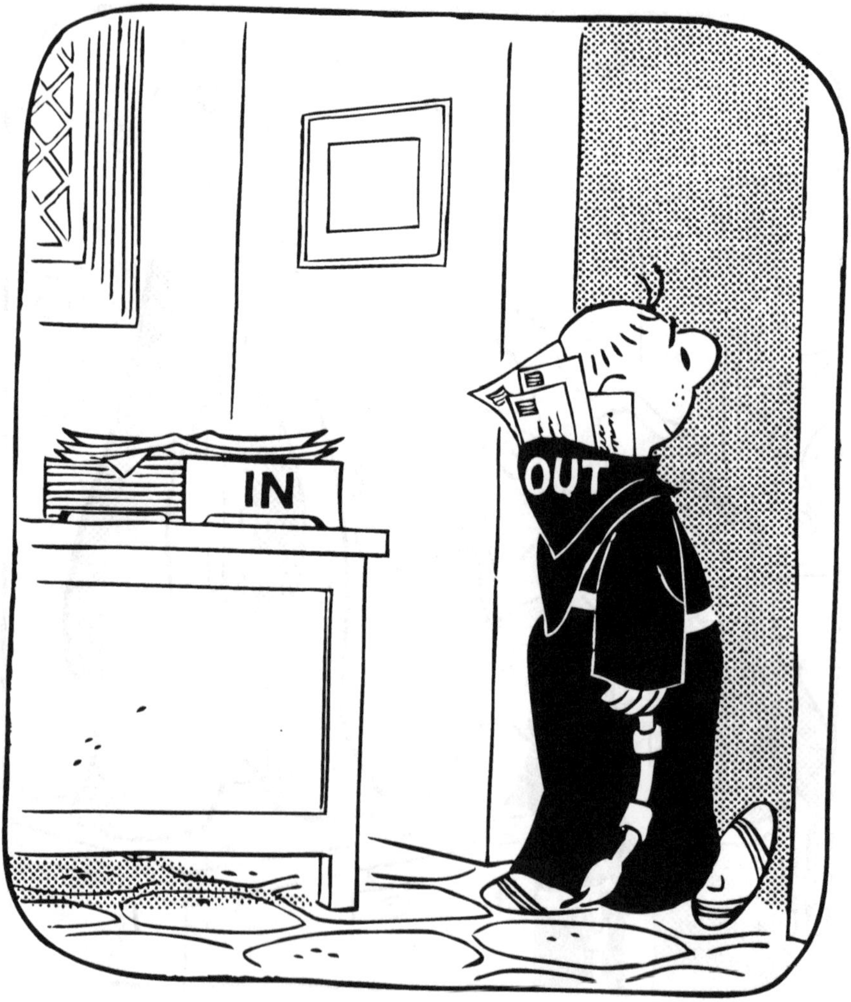
IN
OUT

"I can see now why they call you a beast of burden!"

"Somehow this dampness goes
right through me today."

"Now let's have a nice big frown."

"That new paper boy certainly has a great arm!"

"Around here we always take in the
sidewalks at eight o'clock."

"There were plenty of things you needed more
than a Chinese back-scratcher!"

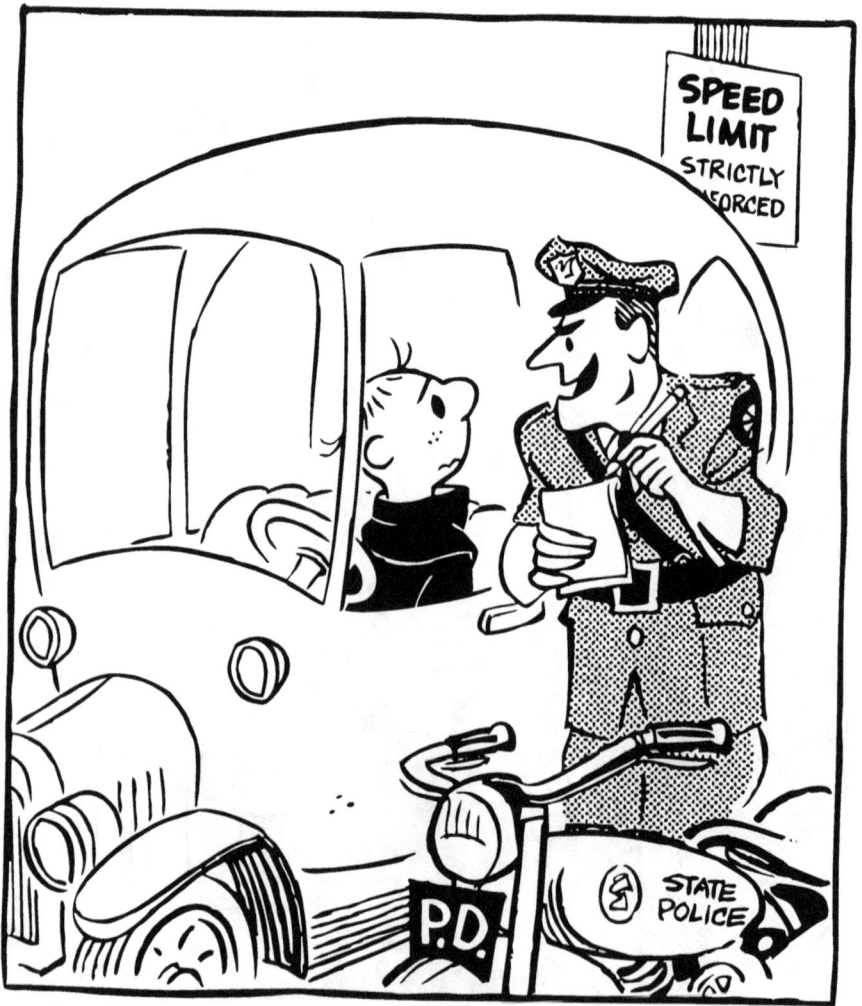

"Brother Juniper, I want you to consider me as a sort of guardian angel."

"We better pay that electric bill. The candle company says no more credit."

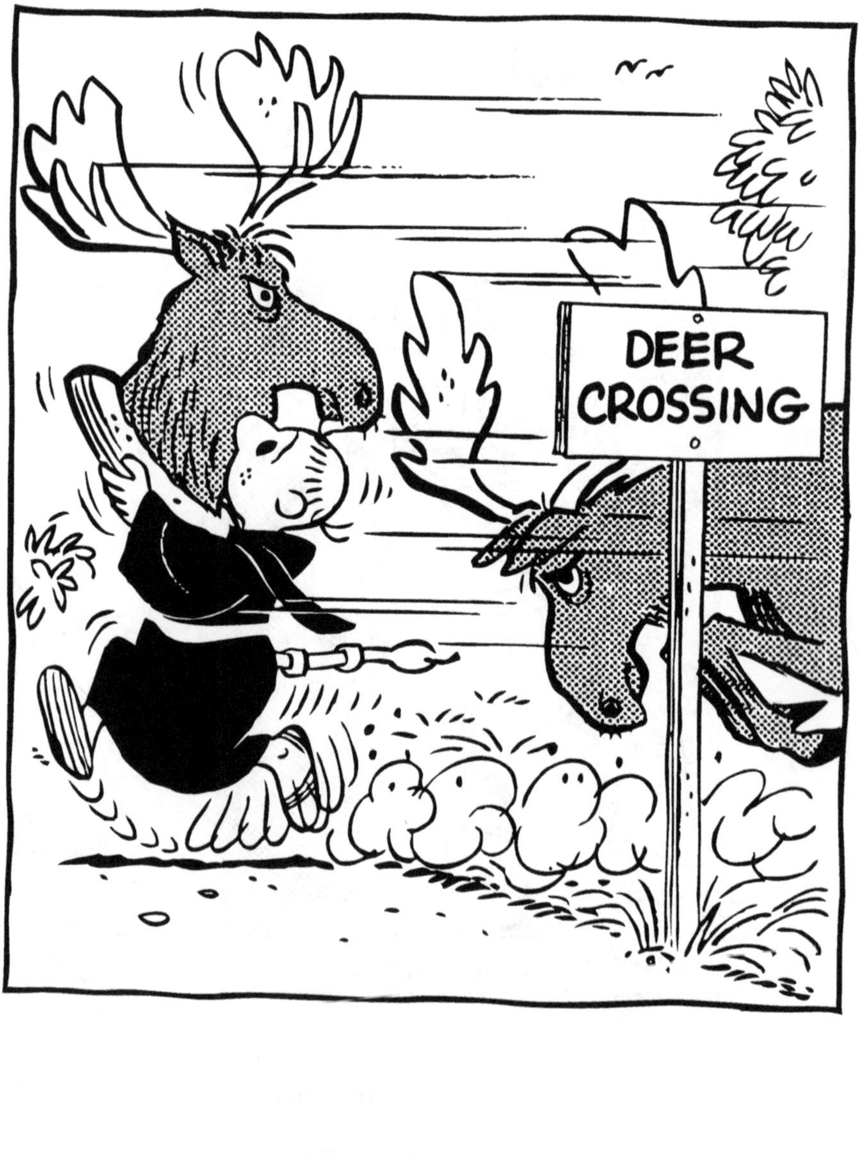
DEER
CROSSING

"Give me a vanilla cone, please, but
don't pack it down tight ... I'm on a diet."

"But, Officer, I know for a fact he's OVER 16!'"

"Take it slow. The life you save may be MINE!"

"Hello, Acme Barbers' College? Would you
please send over one of your seniors?"

"Ain't nobody up here but us chickens."

"I must have taken a thorn out of his foot at some time or another."

"Care to have a drag race, sonny?"

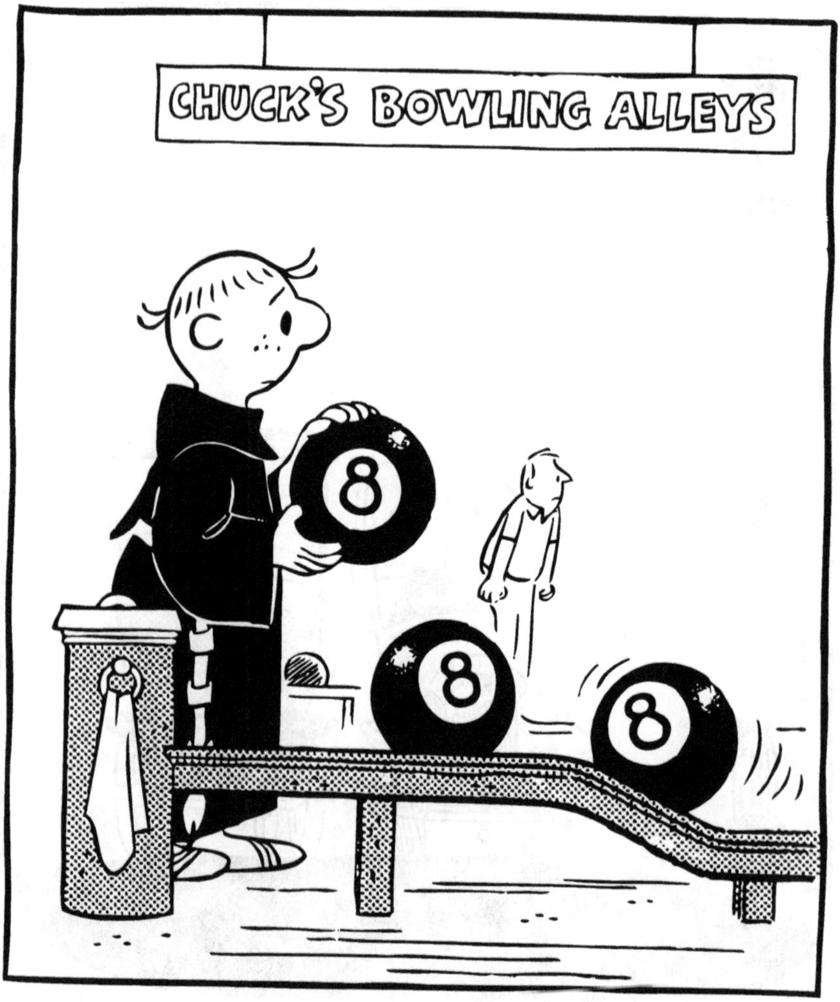
CHUCK'S BOWLING ALLEYS
8
8
8

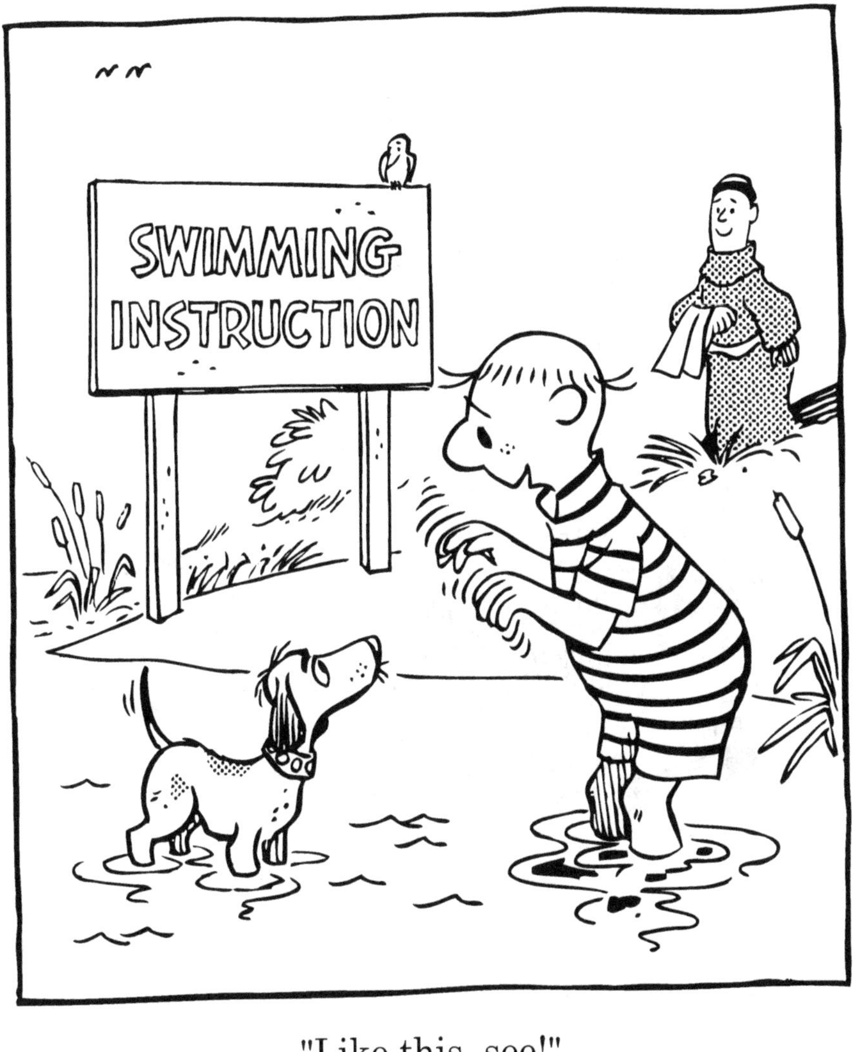
SWIMMING
INSTRUCTION

"Like this, see!"

"Looks like a nervous breakdown to me!"

"I keep telling myself there's no
such thing as a bad boy."

"Canst thou take it off tackle again,
Brother Juniper?"

"Somebody better choose Brother Juniper.
It's HIS tire pump!"

"Do you have any GOODminton sets?"

"Of course we're lost! But we're making
such good time, let's keep on going!"

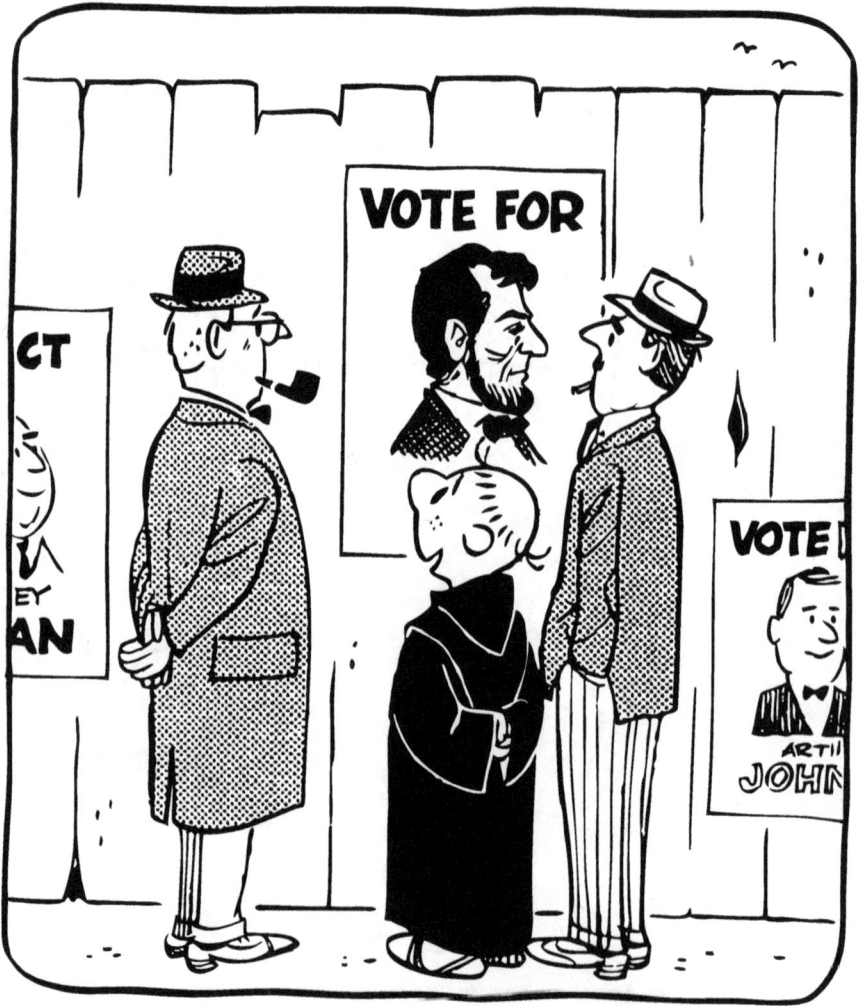

"Personally, I like his looks!"

"Aren't you spreading yourself a bit thin?"

"Either get bigger cups or get a smaller coffeepot!"

"Oh, it's just a spinach sandwich with ketchup, mustard, and strawberries. Why?"

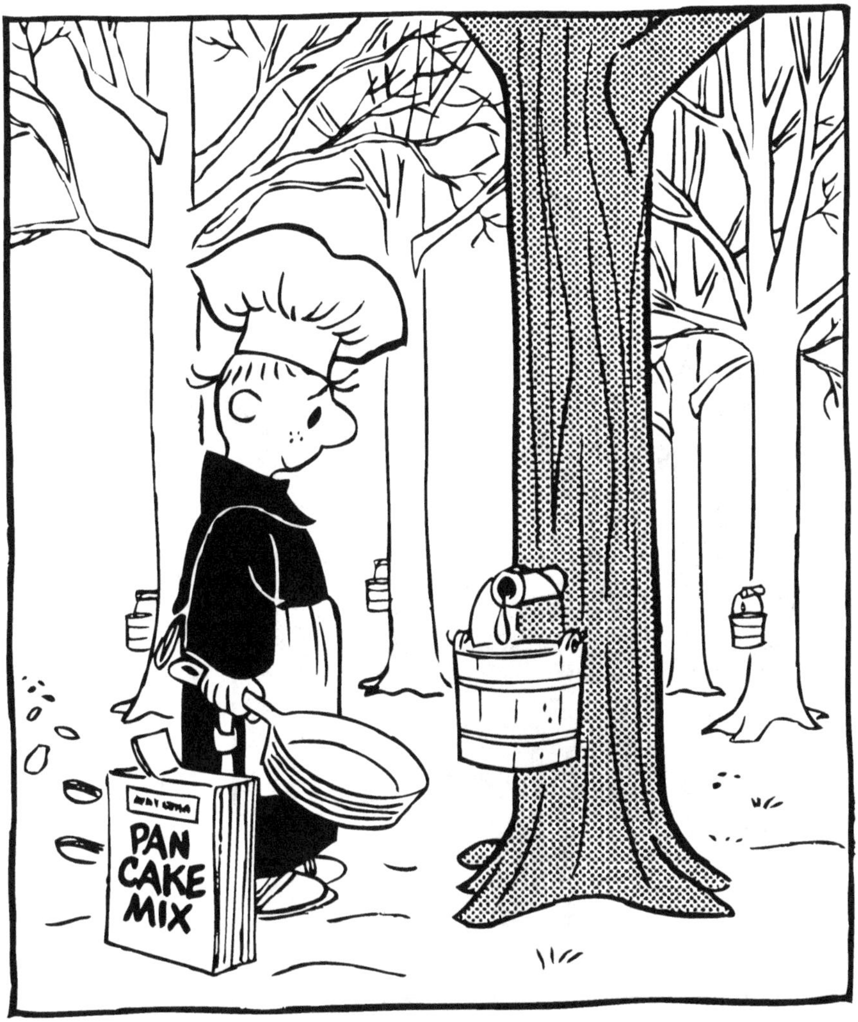
PAN
CAKE
MIX

"Remember, if we get lost, we'll all come in together on 'Mother Machree'."

"This is terrible! We're all out of leftovers!"

"No, thanks. Just sniffing."

"Well, so long. I have to make tracks."

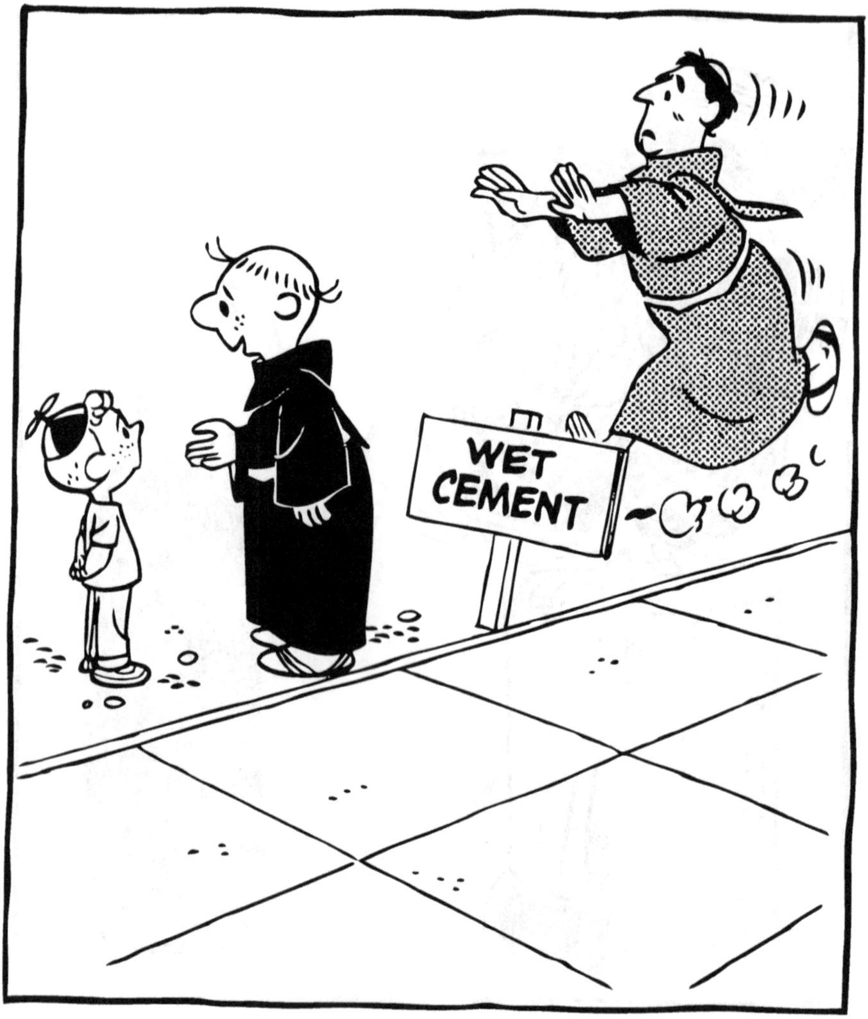
WET
CEMENT

"The cat's safe, but call the Fire
Department to get Brother Juniper down."

"Watch it! I just waxed those flagstones."

"That sticker tells me you bought Girl Scout cookies; it says nothing about having the car inspected!"

"Well, you certainly don't leave
much to Divine Providence."

"I haven't the heart to tell him it's only poison ivy."

"Nice try!"

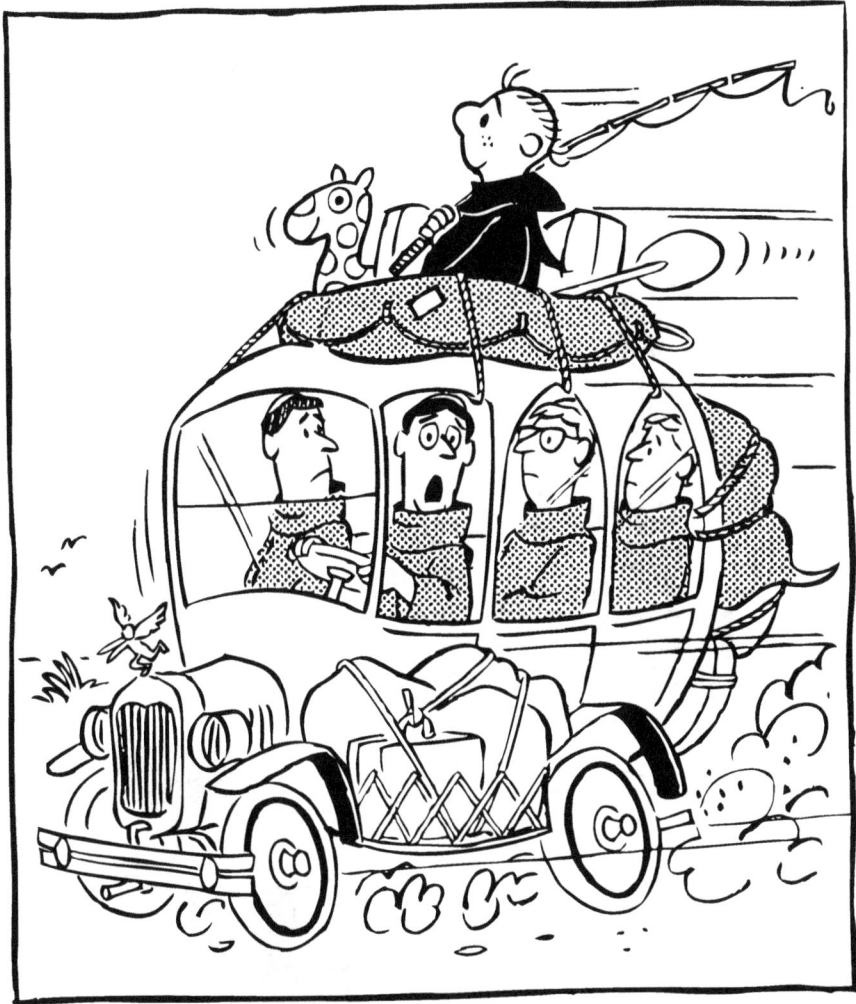

"Good heavens, we forgot Brother Juniper!"

"Excuse me, lady, I thought I was
watering the flowers."

"Here comes God's gift to the corn borers."

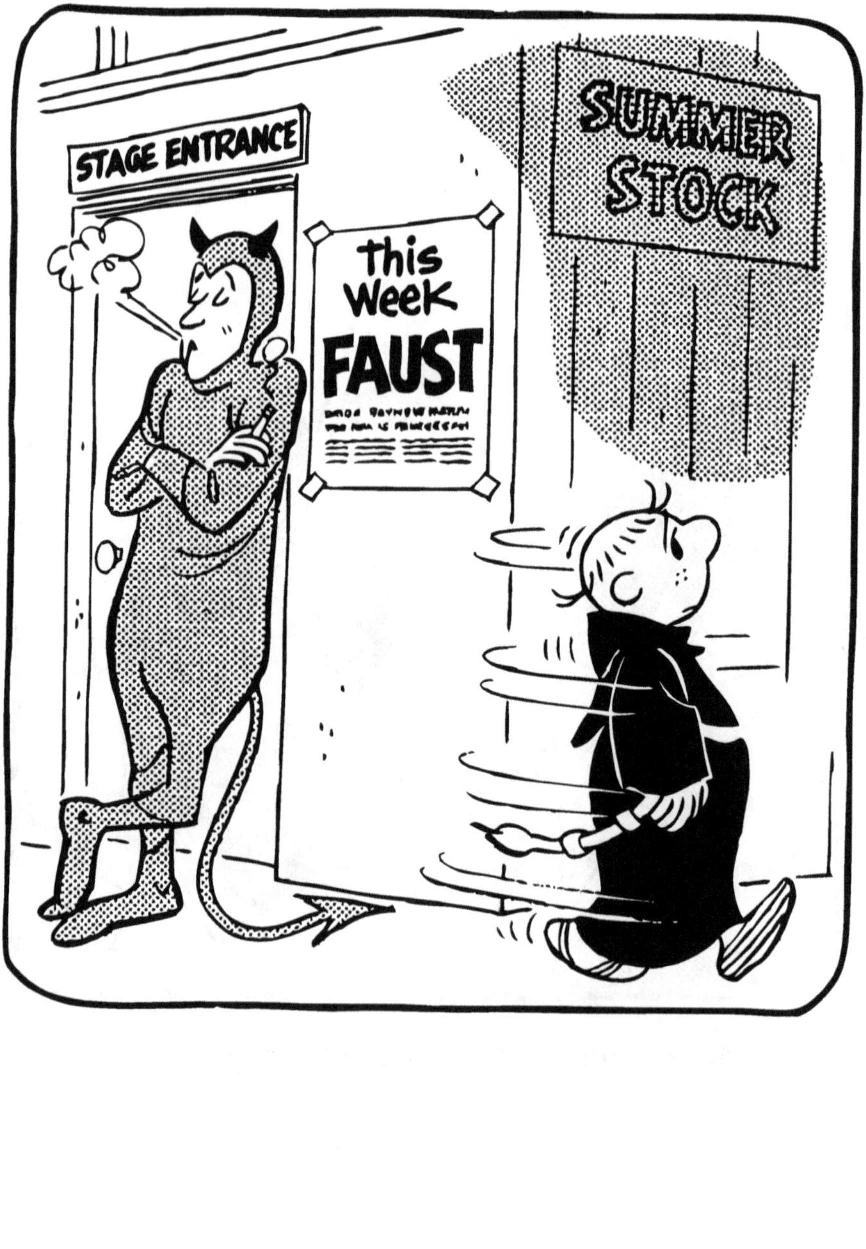
STAGE ENTRANCE
This Week
FAUST
SUMMER
STOCK

"Gee, thanks for listenin' to my troubles."

"It should be just about time to unbend the hose."

GRADE
A
MILK
MILK

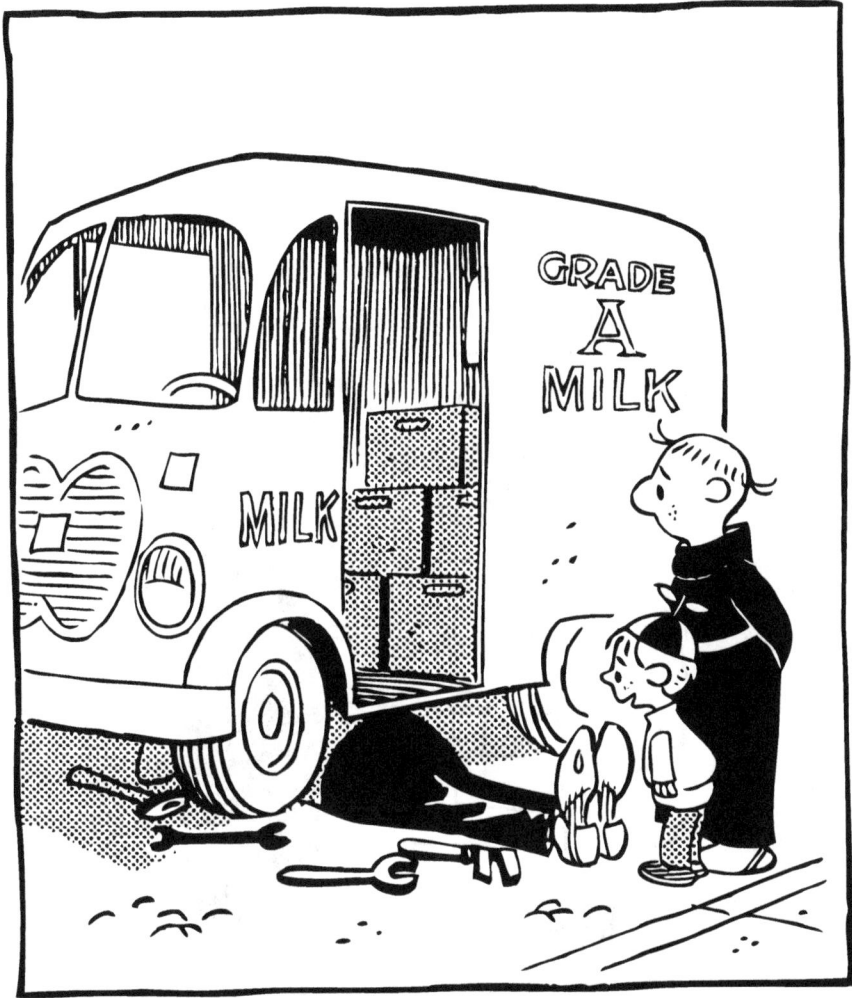

"It must be milking time."

"I'd like something for someone
who is morally bankrupt."

"If you could only pick 'em as
fast as you can eat 'em!"

"Well, be good."

"Him and his lightning bugs!"

"I changed the spark plugs and took
some dents out of the flying buttresses."

"Why not look upon it as an investment
in the future?"

"That's not charcoal. Those are the STEAKS!"

"Hey, Brother Charlie, the Chief's
lawn chair is here!"

"Got everything? Milk, crackers, butter, salt,
crackers, coffee ... crackers?'"

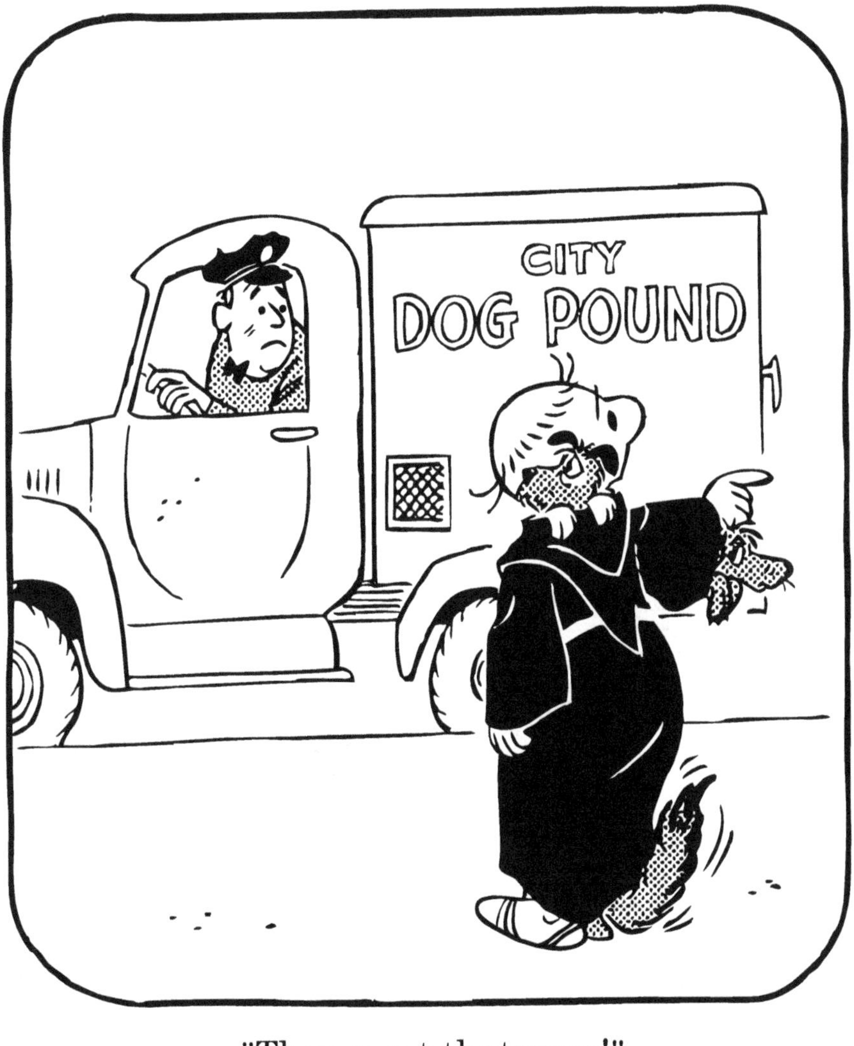
CITY
DOG POUND

"They went thataway!"

MORE
BROTHER JUNIPER

BY FATHER JUSTIN
'FRED' MCCARTHY

Empty-Grave Extended Edition

"Come and get it!"

"You jump over him, then he
jumps over you. Then..."

"Wait a minute! We've caught
you three times already."

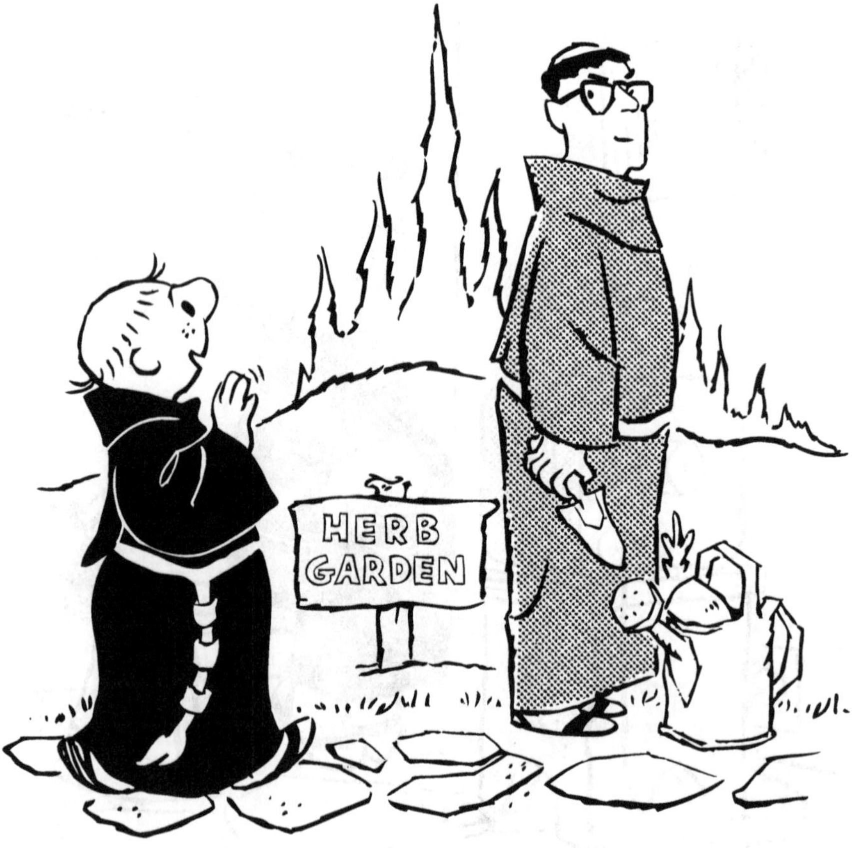
HERB
GARDEN

"Hi, Herb!"

"Two dozen with mustard, Tony ... and hurry!"

"No thanks, Ma'am. I always use my own."

"My health is excellent, thanks. Just dropped in to
read your old magazines."

"Ran into a couple of friends, downtown."

DENTIST

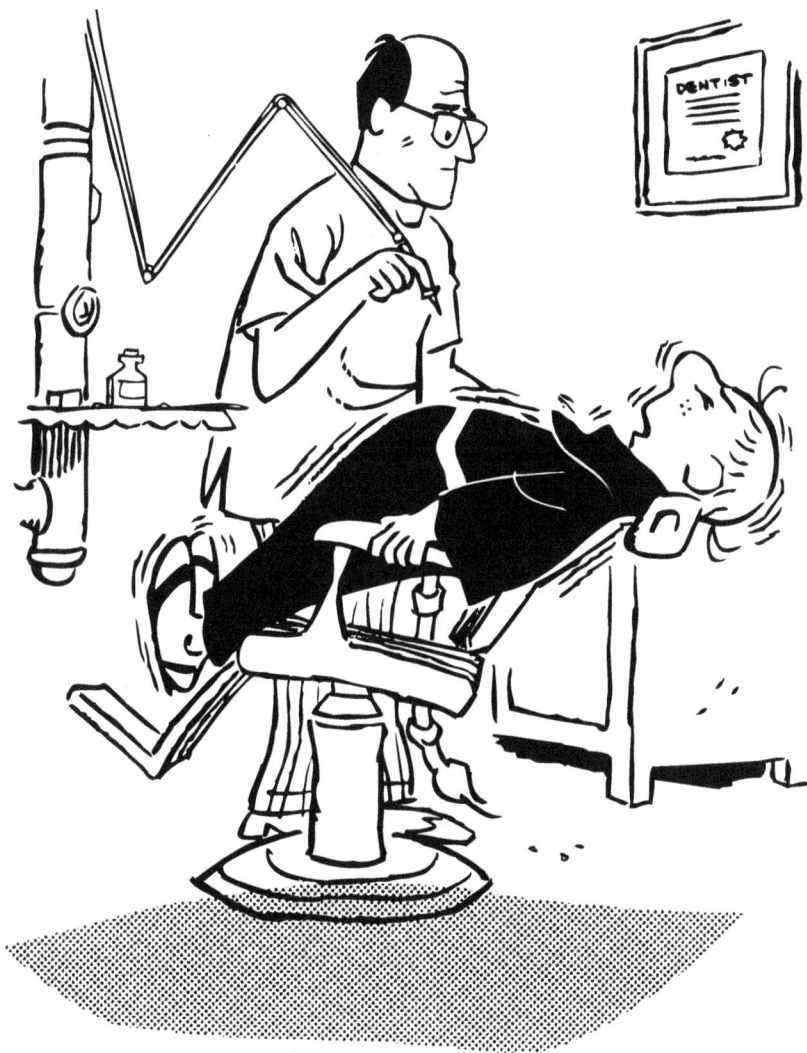

"I am not nervous!"

"And furthermore, stop calling me B.J.!"

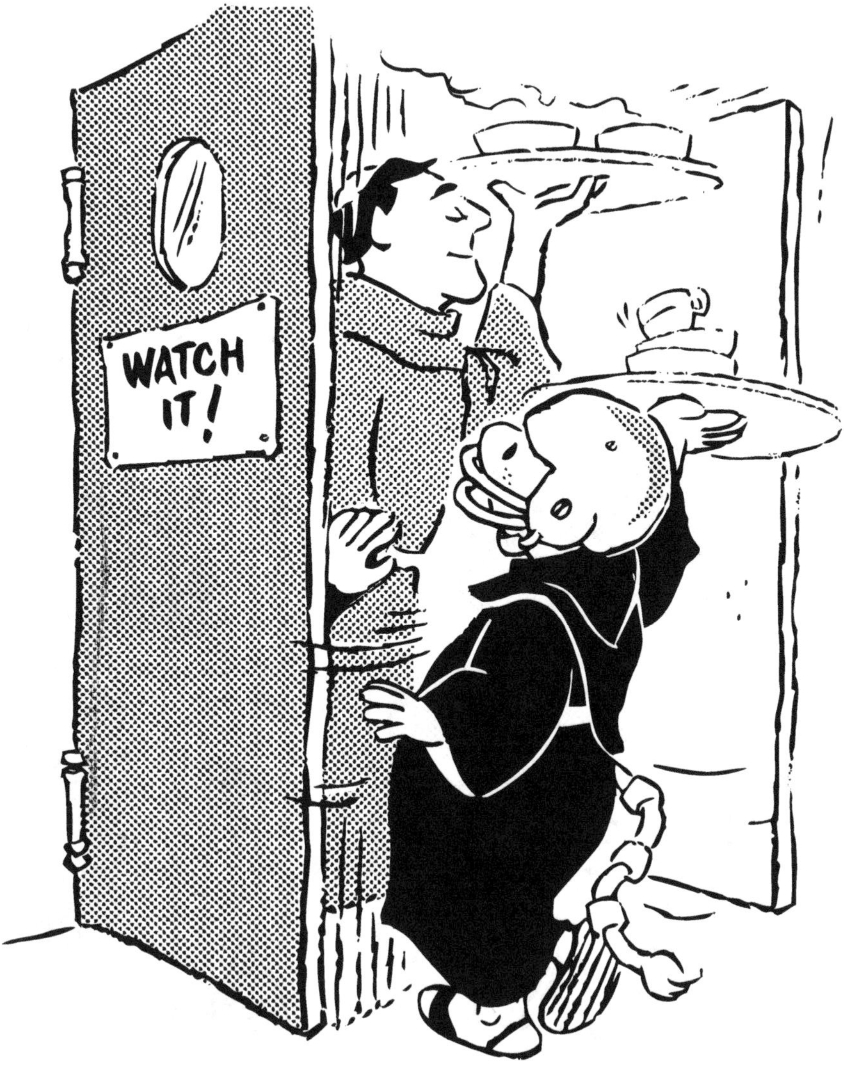
WATCH IT!

"We feel that with a little effort
you can be 'holier-than-thou.'"

"All right, Brother, where's the fire?"

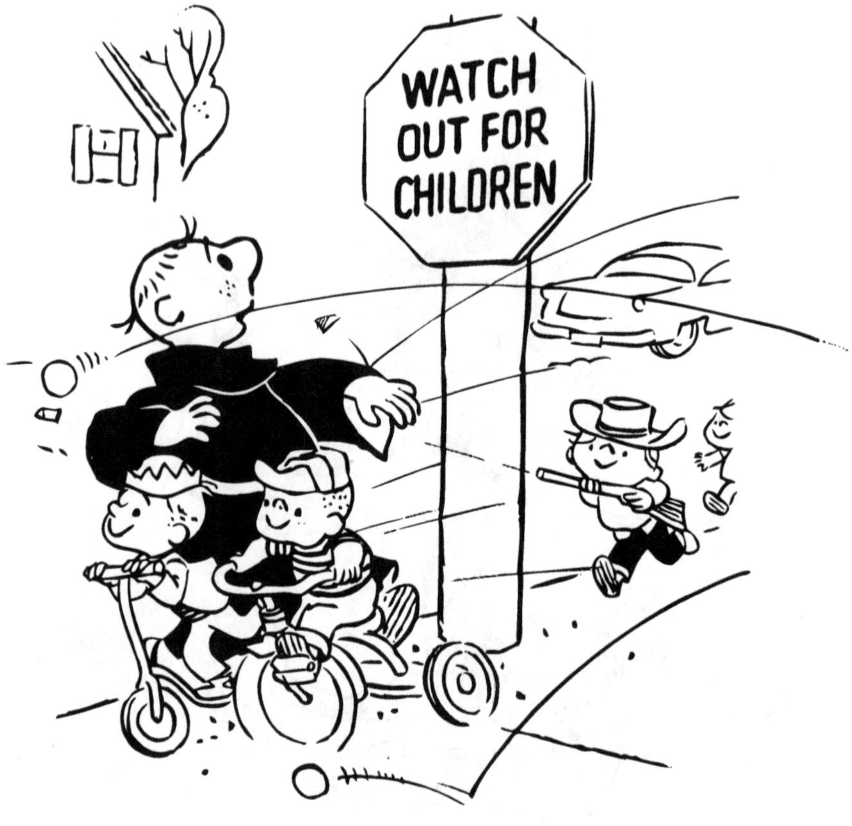
WATCH
OUT FOR
CHILDREN

"Boy, I'll say!"

"What do you mean, they're no good?
They're the same buttons you put in the
collection basket last Sunday."

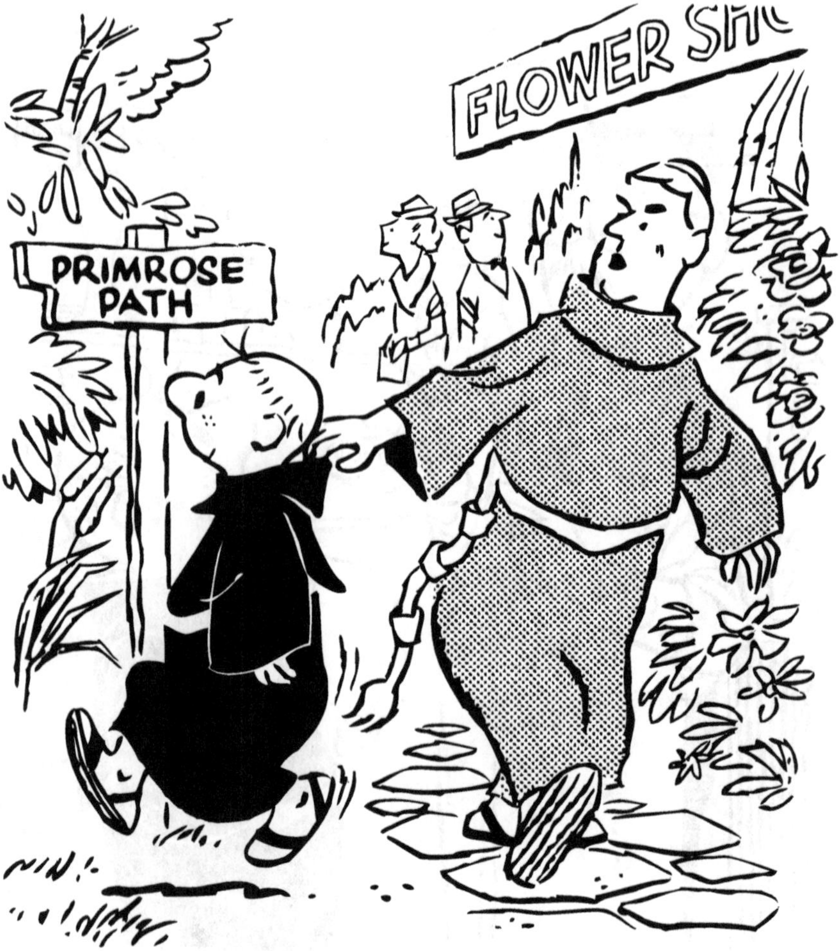
FLOWER SHO
PRIMROSE PATH

"Come back here!"

"For the man who 'has everything.'"

"I'll have three pounds of fingers ... er ... uh ... I mean flounders, Mr. Flanders."

"Let me know if they bother you."

"It must be nice to feel wanted."

"I turned the other cheek like you said, and he let me have it again, like I said!"

"Gets harder to part every year."

"Draw, pardner."

"Excuse me, I thought the Wednesday Nite Bowler
Boys were meeting here."

"I am not trying to hide your light under a bushel!"

"Don't you fellers know smoking
will stunt your growth?"

"While I was busy finding this one,
I lost all the others."

"Have you seen a little fellow
shoveling snow around here?"

"Don't worry, Dobbin, you'll get 'em back."

"Hey, Juniper, the ice box is locked!"

"Wish someone would send me a CARE package."

"That's all right. I was just coming down, anyway."

INFIRMARY

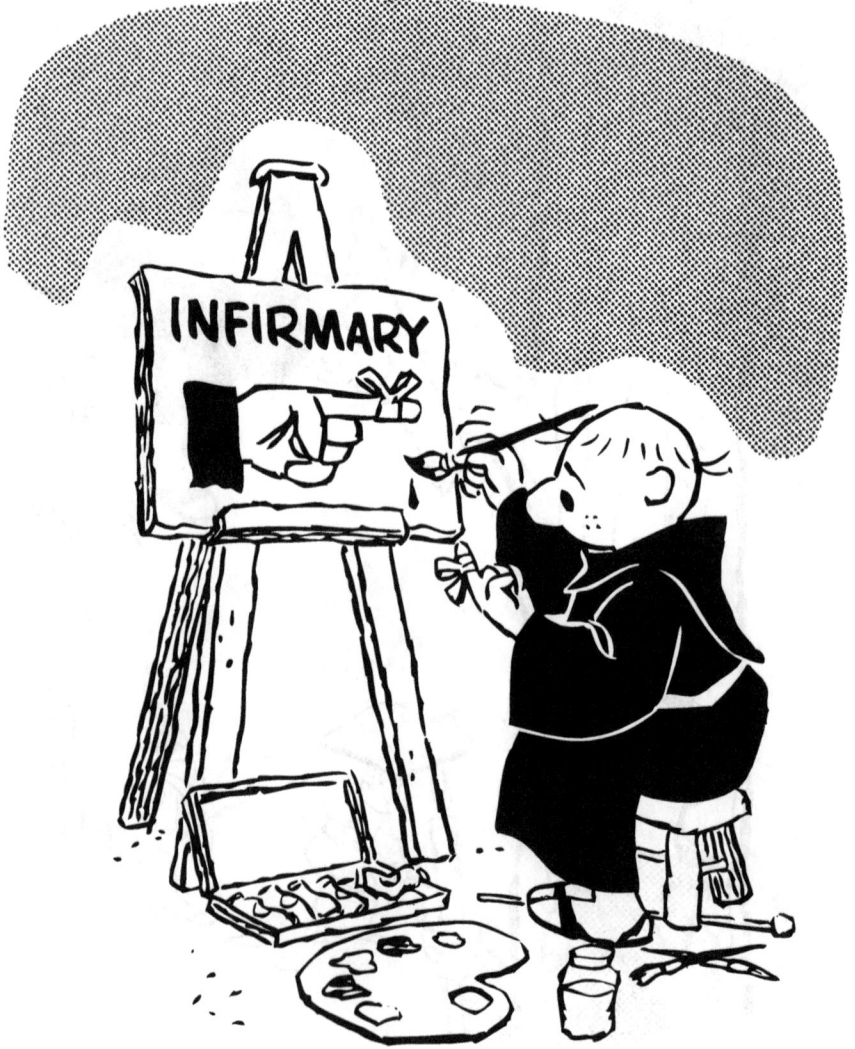

"Hey, Charlie, I'm fixing that
ol' door. Hey, Charlie!"

"Confound it, come back with the sports section!"

"Seems like George Washington comes to church oftener than Abe Lincoln."

"Let's have a little quiet, please!"

"Don't draw on me, son. I'm the
fastest gun in the East."

"Are you the 'Pizza Deluxe'?"

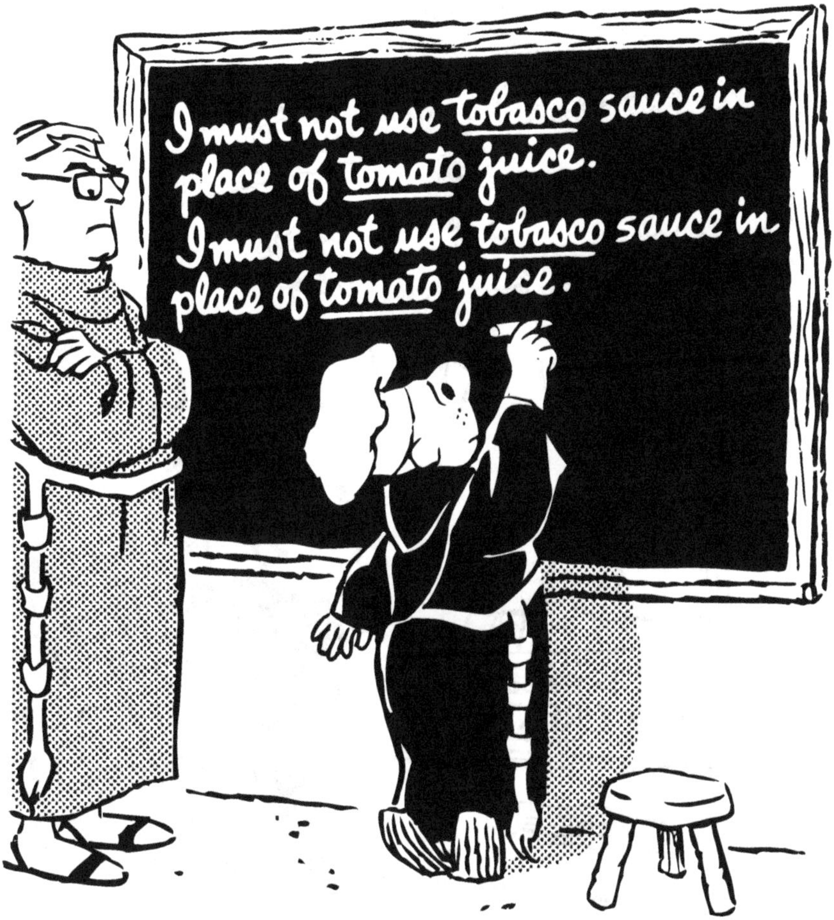
I must not use tobasco sauce in place of tomato juice.
I must not use tobasco sauce in place of tomato juice.

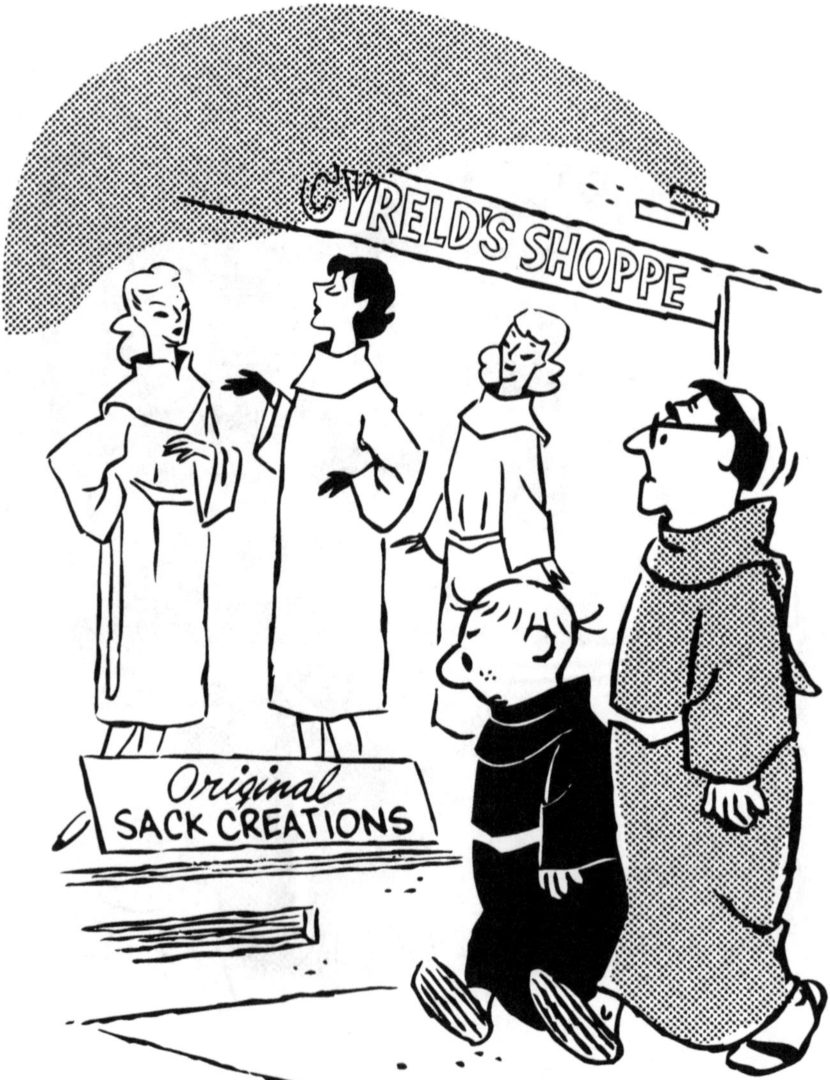
CYRELD'S SHOPPE
Original
SACK CREATIONS

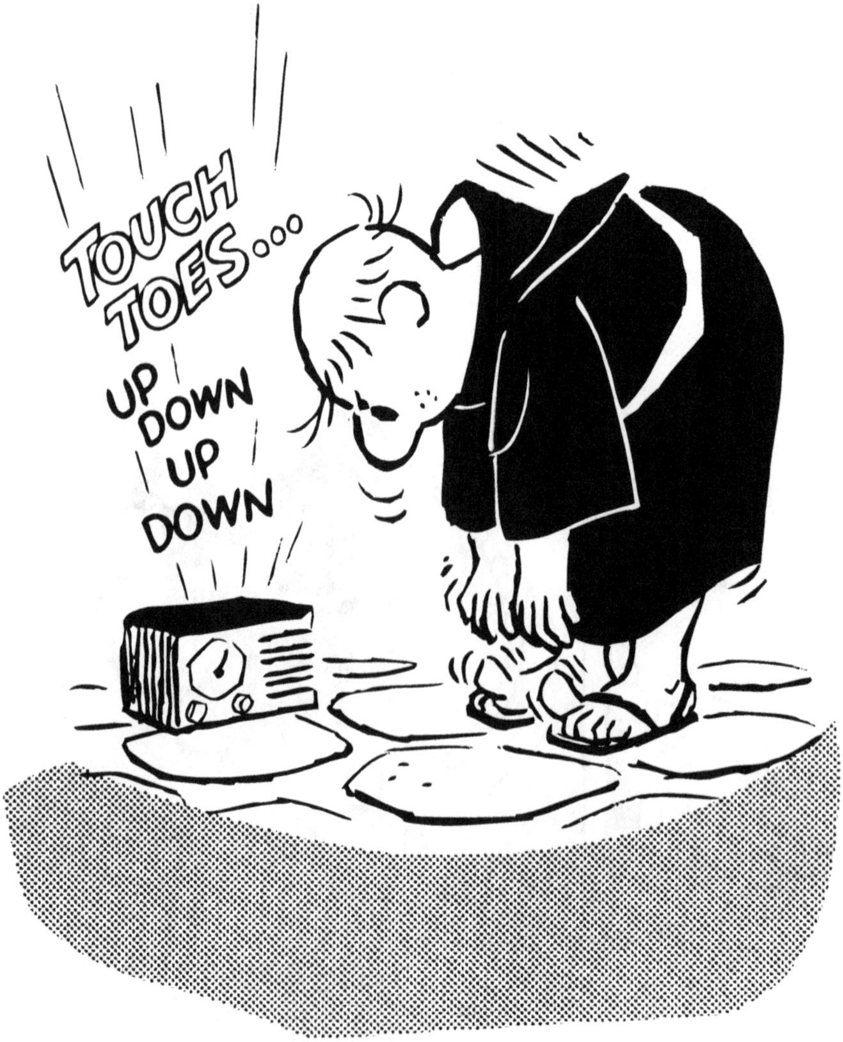
TOUCH TOES...
UP
DOWN
UP
DOWN

"Don't forget what happened in the
Garden of Eden, Officer Clancy."

"We have to economize, men. Tighten those belts!"

"This one is our Ivy League model.
It has a belt in the back."

"A little lower ... to the left ... there. Now, scratch!"

"... and I usually throw in a pinch
of soda-bicarb ... for luck!"

"By collateral we mean something more
than just an honest face."

"Isn't everyone entitled to one mistake?"

"We don't allow no gun-totin'
on the premises, pardner."

"Aw, he's a good guy. Why don't we
let him win once in a while?"

"I promised his mother I'd keep an eye on him till she got back from the store."

"We're going into this game with identical records,
men. They haven't lost and we haven't won."

"I almost lose my mind at daylight-saving time."

"How come I always have to be the good guy?"

"Quick, Joe, hide the devilfish!"

"Not that little one down there,
this little one up here."

"You're spoiling him with those baked apples!"

"So that's why he took out a library card!"

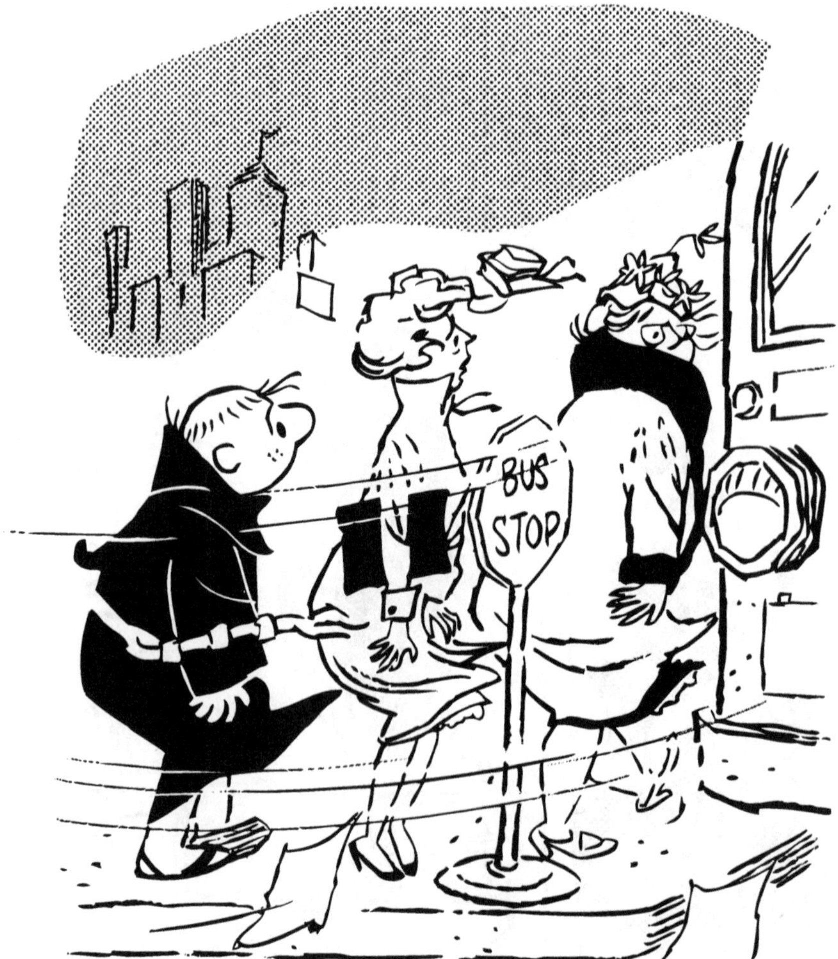
BUS
STOP

"For Pete's sake, get him a taller candle.
He's ruining the formation."

"Now try it!"

"This may be the chief's idea of spring training, but it's not my idea of spring training!"

"I'm dog-tired. Think I'll turn in early."

"Please hurry. I have a roast in the oven."

"Come now, where's that brave little smile?"

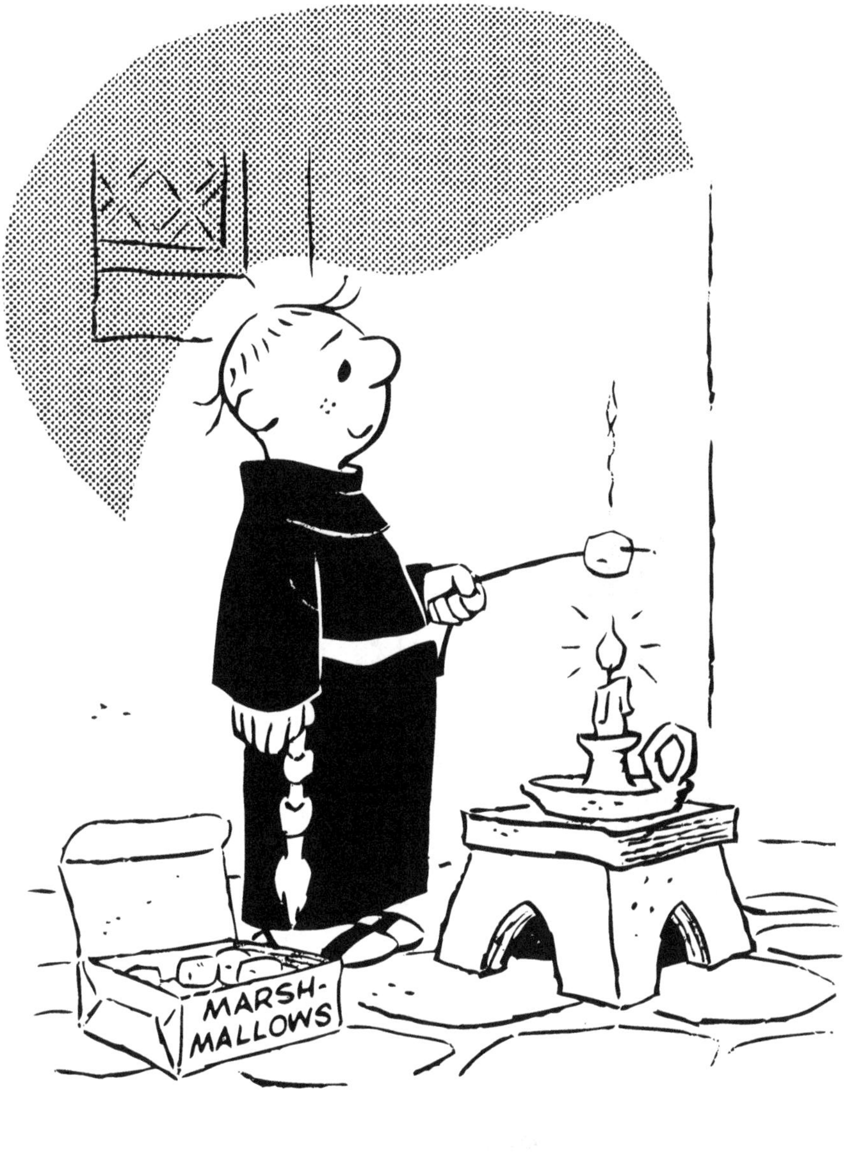
MARSH-
MALLOWS

"Bulbsnatcher!"

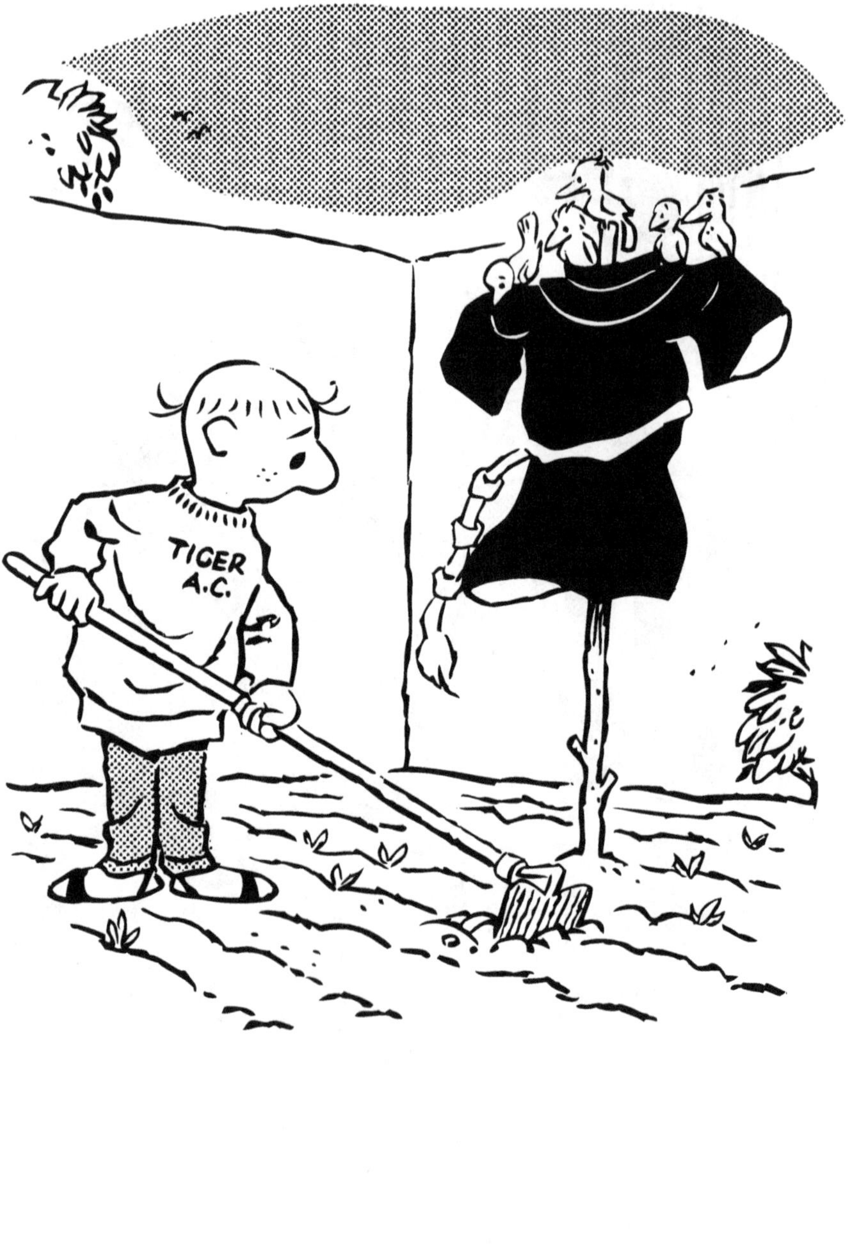
TIGER
A.C.

"It says: You like people and
have a host of friends."

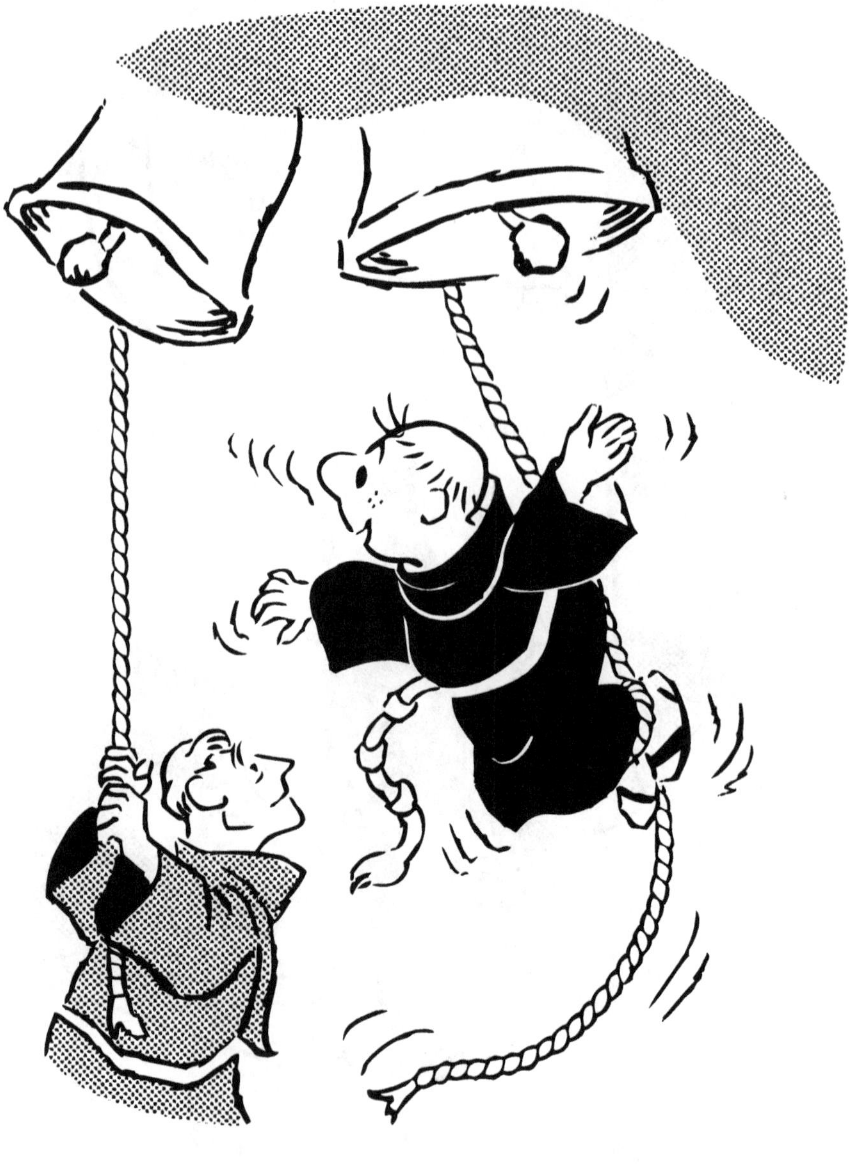

"Look, Charlie. No hands!"

"Well, that's your good deed for today!"

"No, this isn't your Aunt Mamie!"

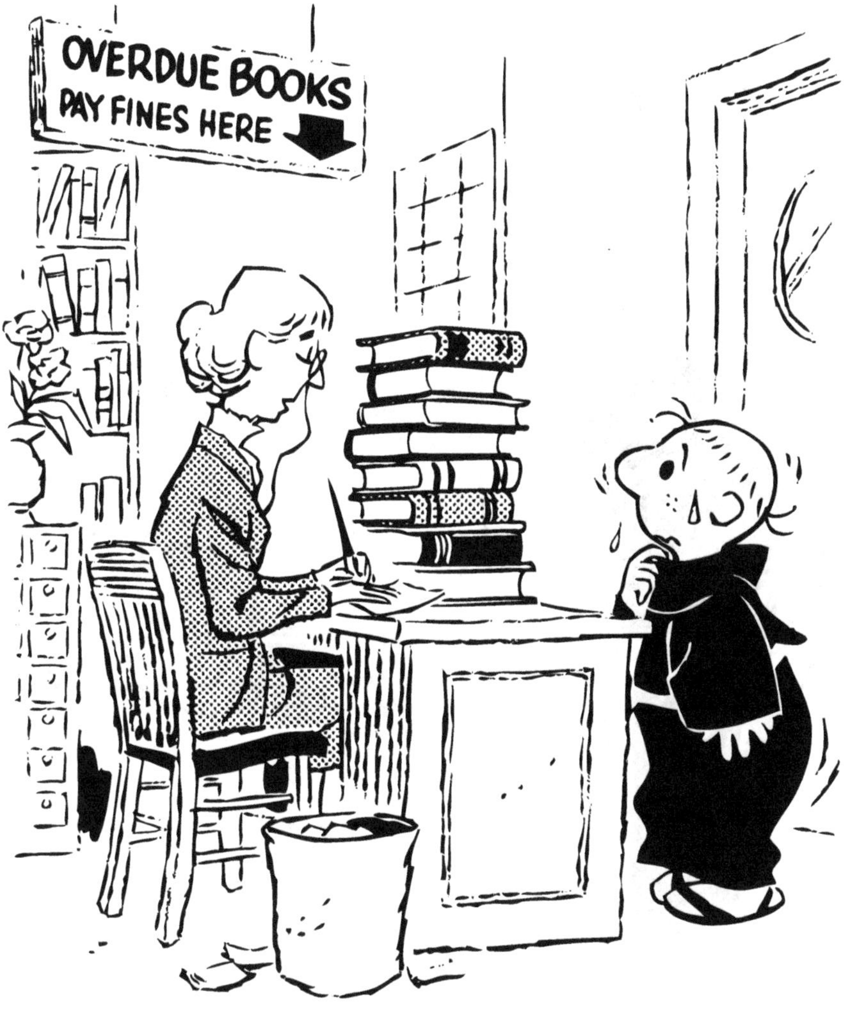
OVERDUE BOOKS
PAY FINES HERE

"That comes to $37.00 ... even."

"It's our 'Company Car.'"

"Thank goodness, the Ten Commandments
finally arrived."

"I'll tell you one thing, Rocky, you can't solve your problem by running away from it."

"Please, lady. Off the toes! Off the toes!"

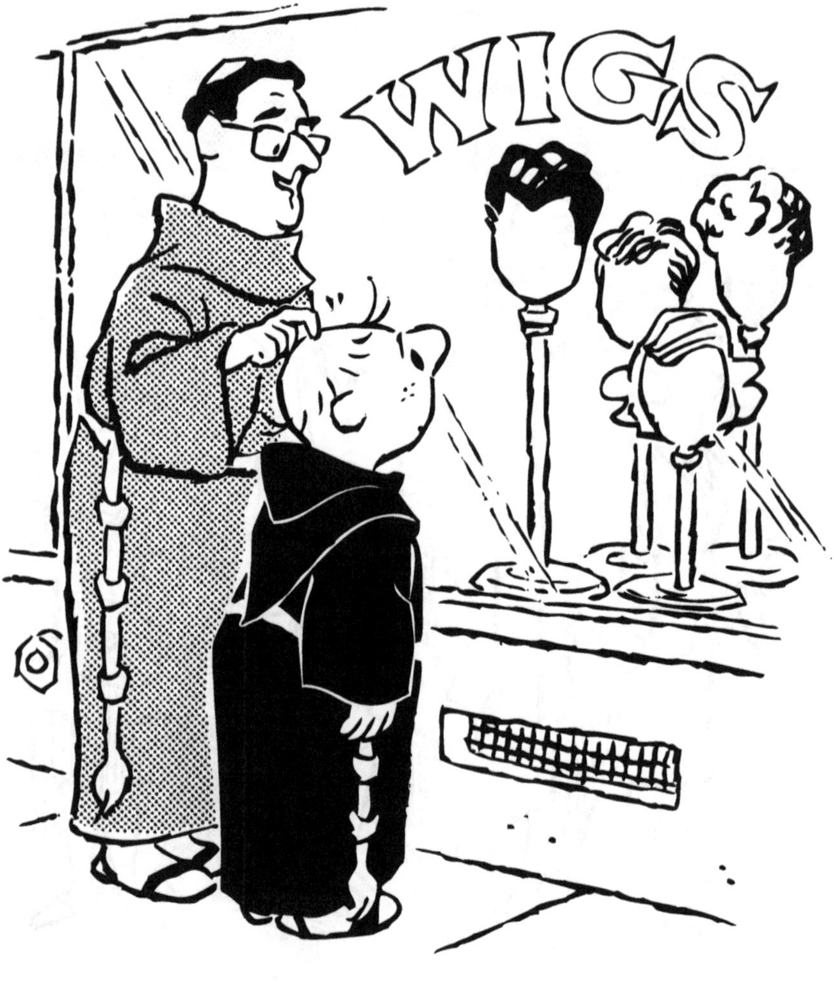
WIGS

"Eat your heart out."

"If I get my license it'll be a miracle, huh?"

"See that Brother Juniper takes
these pills religiously."

"You mean you don't give clerical discounts?"

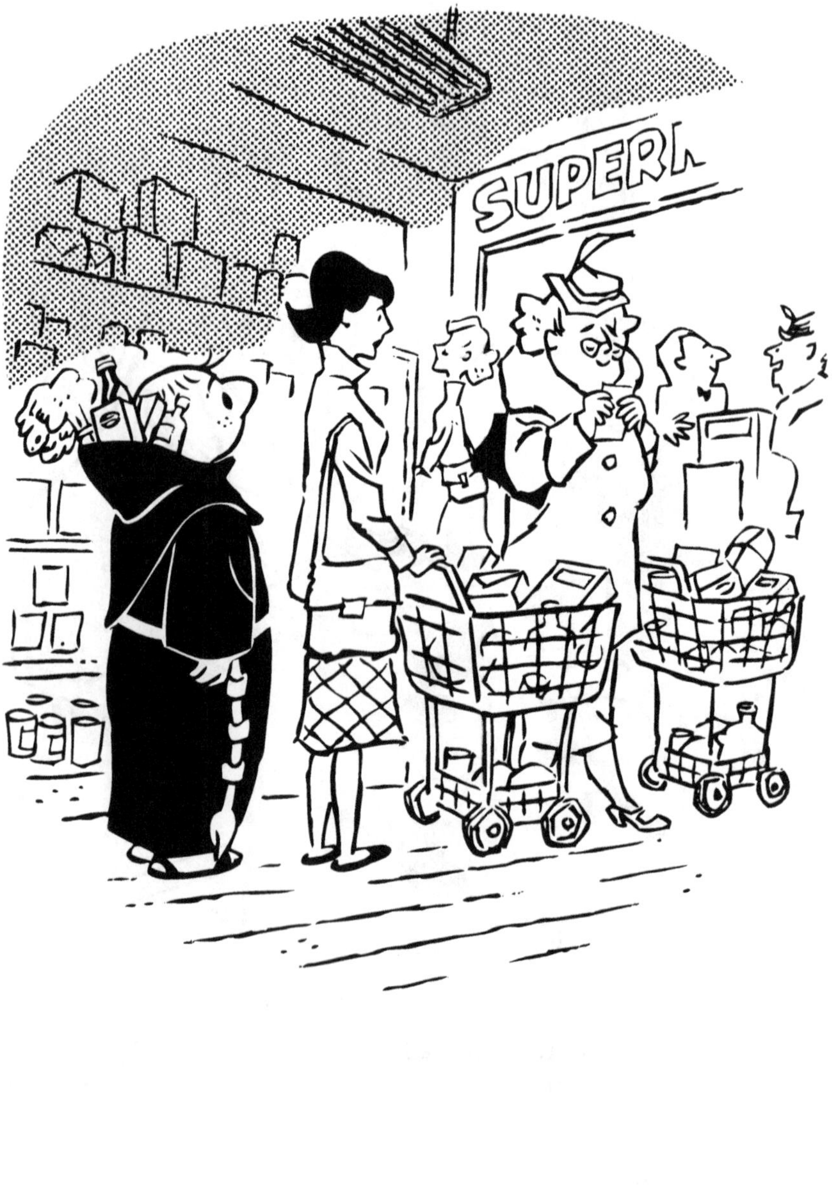
SUPERM

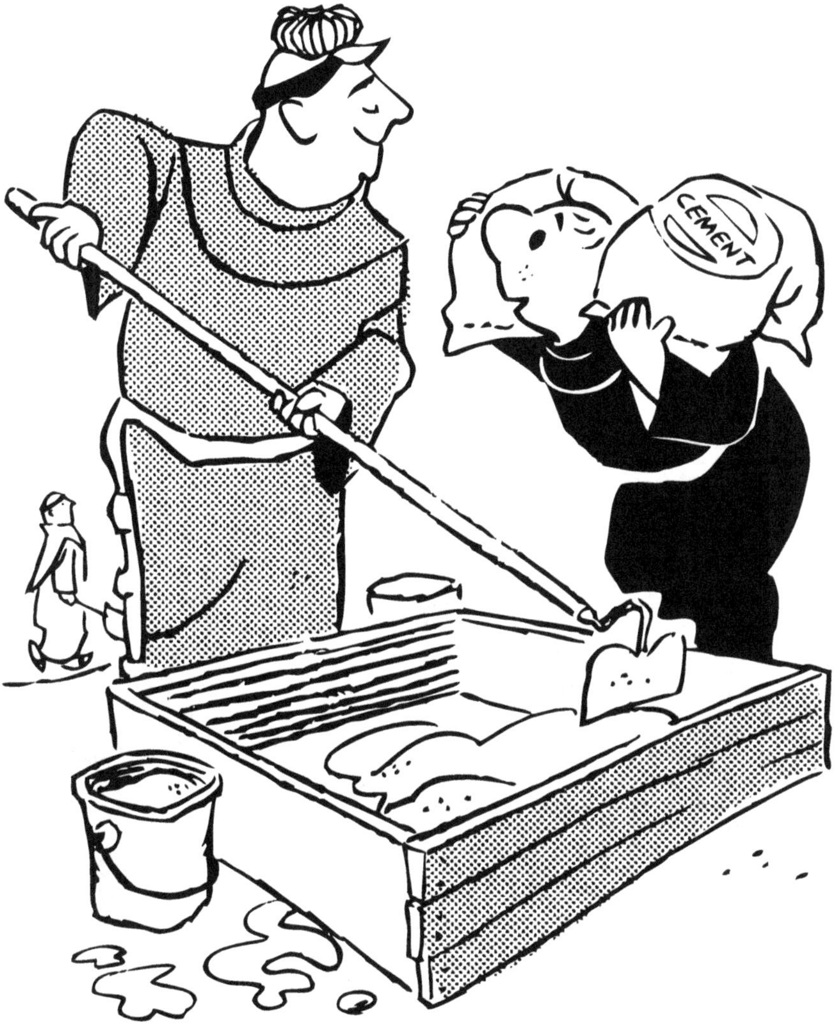
CEMENT

"One lump or two?"

"Something in a stylish stout?"

"Where's that feller who said I couldn't
hit the side of a barn door?"

"Well, that's the way the ball bounces."

"Bring me the Business Man's Lunch, please."

"I'll spot you twenty points, okay?"

"It's either the onions or Young Widder Jones."

"What in heaven's name is Brother
Juniper doing on Alcatraz?"

"Will you please lift me up, sir?"

"Wait up. I left my sandals under the seat!"

"Which troop do you belong to, young man?"

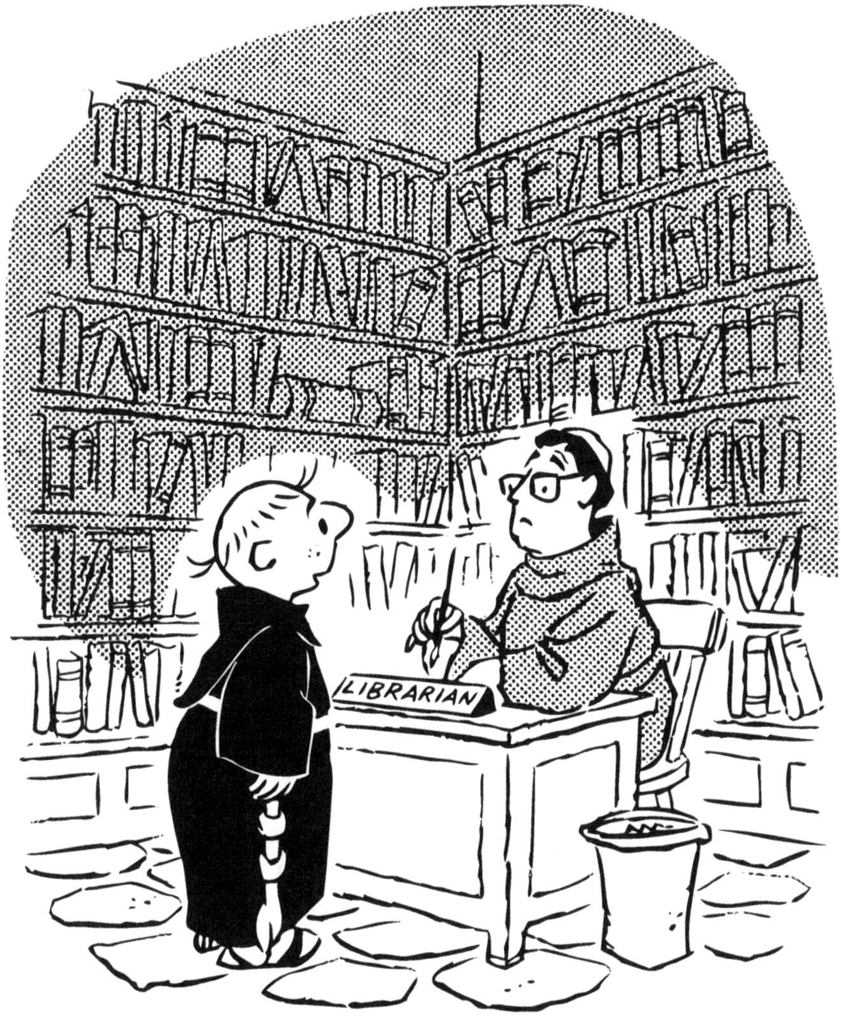
LIBRARIAN

"Got anything to read?"

"... and to make my crust crispy,
I add a little plaster of paris."

"Why do I hafta tuck in my shirt? Look at him!"

"Brother Juniper, will you be our den mother?"

"I don't know who he is. He came with the cereal."

"Brother Juniper is away. This is his answering service."

"I don't know about those headaches, but I feel sure
I can clear up that stiff neck."

"Do praying knees hurt as
much as scrubbing knees?"

"How much is a scared prayer worth?"

"He was bad enough when he could only talk."

"This going to bed with the chickens is a hard life!"

"Of course, monkscloth is always very dependable."

"Now that you mention it, there
is a family resemblance."

"I always carry a spare."

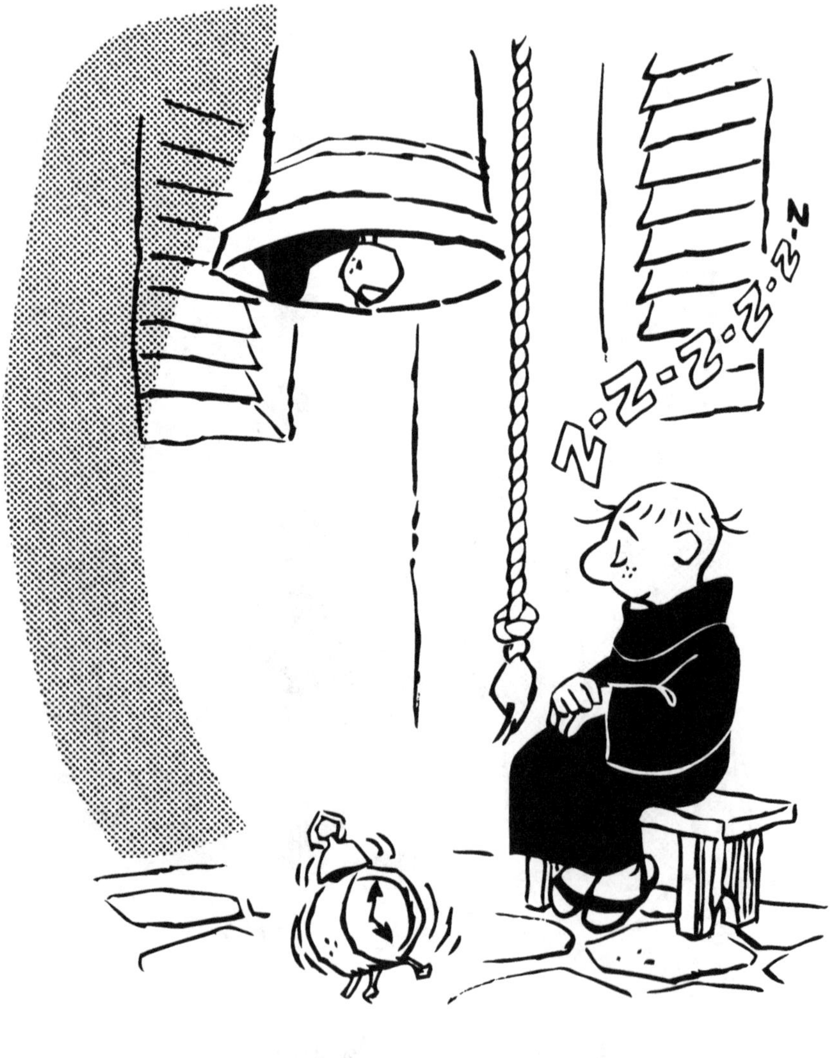

Z-Z-Z-Z-Z-Z-Z

"Isn't this where we came in?"

"We can help a lot of people 'cause
we have such a low overhead."

"This looks like a good place to stop."

Complimentary eBook Downloads

Due to retailer restrictions it is not possible to bundle an eBook with a physical book. However, I believe anyone purchasing a brick-sized "Definitive" collection of cartoons should also be able to enjoy those cartoons on their computers and eReader devices without having to buy the same book in a different format. I will eventually release the eBook version of this collection but until then owners of the physical hardback will be able to download the non-DRM electronic versions of each of the eight books in the Brother Juniper series in the formats of their choice through the website www.BrotherJuniper.com for free. The eBook version of *The Definitive Brother Juniper* will also be available to hardback owners for free when it is released.

If you would like to be notified when the eBook version of *The Definitive Brother Juniper* is released please visit www.BrotherJuniper.com and sign up for the email newsletter or "Like" us at www.facebook.com/BrotherJuniperProject.

To receive your free eBook downloads visit **www.BrotherJuniper. com/definitive** . You will be prompted to flip to a page in this book and type in the specified word (example: What is the 3rd word on page 485? Answer: like). Then download the password-protected ZIP files containing the eBook format of your choice. Unzip the ZIP files using the following password: definitive486

Then simply transfer the unzipped files to your electronic devices and enjoy a slightly more portable version of everyone's favorite monk.

Thank you for supporting the Brother Juniper Rejuvenation Project!

Sincerely,
Adam Nicolai

Inside Brother Juniper

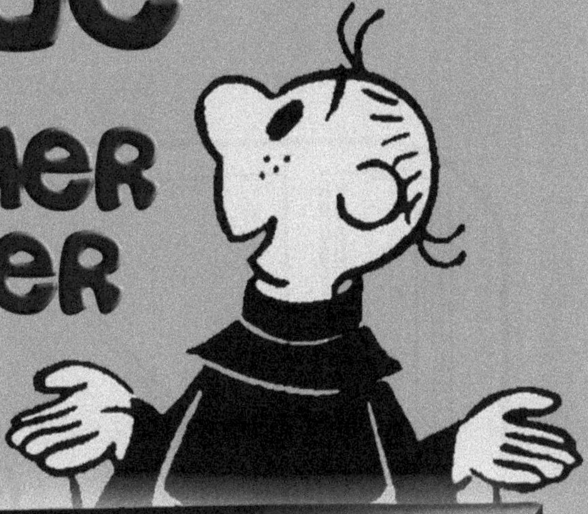

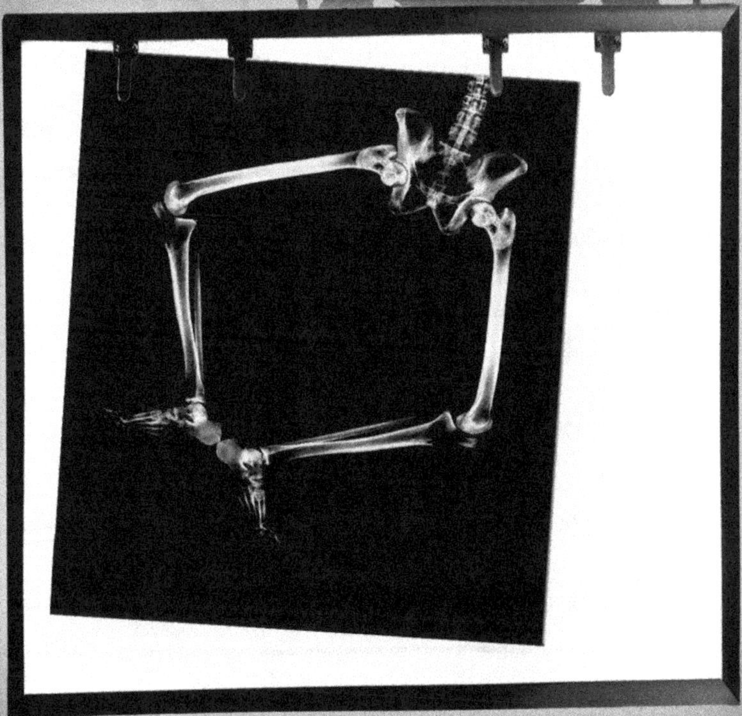

By Father Justin 'Fred' McCarthy

Empty-Grave Extended Edition

"Well, if it isn't the last of the big spenders."

"You don't LOOK like a dry cleaner."

"Let's keep looking till we find
one that cheats a little."

"Best places in town for an eye for an eye,
and a tooth for a tooth."

"Good ol' Brother Juniper. Right
down the groove every time."

"Ever have a feeling YOU'RE being watched?"

"Don't just stand there; GET LOST!"

"Been out playing with the kids again, I see!"

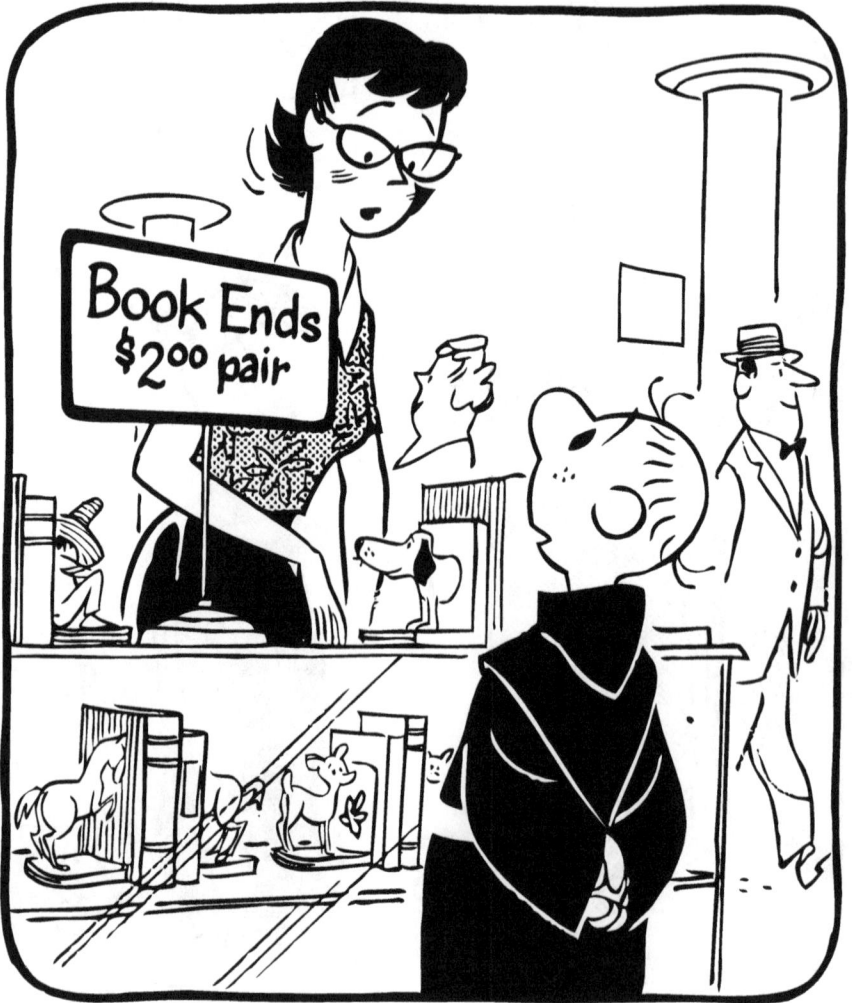

"How much for ONE bookend?
I only have one book."

"What position do I play?"

"I only taught him to sit up and beg.
Panhandling on corners was his own idea."

"I'd be ashamed to ring the big one.
I only fixed them a light lunch."

"This ought to be a good attention-getter."

"Don't bark at me, young man!"

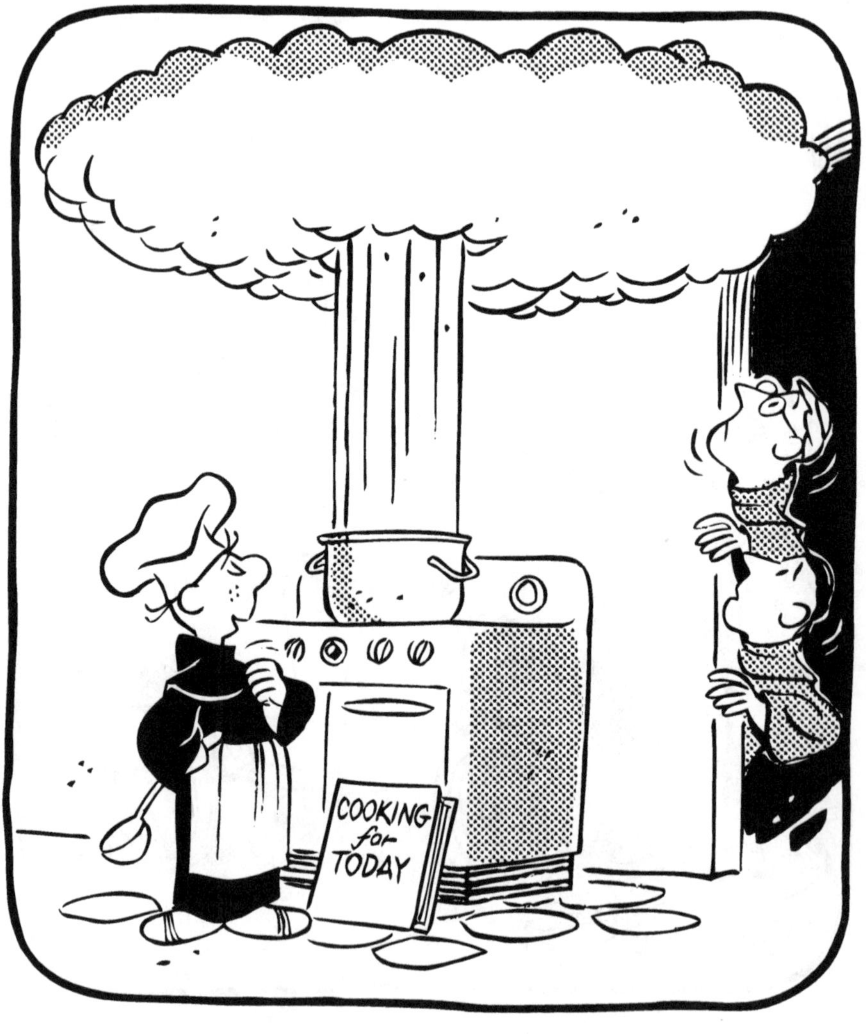
COOKING for TODAY

"It's mushroom soup, why?"

"In a good year, I'll average over
a hundred crows to the acre."

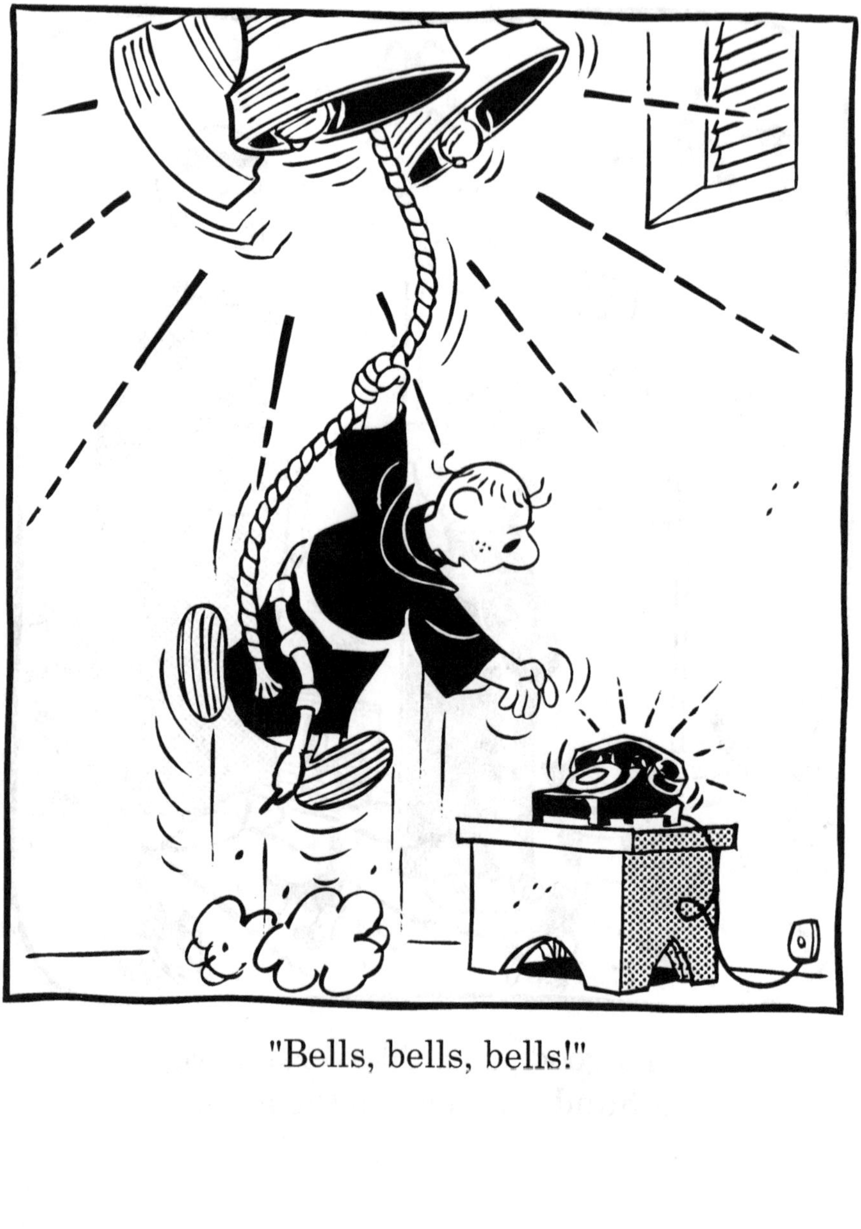

"Bells, bells, bells!"

"Well, he finally did it: crossed
an apple tree with a pine tree!"

"There's too much audience participation
around here to suit me."

"April showers bring May flowers!"

"See if there's moss growing on his north side."

"Aw, go climb an Alp!"

"No, that isn't when it was built;
that's the license number!"

"Aw, you can refund it more
cheerfully than THAT!"

"All right, who put the coconut
in my bowling bag?"

"It's not really a bad umbrella...
except when there's an east wind."

"The grass doesn't just SEEM greener in
the other fellow's yard ... it IS greener!"

"All right, you can go to the ball game...
but don't let me catch you sneaking
off to visit your grandmother instead."

"... greatest invention since the wheel.
It's called 'The Hammock.'"

"Something tells me Brother Juniper
may have said more than his prayers."

"If you don't WANT to be helped across the street, ma'am, I'd advise you start running."

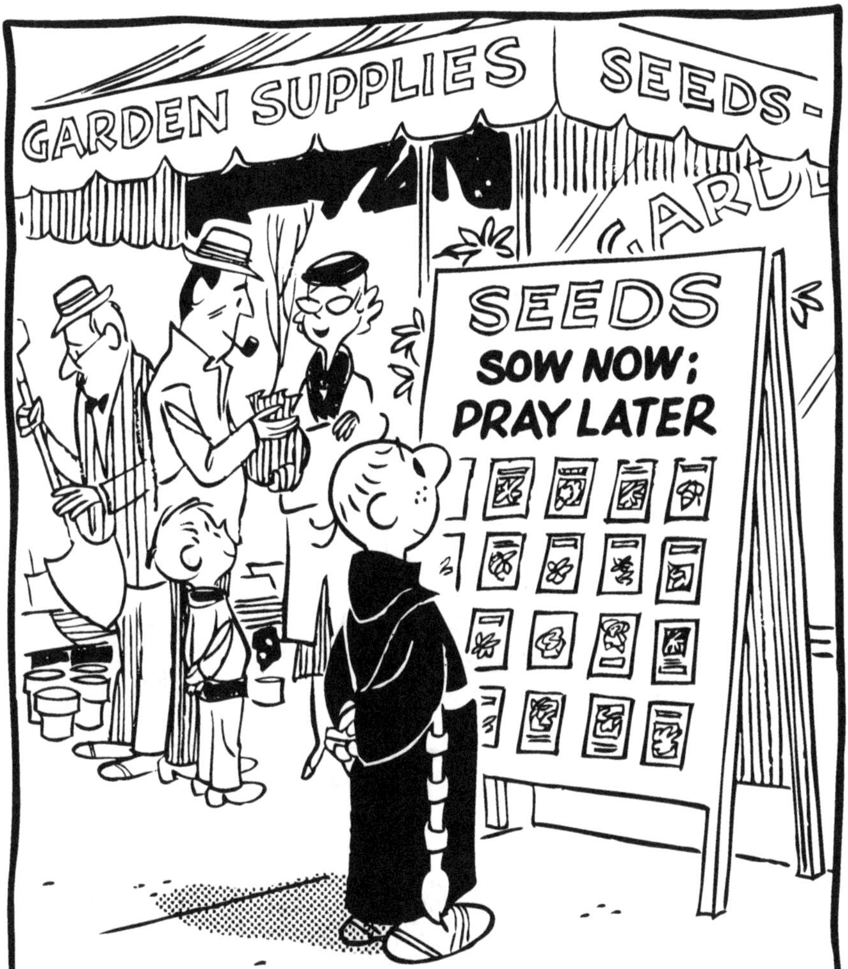
GARDEN SUPPLIES
SEEDS-
SEEDS
SOW NOW;
PRAY LATER

"His spring fever has broken, but I'm
afraid he's contracted summer lethargy."

"WHO are you calling a statistic?"

"Funny, you don't look a bit like your pictures."

"Wouldn't it be keen if they'd let us
do our HOMEWORK in cement?"

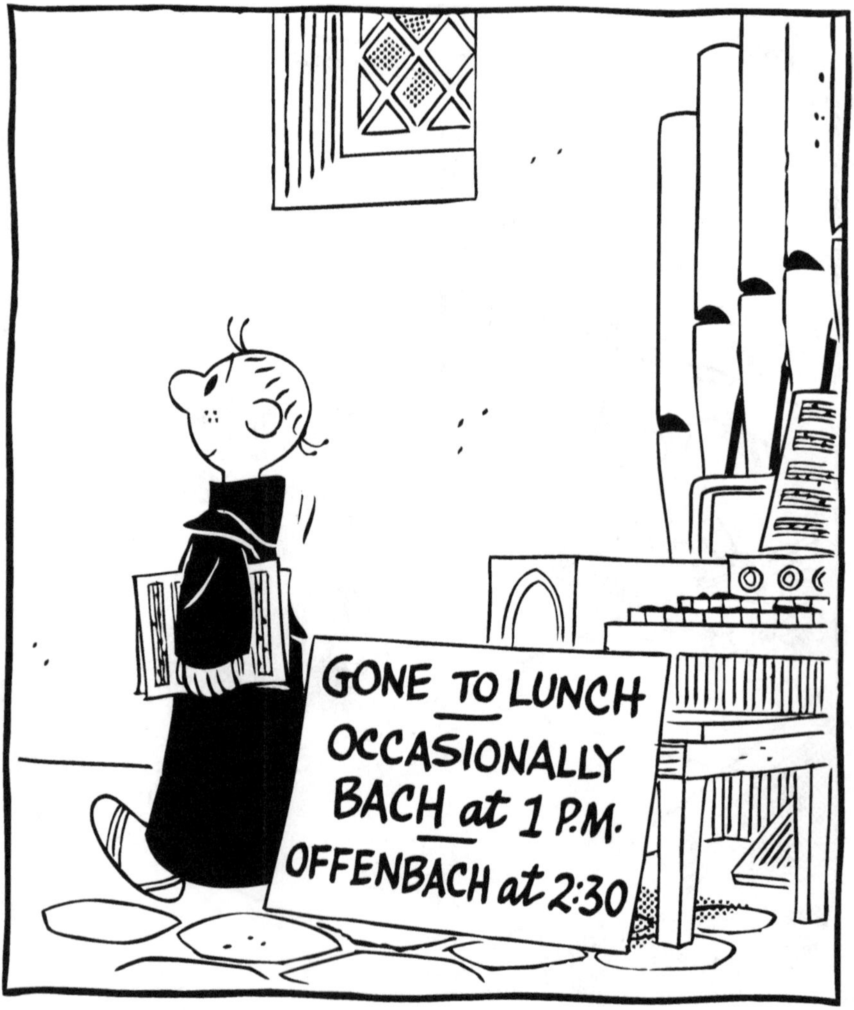
GONE TO LUNCH
OCCASIONALLY
BACH at 1 P.M.
OFFENBACH at 2:30

"Well, anyway, we played our usual
conservative brand of baseball."

"To err is human, but this is ridiculous!"

"Nice to see you, Ed. Sorry I forgot
to return your golf clubs."

"Say, this should be good!"

"An anonymous letter? Who from?"

"You can always tell by the number of dents
in the wing if the pilot is any good."

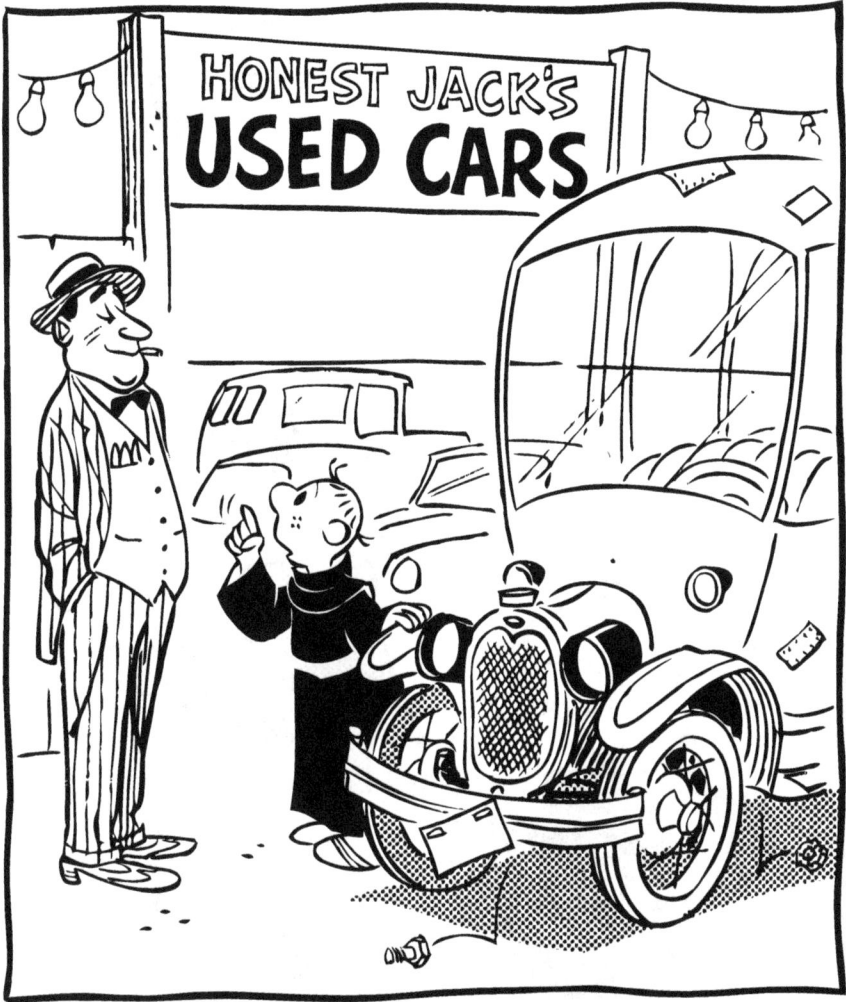

"Before I agree to sell, will you promise
to see that it gets a good home?"

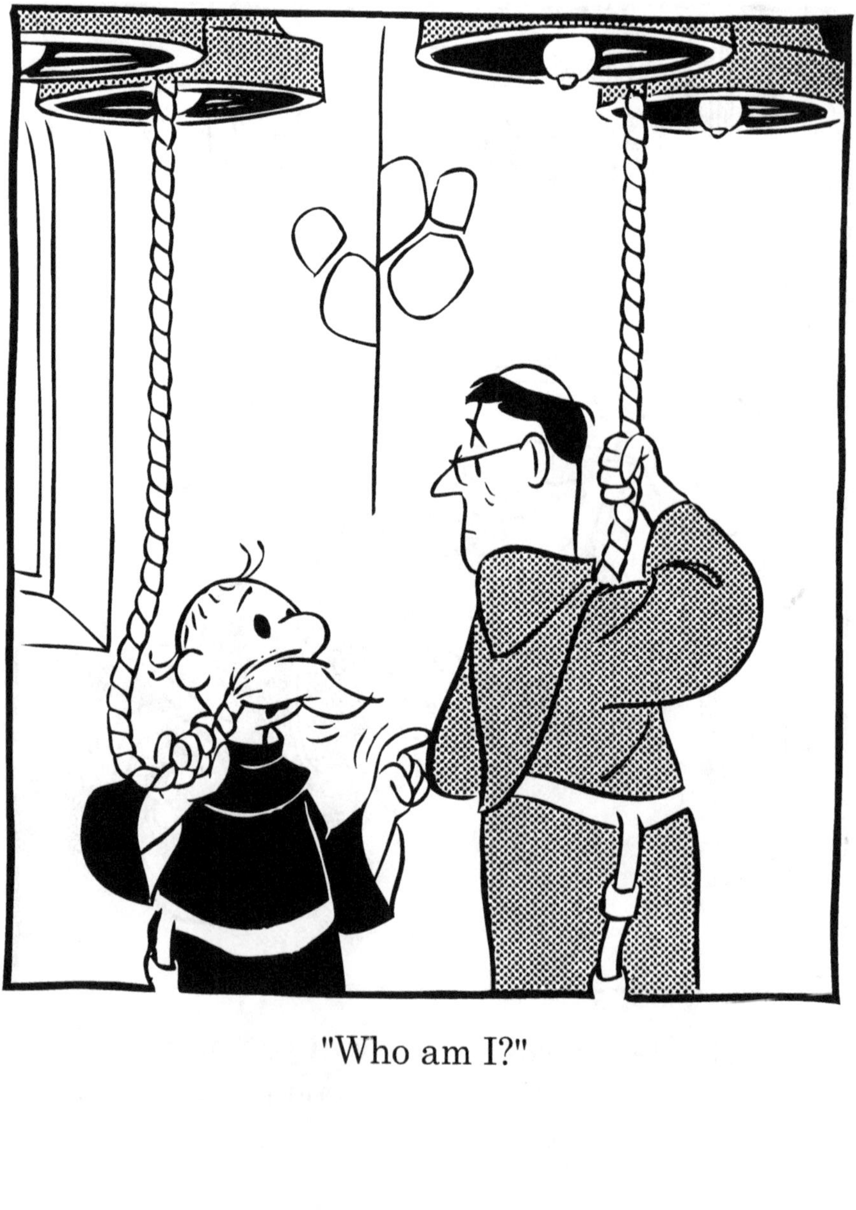

"Who am I?"

"If he could only hit half as hard as he can pray."

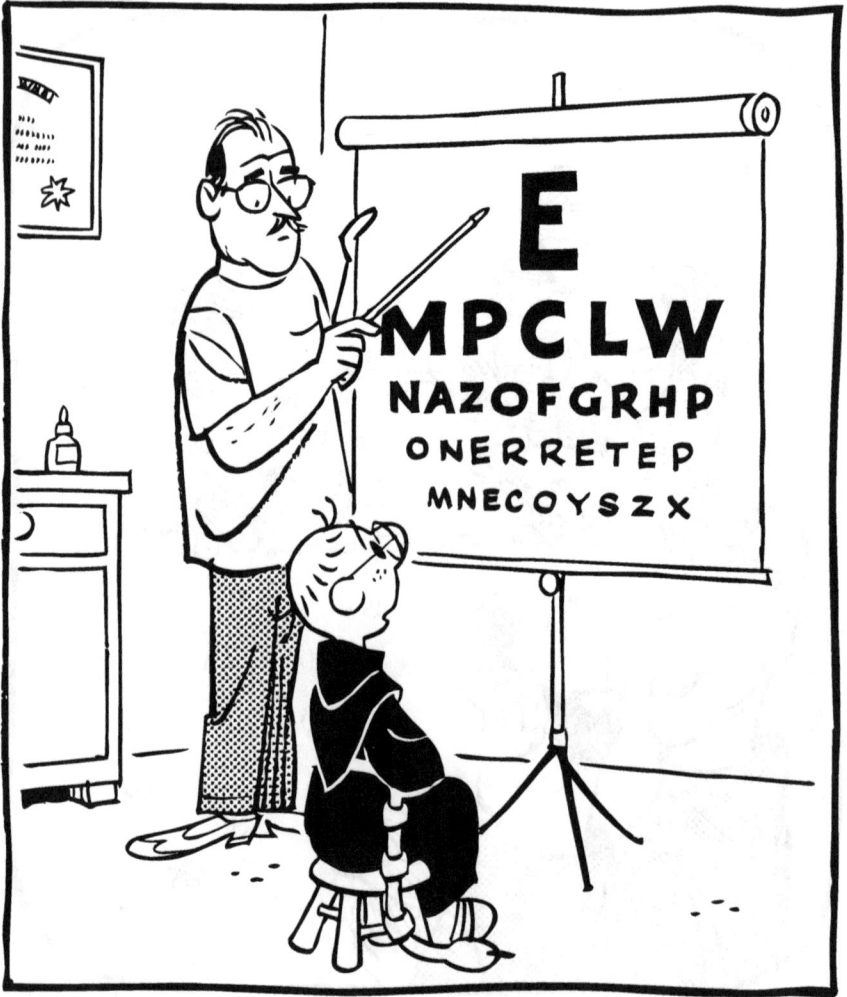

"Honestly, the message seems a bit garbled."

"What this country needs is a
good 5-cent ANYTHING!"

"...where angels fear to tread."

"Looks like the 2:05 is running ahead of schedule!"

"Last year I planted chrysanthemums,
but they were too hard to pronounce."

"You're in more of a hurry to reach the
pearly gates than the law allows."

"You just add water and...
bang! 'INSTANT WEEDS!'"

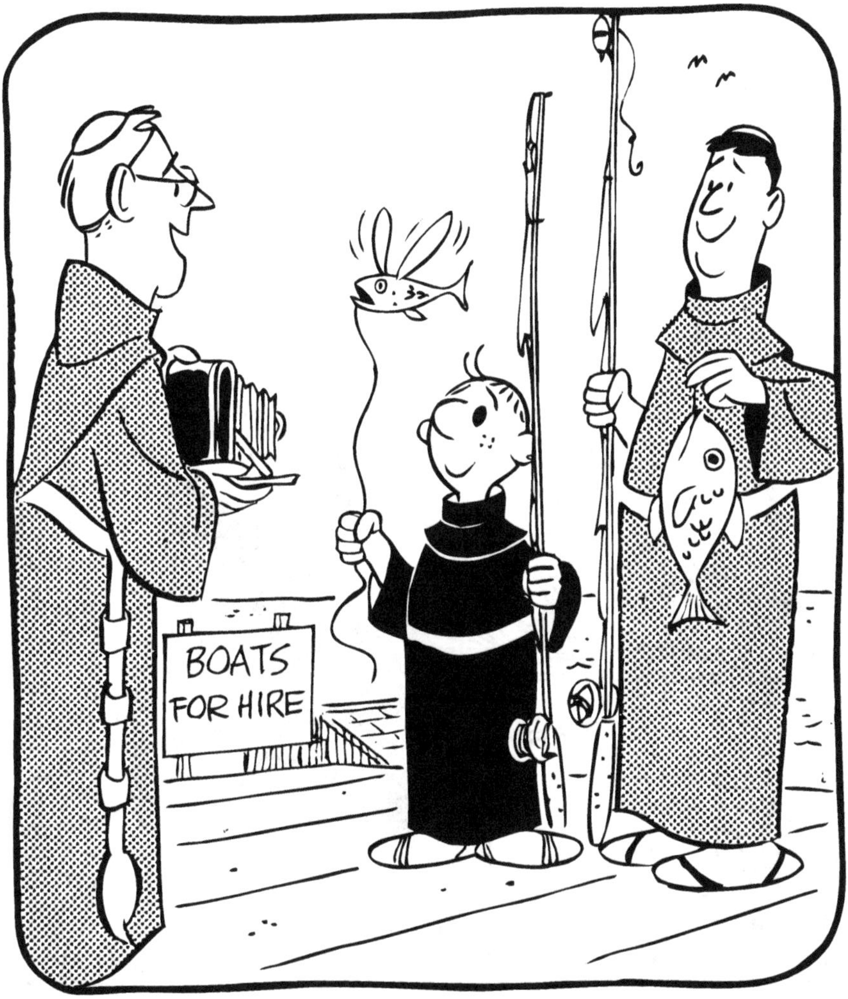
BOATS
FOR HIRE

"Smile!"

"Like they say, one picture is
worth a thousand words."

"I always put in quicksand.
It makes the days fly by."

"This is the part I hate: having to go
back and face the cats empty-handed."

"Somebody must have forgotten
to feed the mosquitoes."

"Oh, excuse me sonny. I thought
YOU were the litter basket."

"The reason it costs so much is
because the sand is IMPORTED!"

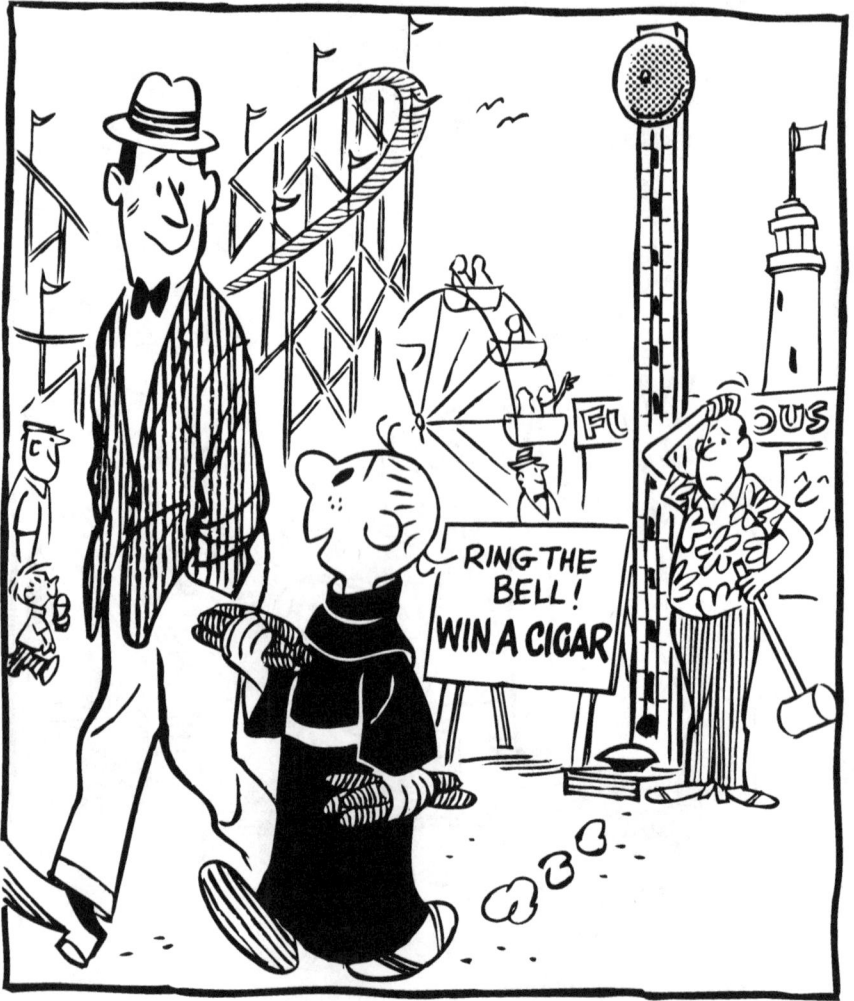

"That was a CINCH. Where I work,
we have to ring TEN bells at once!"

"Well, that makes the tenth straight year I've been
left off the best-dressed men's list."

"Funny thing, in my profession we
have to tell 'em to come UP FRONT."

"Know any good hymns?"

"Not NOW! I'll tell you when."

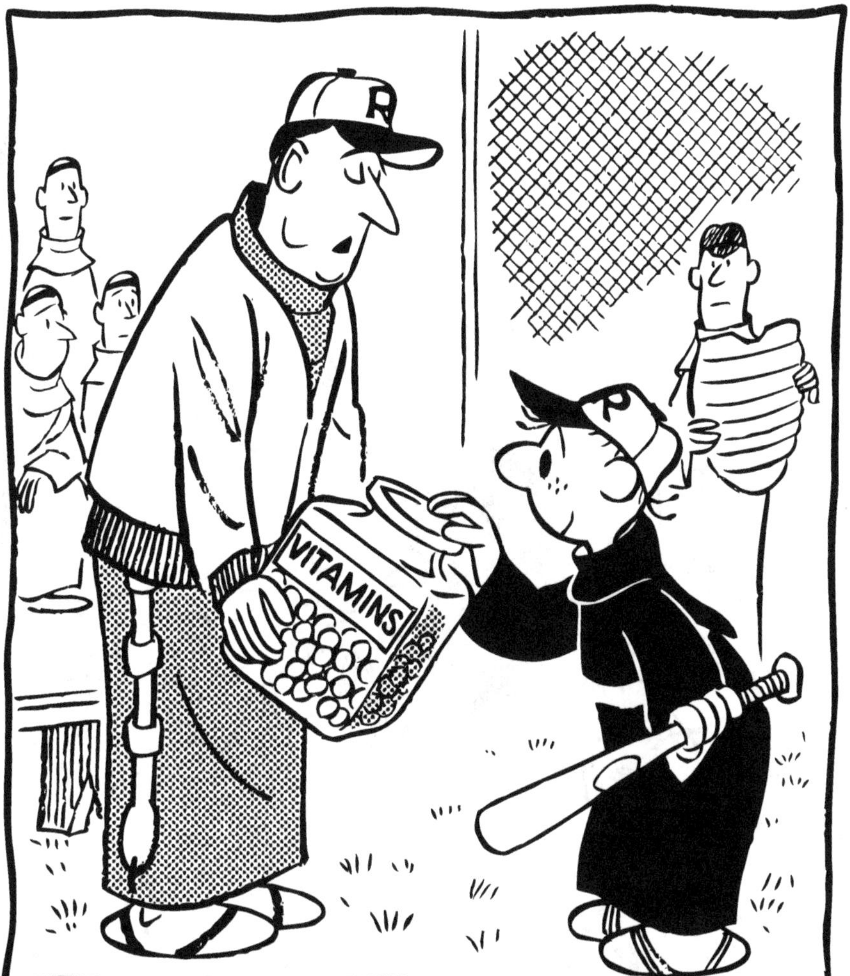
VITAMINS

"Take two, and hit to left."

"Wait'll next year!"

"That's enough. That's ENOUGH!"

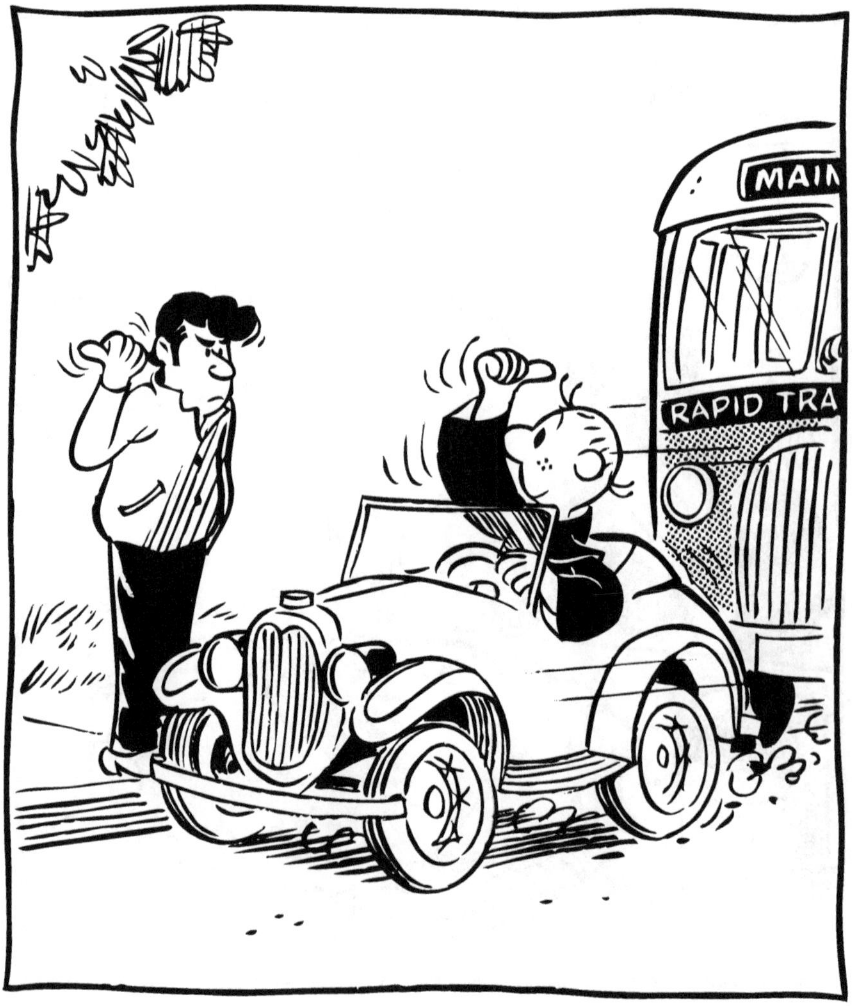
MAIN
RAPID TRA

"But I'd make a terrible angel. I
haven't even had pre-flight training."

"Well now, let's just take a look
at that little ol' rule book."

"Will you please stop defying gravity!"

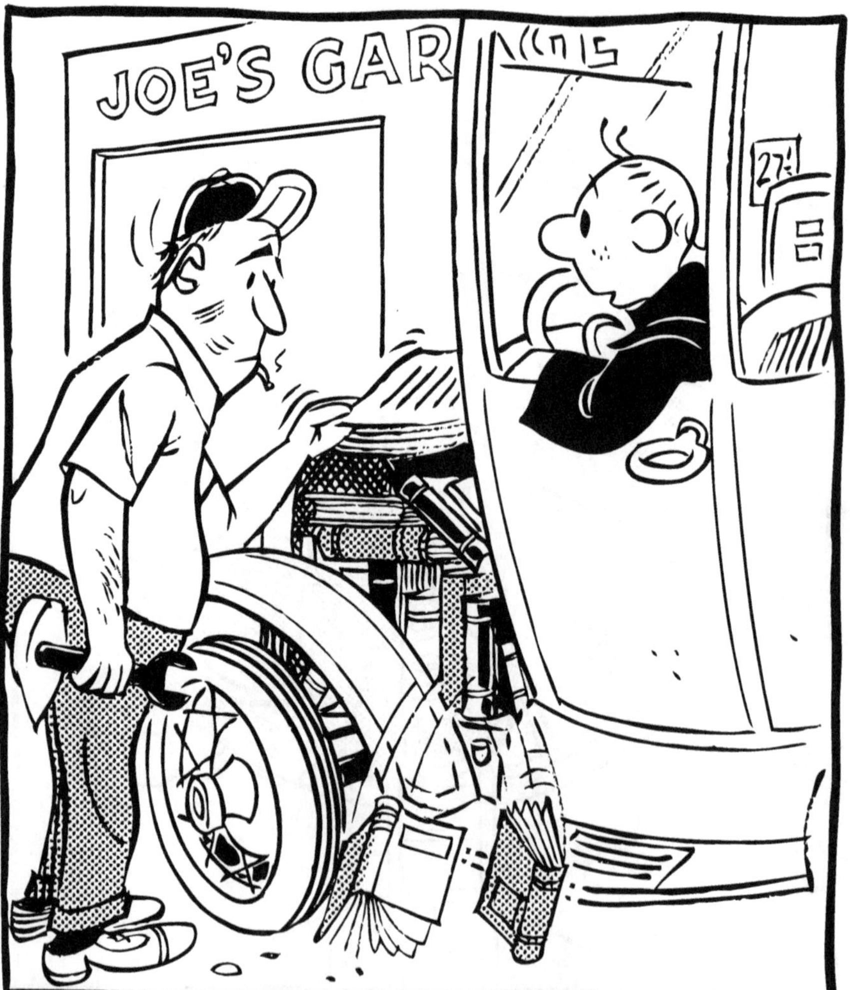
JOE'S GAR

"The engine's in the back."

"Oh, thank goodness, the angels'
costumes have arrived!"

"How much do you charge for sick calls?"

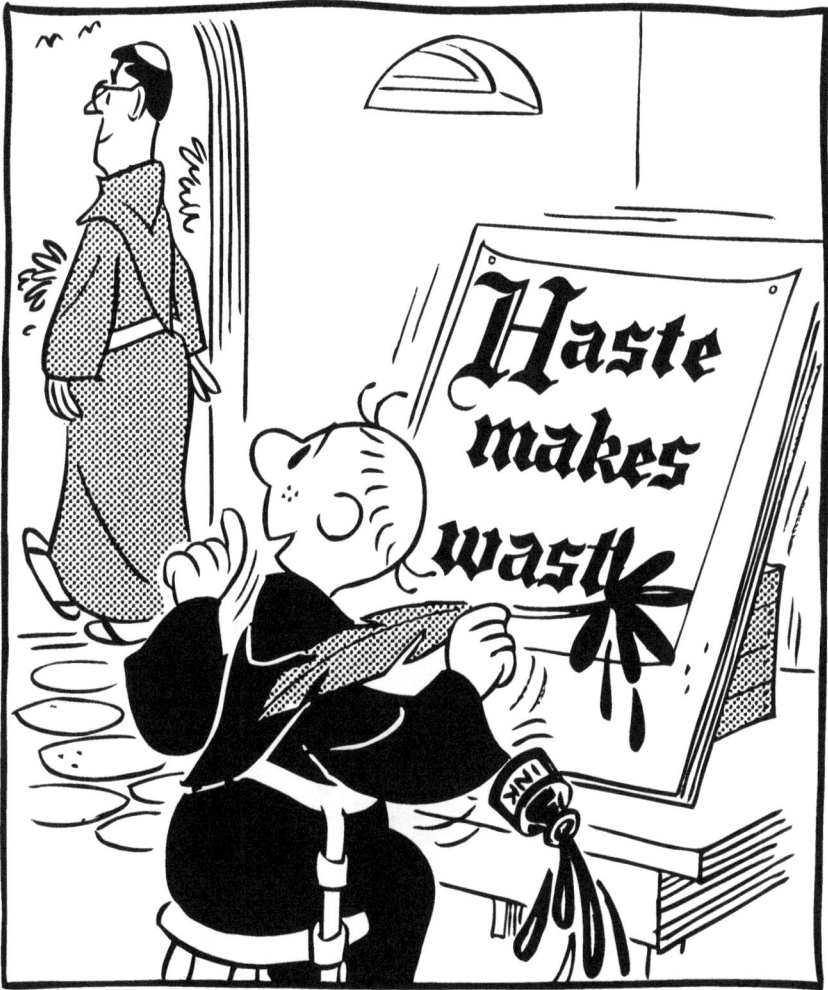

"Wait for me, Brother Egbert,
this won't take a second!"

"Mirror, mirror on the wall, who's
the baldest of them all?"

"I'd like a bottle of unsocialized medicine."

"... been an epidemic or something?"

"What do you mean, 'Is the sap still running?'"

"I've been calling 'Dial-A-Prayer,' but I keep getting the 6th Avenue Delicatessen."

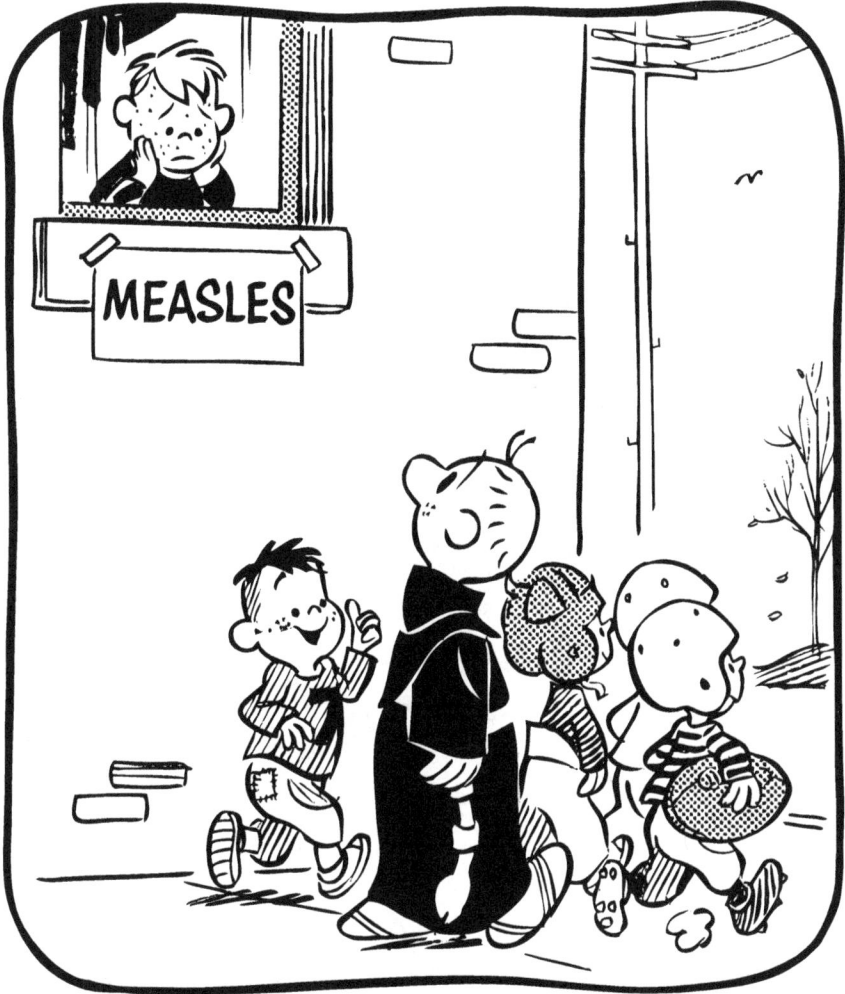

"Him? Oh, he's our lonesome end!"

"Reaching the bowling alley is easy;
it's the trip BACK I dread."

"... and don't forget to put the cat out."

"These aren't bad pennies, but they
keep coming BACK just the same."

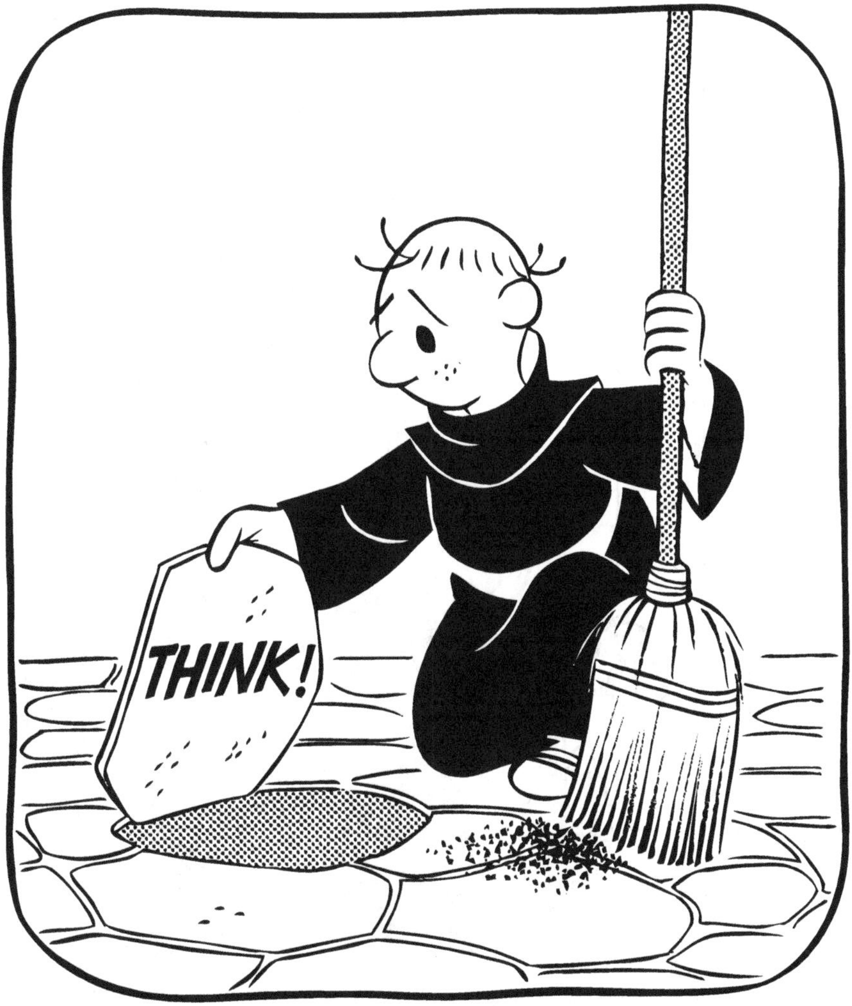
THINK!

"That refers to anybody over sixteen."

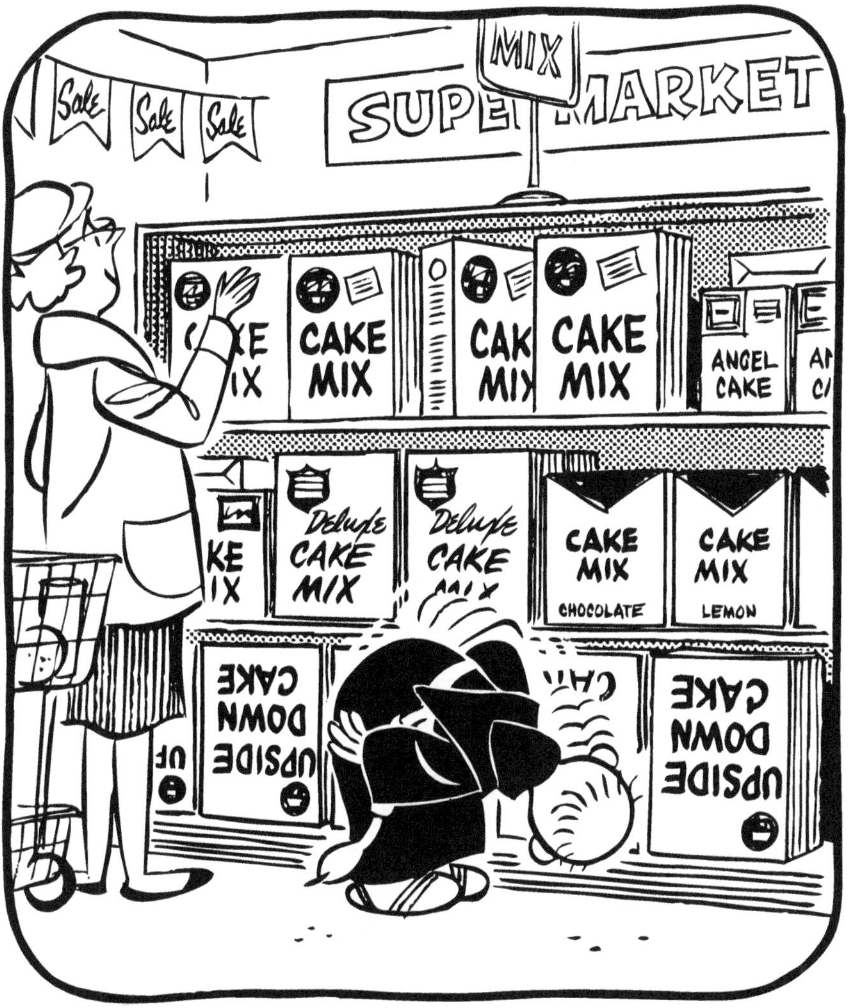

Sale
Sale
Sale
MIX
SUPER MARKET
CAKE MIX
CAKE MIX
CAKE MIX
ANGEL CAKE
Deluxe CAKE MIX
CAKE MIX CHOCOLATE
CAKE MIX LEMON
UPSIDE DOWN CAKE
UPSIDE DOWN CAKE

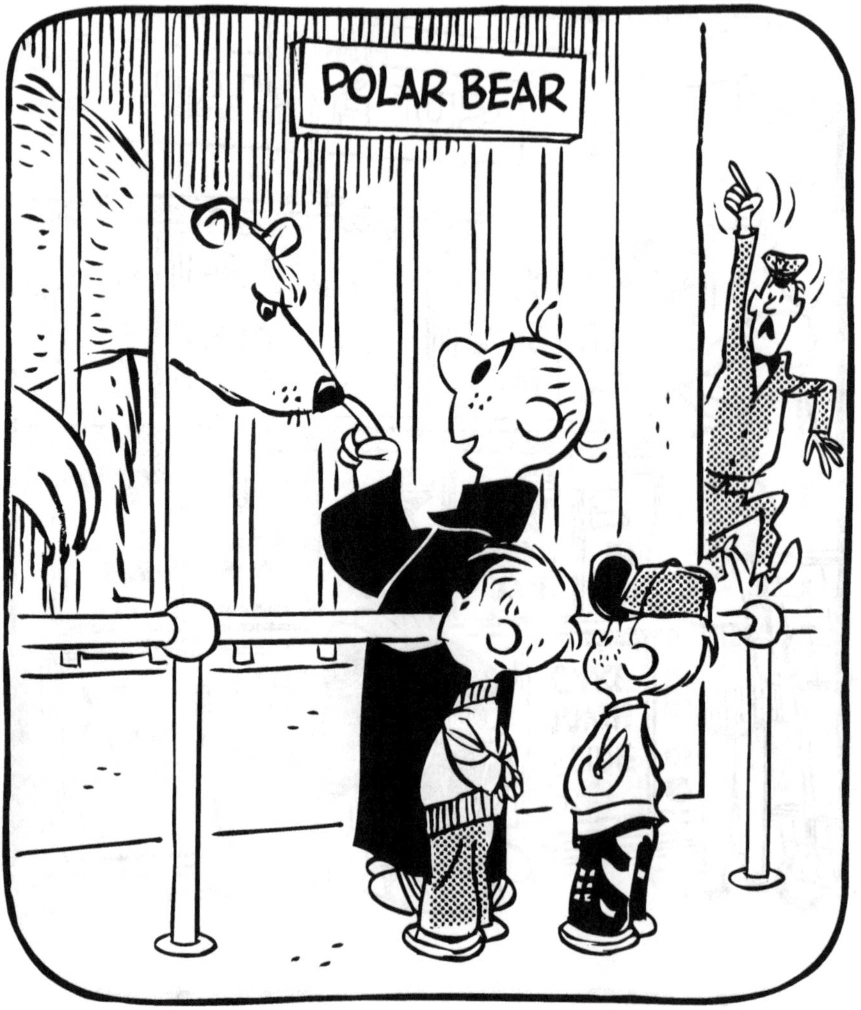
POLAR BEAR

"Cold nose; warm heart."

"When you order the 'chef's surprise'
that's the chance you take."

"But in this case, you're SUPPOSED to let
your left hand know what your right is doing."

"Let's see now ... have we forgotten anybody?"

"Now remember, just ONCE around the block."

"... or in the language of the layman ..."

"Ever notice when the sermon is
moving the people aren't?"

"Brother Juniper? Oh, he's out back
jacking up his status symbol."

"He's not much for feeding a cold, but
he's awful good at starving a fever."

"You show me a 'home where the buffalo roam,' and
I'll show you a messy living room."

"All right, you two. Turn in your halos!"

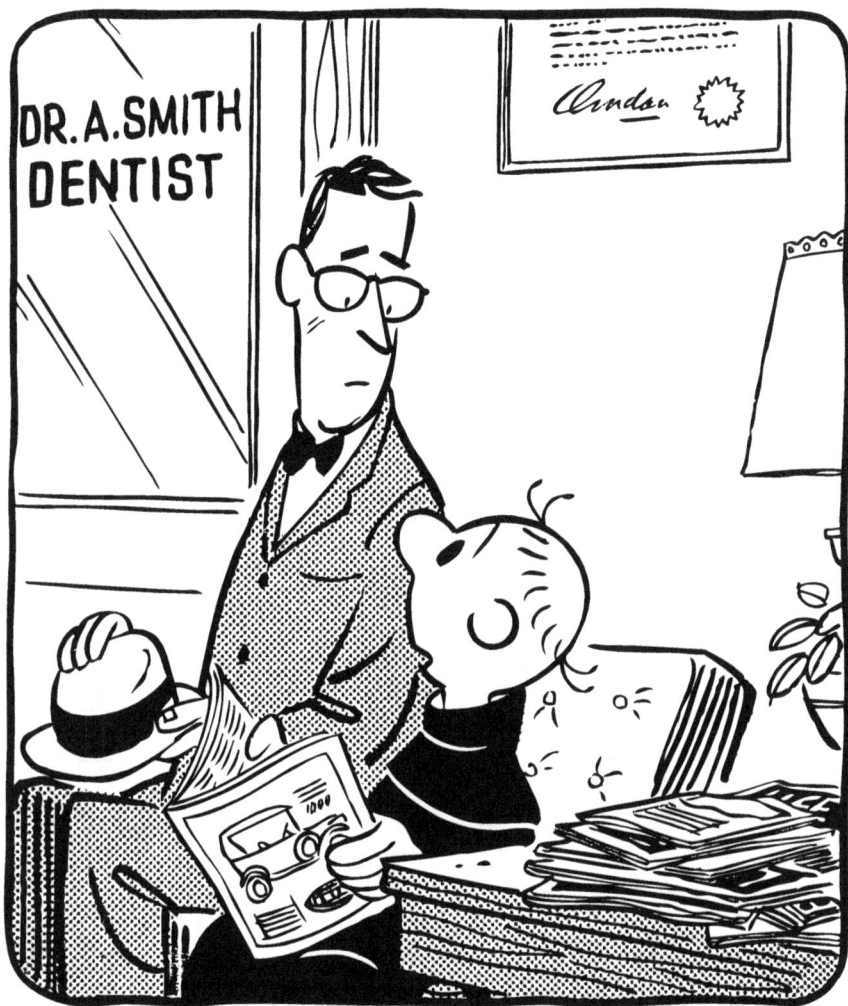

"I see where Calvin Coolidge
may run for President."

"I may have had my hand out, but I
certainly didn't intend to shake hands."

"Never mind which are stalactites and which are stalagmites. Did YOU leave the water running?"

"How do I know? Oh, just say a little bird told me."

"Reading comics around here
is NO LAUGHING MATTER."

"Brother Juniper would like to come
out and play basketball, kids, but
he has a pressing engagement."

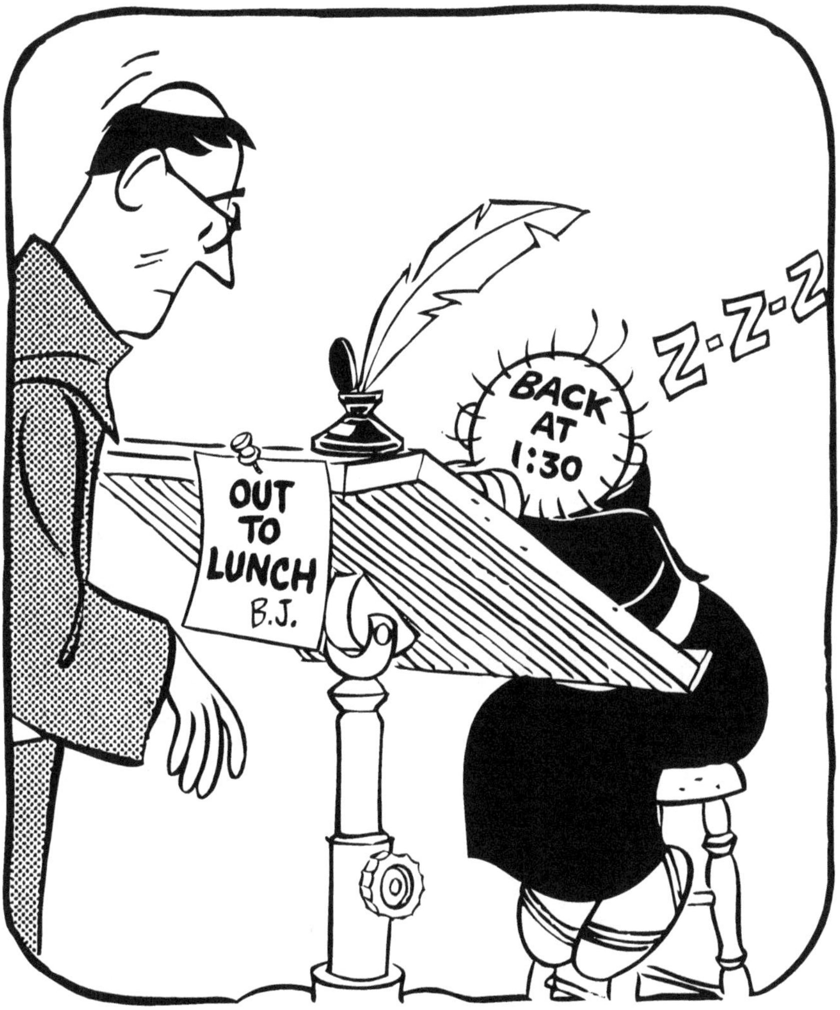
OUT TO LUNCH B.J.
BACK AT 1:30
Z-Z-Z

"I forgot to turn mine off last night!"

"What program am I watching?
Why I'm watching...er, uh...it's, uh...!"

"This is a fine time to lose your contact lenses!"

"Snow tires!"

"Looks like a victory for labor over management!"

"His first name's Ned, operator. 'N' as in
Nebuchadnezzar, 'E' as in Epaminondas,
'D' as in disestablishmentarianism.
Last name's...what's that, operator?"

"Not today, thanks. I'm expecting the doctor."

"Something tells me this is
the softest touch in town."

"I know, but they revoked his license.'"

"Praise the Lord and pass the ammunition!"

"Well, that's another year shot to heaven!"

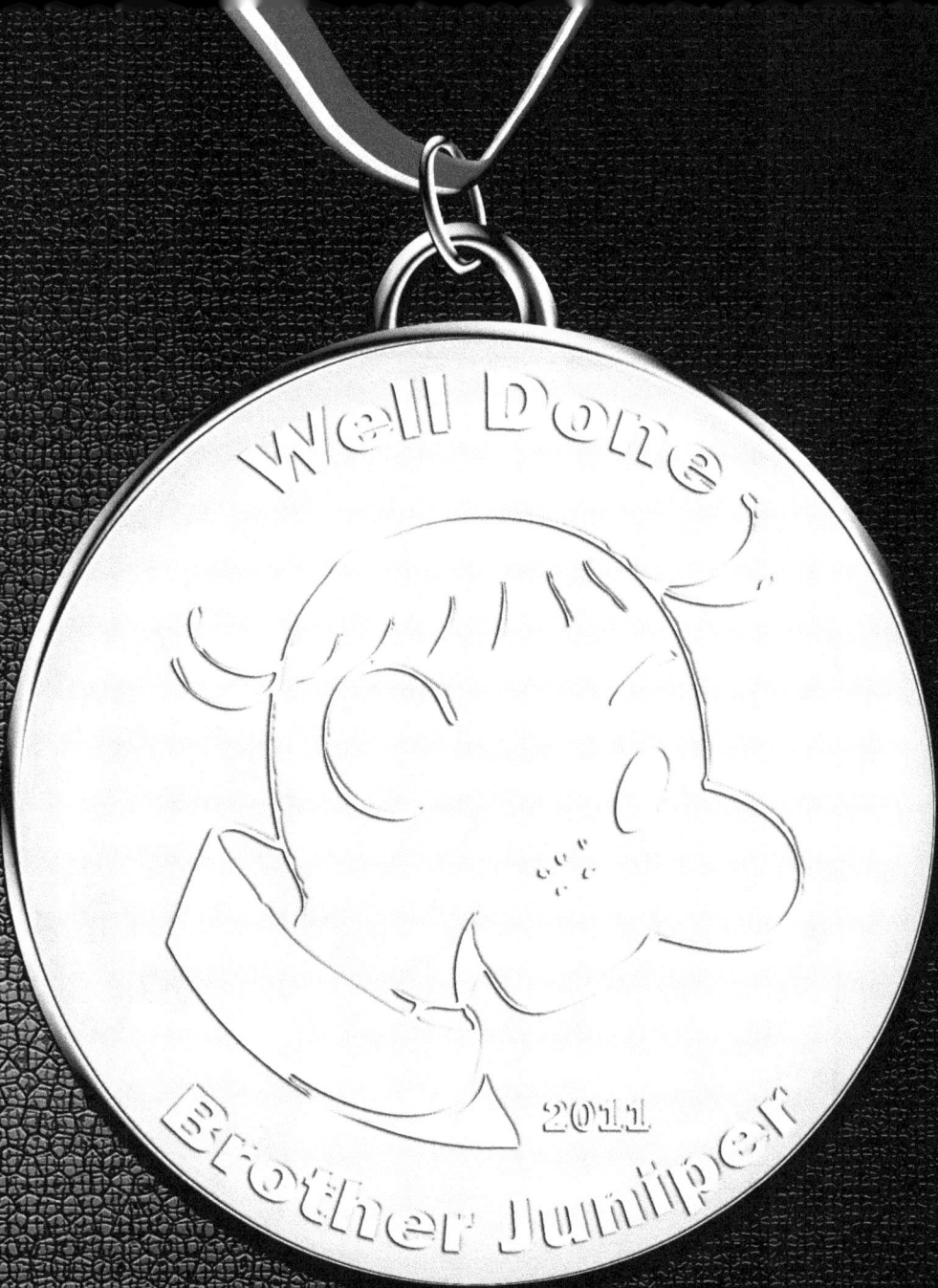

Well Done, Brother Juniper

2011

BY FATHER JUSTIN
'FRED' MCCARTHY

Empty-Grave Extended Edition

"Hiya, bud!"

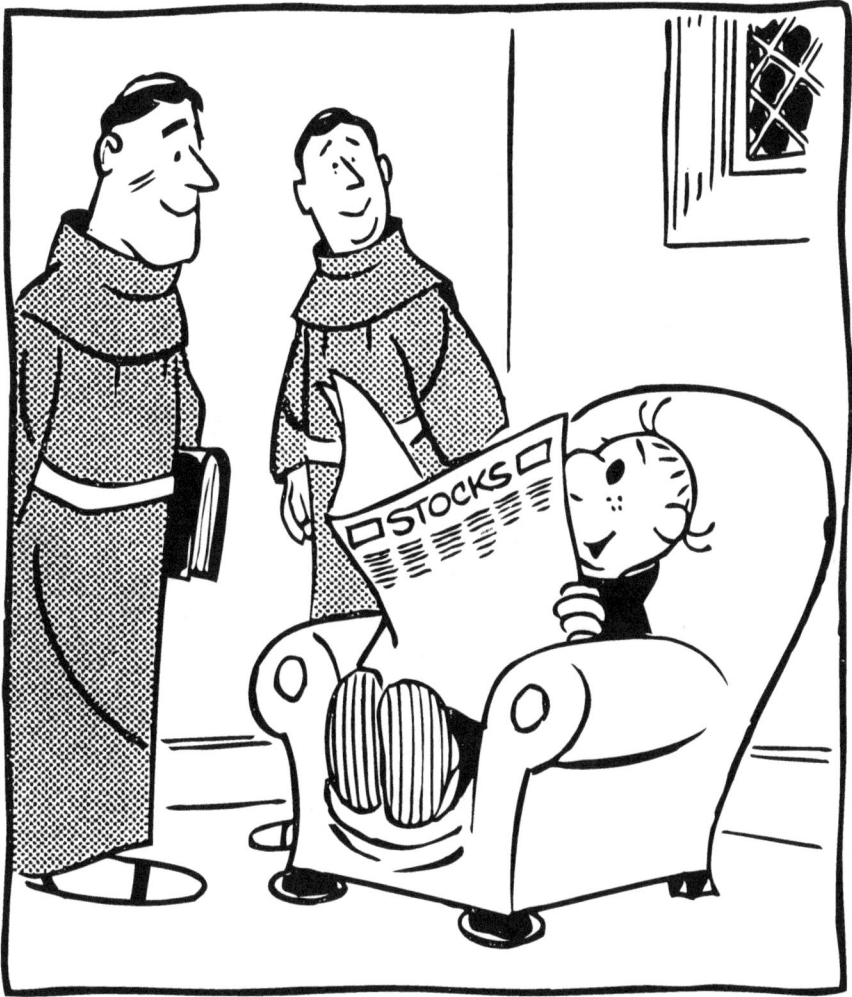

"If I didn't have a vow of poverty I estimate I'd have lost a cool half million on the stock market!"

"Chicken!"

"This is the job I hate. Giving him NOSEDROPS!"

"Don't blame me, chief. It was HIS idea!"

"Take two and hit to the left!"

"I think he's lost; THIS isn't
the way to the lion house!"

"Is it more blessed to kick than to receive?"

"Are you aware that there is no bounty on
pedestrians this time of year?"

"All right, I give up. How did it get there?"

"Nobody, but NOBODY, kicks
field goals against us!"

"Never mind that 'lick and a promise' stuff.
We need the milk right now!"

"...and if you should happen to run out of gas..."

"No, no, your head's all right. It's
the mirror that's cracked!"

"Hold tight to my hand, Pete!
A zoo is a dangerous place!"

"Where were you last winter when
I NEEDED an extra blanket?"

"...Then he says 'Here's a denarius.'
Say, Joe, how much IS a denarius?"

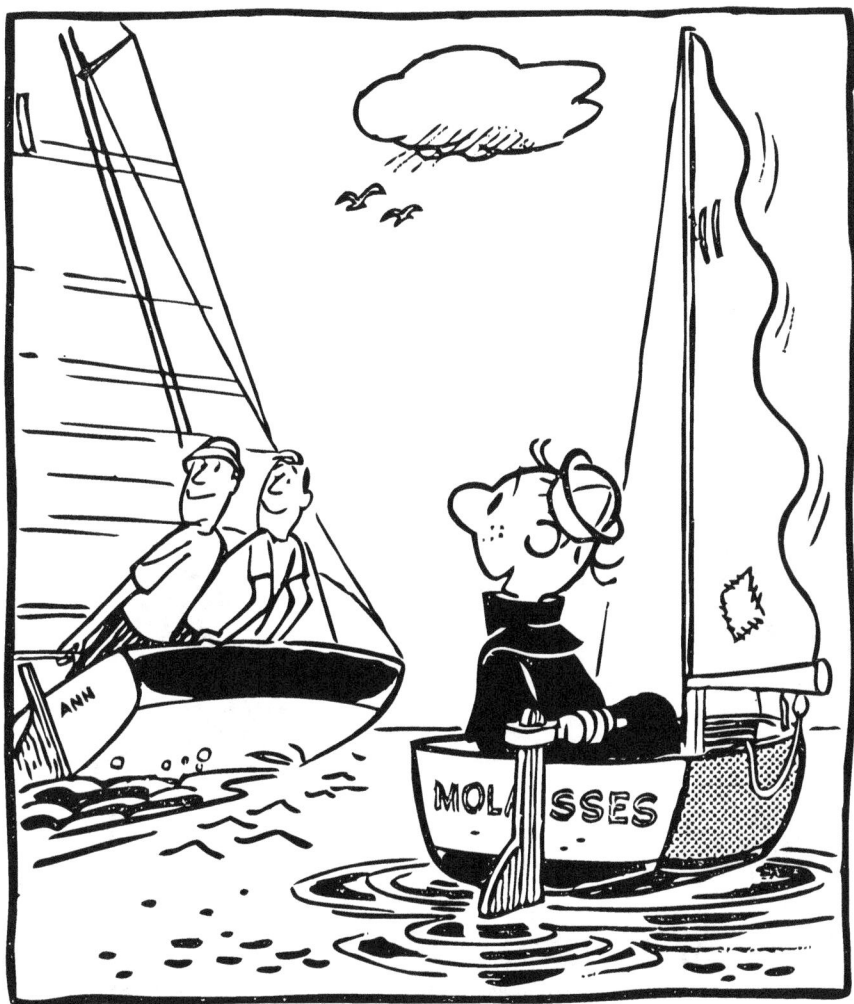

"I'm waiting till I get my second wind!"

"It's the thought behind the card
that counts—fifteen cents!"

"Yes, we had high hopes for that one!"

"His cooking almost makes grace
at meals uncalled for!"

"Oh, put me down for a couple of gallons.
After all, it's only blood!"

"Goodness, you're coming all unraveled!"

"How do you know you don't like cabbage
sandwiches if you've never tried one?"

"I didn't know you spelled your name
that way, Mister Shea!"

"Oh, oh! Fasten your seat belts!"

"A great sermon...lifted from Chapter Six
of your best-selling book, wasn't it?"

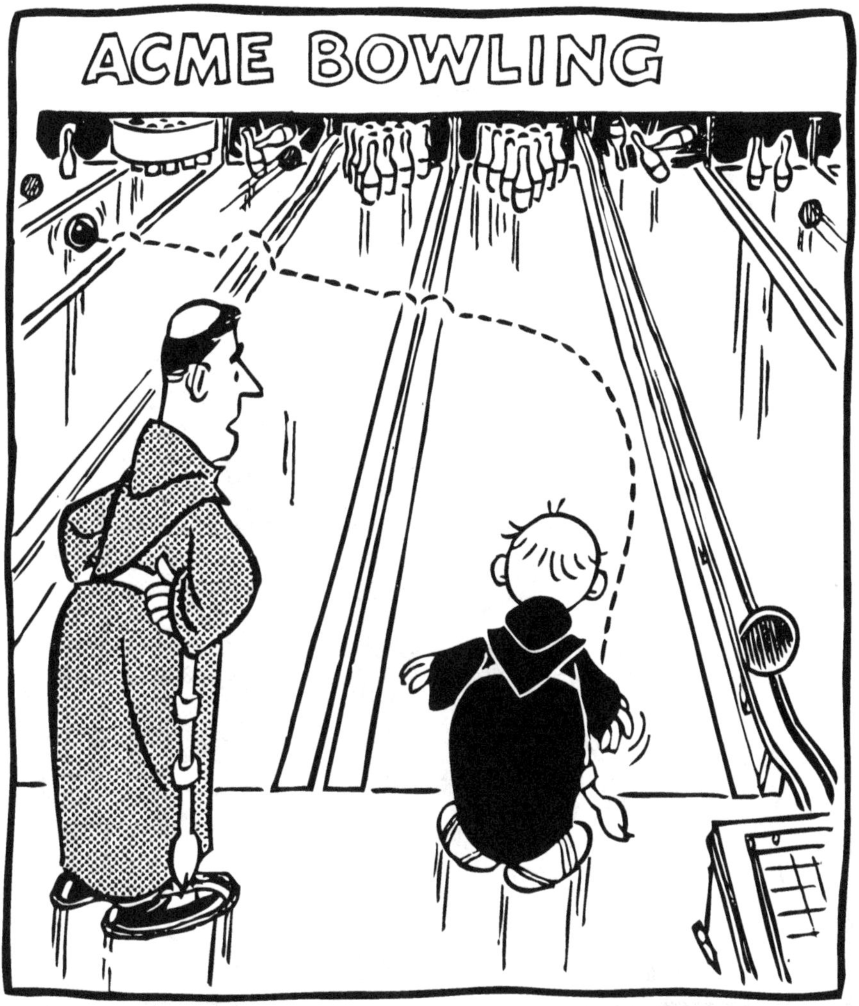
ACME BOWLING

"A little too much hook!"

"If you ask me, I'd say they built the
whole course entirely too low!"

"Actually, YOU'RE the worst pest
in this whole garden!"

"For Pete's sake! Don't tap the plate so hard!"

"These high school kids don't give it
the 'ol' college try'...like the PROS!"

"Yes, I got your bill, Doc, but I figured
it was probably psychosomatic!"

"Spare a dime for a cup of – puff –
instant coffee, sir?"

"Repositories of learning to you, maybe —
DUST COLLECTORS to me!"

"Parrots are okay in comic strips, but
in real life they're ridiculous!"

"I didn't have on my READING glasses!"

"Expecting a frost? I see you've
started the smudge pots!"

"Celery and peanut brittle, now that's
what I call a deafening meal!"

"Why shouldn't he be our mascot?
He's a CHURCH mouse, isn't he?"

"Running away leaves me cold, but
my parents seem to think it's cute!"

"Looks like we've finally worn out our welcome!"

"Brother Egbert? Oh, he's bringing up the rear!"

"Say, isn't that the turtle we passed an hour ago?"

"Saint Christopher leaves when the speedometer passes sixty, but me...I'm leaving RIGHT NOW!"

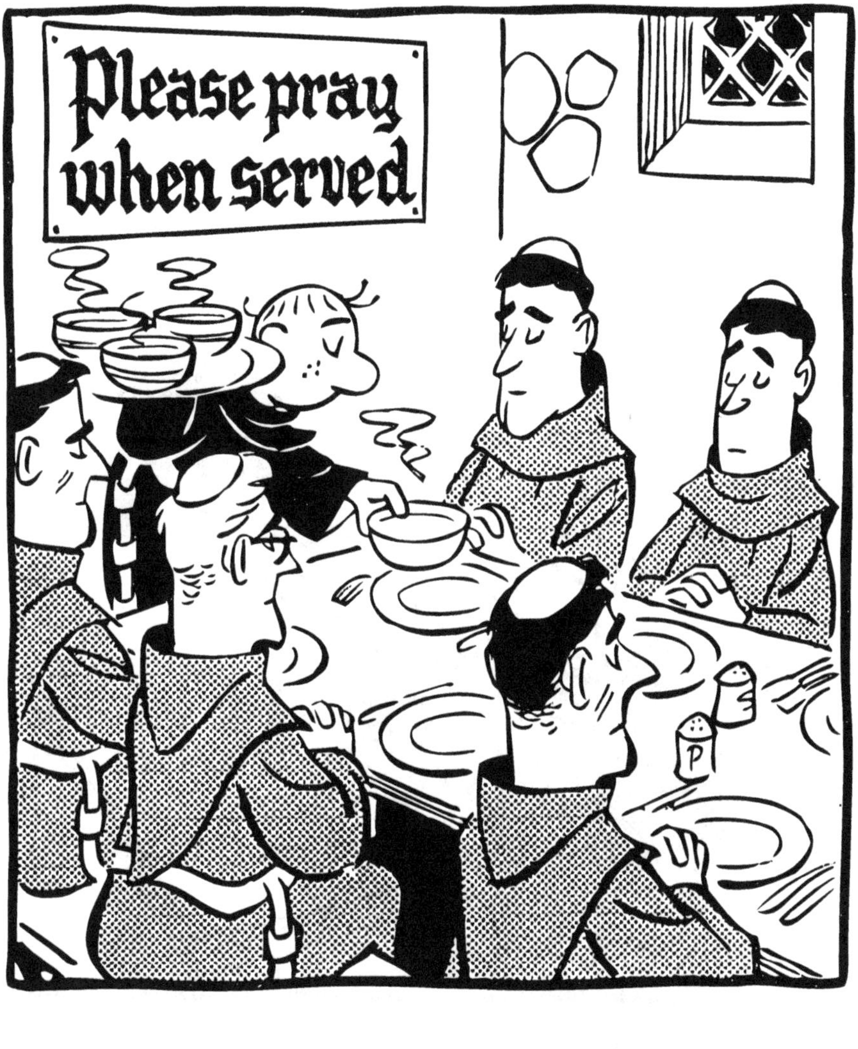
Please pray when served
P

"Y'know, when you come right down to it,
our church is COIN-operated!"

"It's so noisy in here you can't hear yourself..."

"Don't look now, but the abominable
snowman is right behind you!"

"Sounds like music to hook rugs by!"

"Things can't possibly be as bad
as they're painted!"

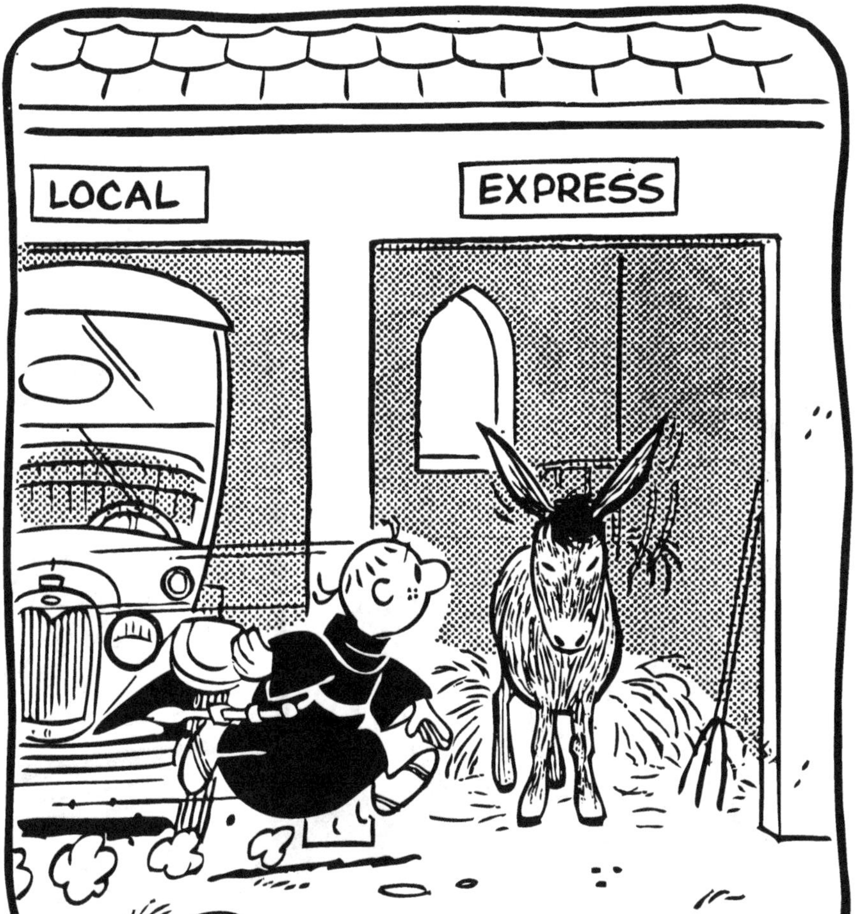
LOCAL
EXPRESS

"Pssst! Opera glasses yet!"

"My advice to you, sir, is get
rid of those water skis!"

"We find the defendant 'Guilty as sin'!"

"If we don't like this highway, will our
money be cheerfully refunded?"

"The ladies all said your sermon was inspiring;
the men looked well rested!"

"Gee, Officer Krupke, I thought
you just wanted a LIFT!"

"I'm a heavy sleeper. What I really
need is a launching pad!"

"How do they expect us to catch up with the
Russian kids if they keep flunking us?"

"This may turn out to be the heaviest
snowfall of the year!"

"Go tell 'Walky-Talky' to get back on the job!"

"Give a man enough rope, I always say!"

"Yes, yes! I haven't forgotten
when your vacation starts!"

"You had everything today, Lefty: speed, control. How they ever managed to hit those thirteen home runs, I'll never know!"

"Red-headed woodpecker nothing:
That's a FIRE-HYDRANT!"

"A-okay!"

"Where do elephants go with they die?
Listen are you trying to get me involved
in a theological argument?"

"Thirty-six hairpins and three sets of false teeth!
Must have been QUITE a sermon!"

"Something tells me I took the
wrong tack at Montauk!"

"Admit it. The door is warped and you can't shut it!"

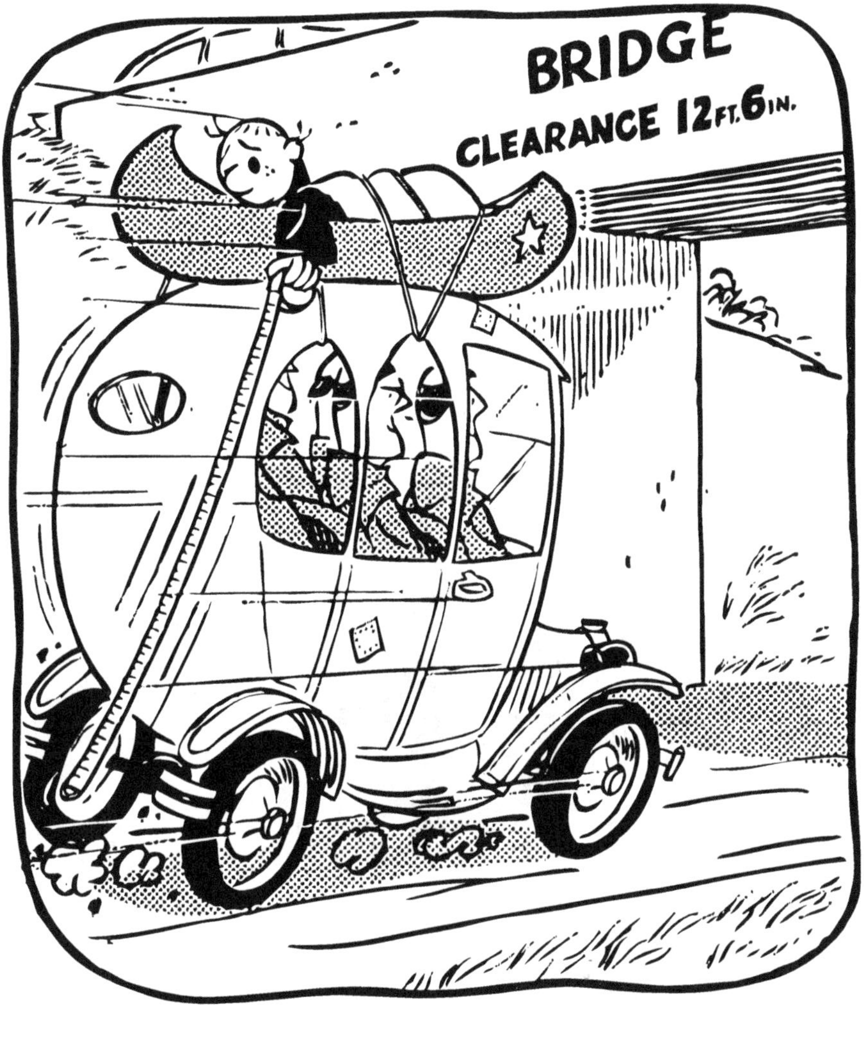
BRIDGE
CLEARANCE 12 FT. 6 IN.

"Wait, I haven't finished my REBUTTAL!"

"Do you think the day will ever come when we
can beat our missiles into ploughshares?"

"That job is slowly turning him into a fiscal wreck!"

"Gee, mister, maybe your picture tube is shot!"

"...but I don't have a bone. Here,
gnaw this till we get home!"

"You're not supposed to cry at
'Coming Attractions'!"

"What I wouldn't give to be
mowing a nice hot lawn!"

"Get up on the wrong side of
the bed this morning?"

"...and we do NOT refer to the
rear of the church as the 'end zone'!"

"Don't look at me. I'M lost, too!"

"How would I like my hair cut? In SILENCE!"

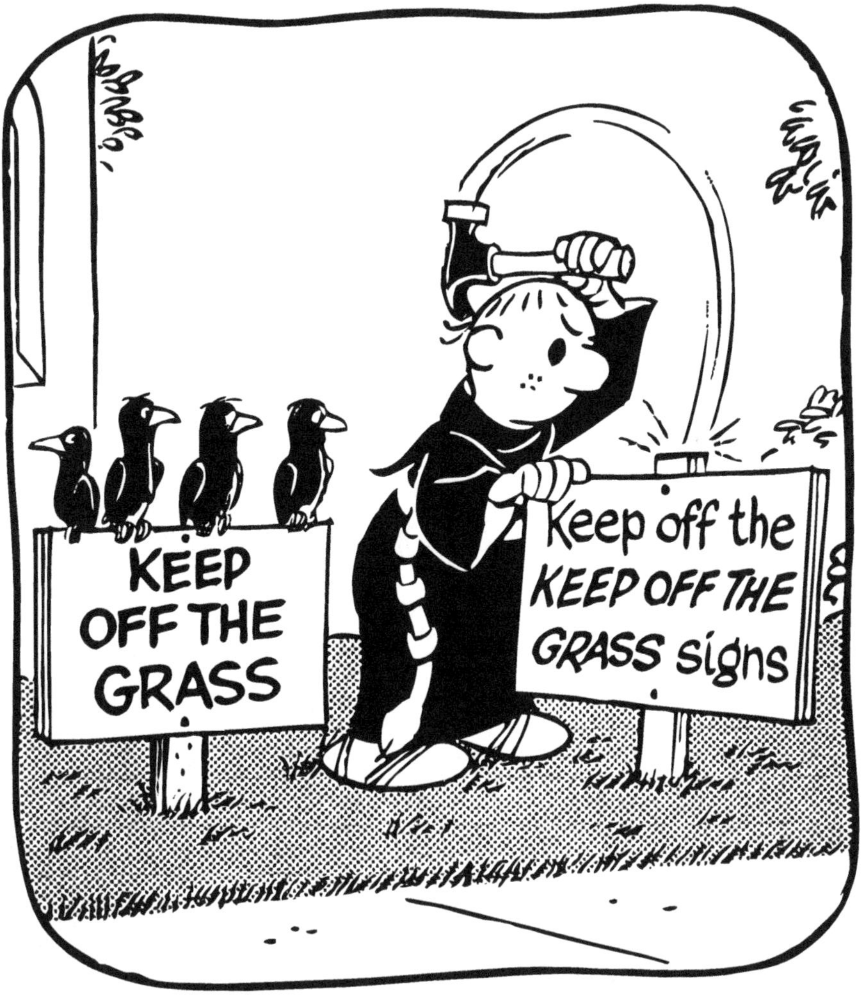
KEEP
OFF THE
GRASS
Keep off the
KEEP OFF THE
GRASS signs

"...but what do you feed 'em when it isn't FRIDAY?"

"Personally, I would have let him take the lunch!"

"Dust off that ol' recipe for shark fin soup!"

"Brother Juniper signing off! Over and out!"

THE WHIMSICAL WORLD OF BROTHER JUNIPER

Father Justin
'Fred' McCarthy

Empty-Grave Extended Edition

"Now, don't you worry. It's in here SOMEPLACE."

"This is my favorite mystery.
It's about a Holy Terror."

"Around here we have to 'work like heaven,' but you wouldn't know about that."

"It says, 'The family that prays
together stays together.'"

699

"There are those who sneer at buttons in the collection, but I'm not one of them."

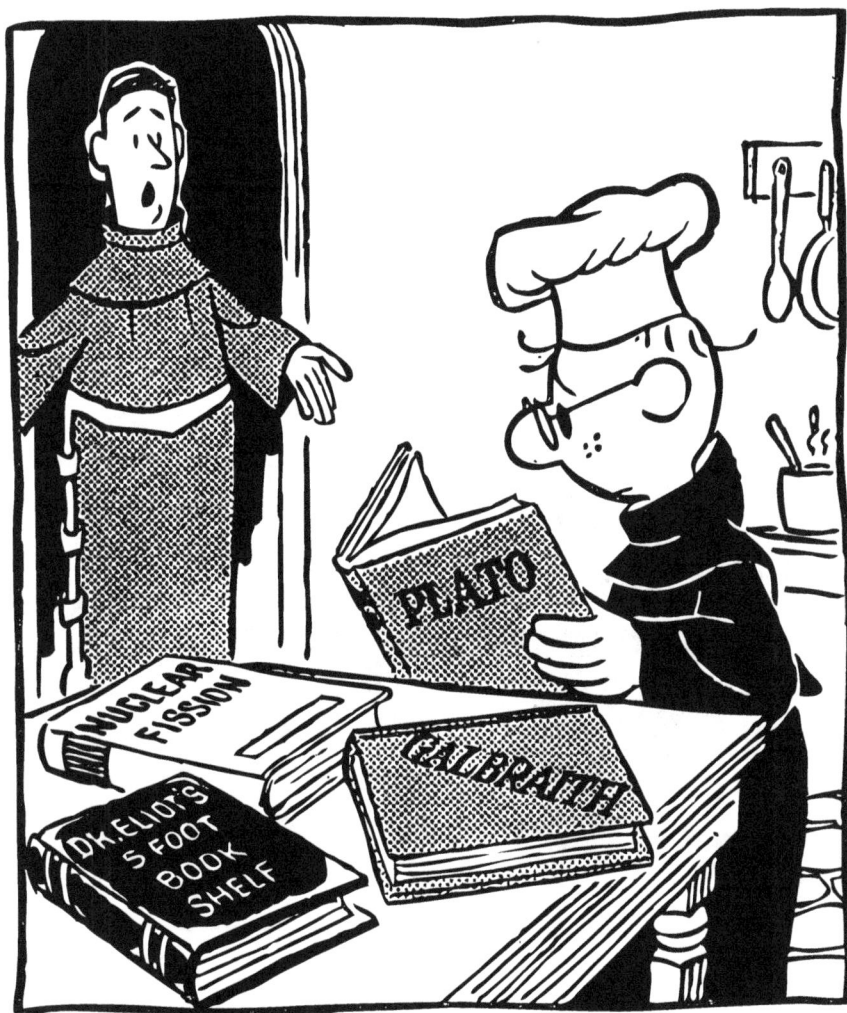

"All this research just for a
side order of Harvard beets?"

"I'm trying to meditate on heaven, but I can't seem to get past Cape Canaveral."

"Chief, just what you've been
looking for: Executive Gothic!"

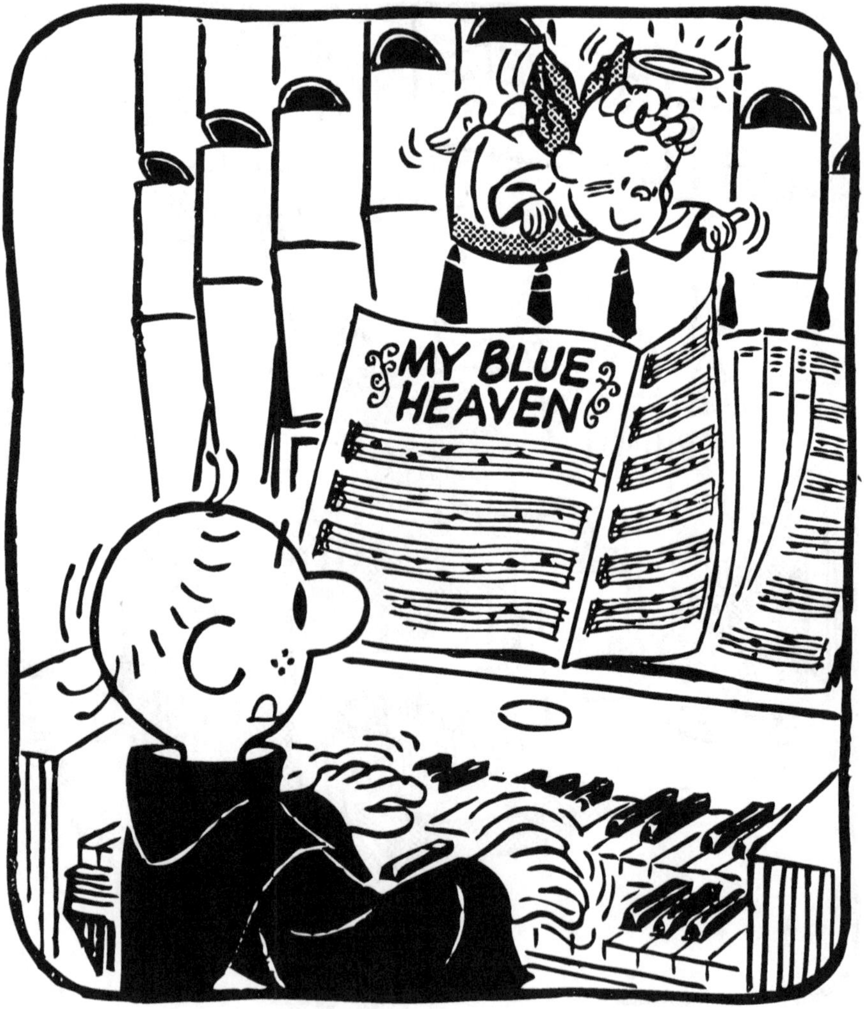
MY BLUE HEAVEN

"He said 'Whom.' I distinctly
heard him say 'Whom!'"

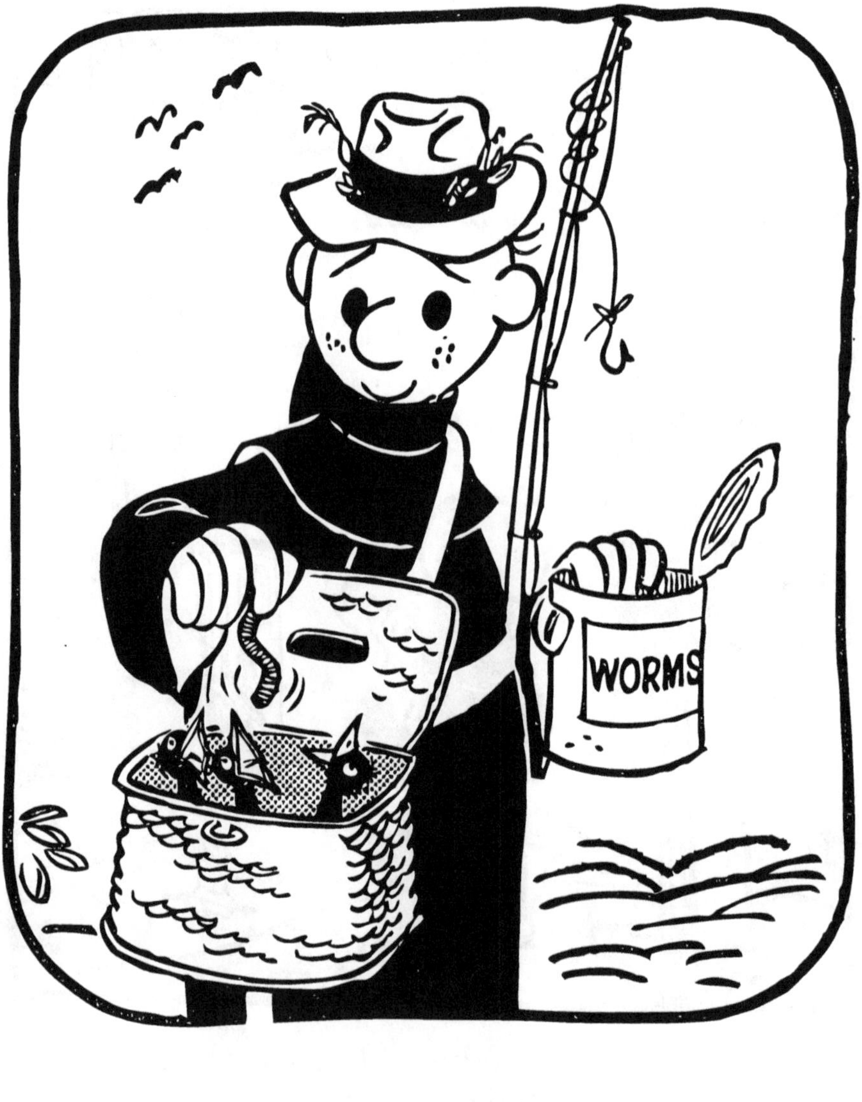
WORMS

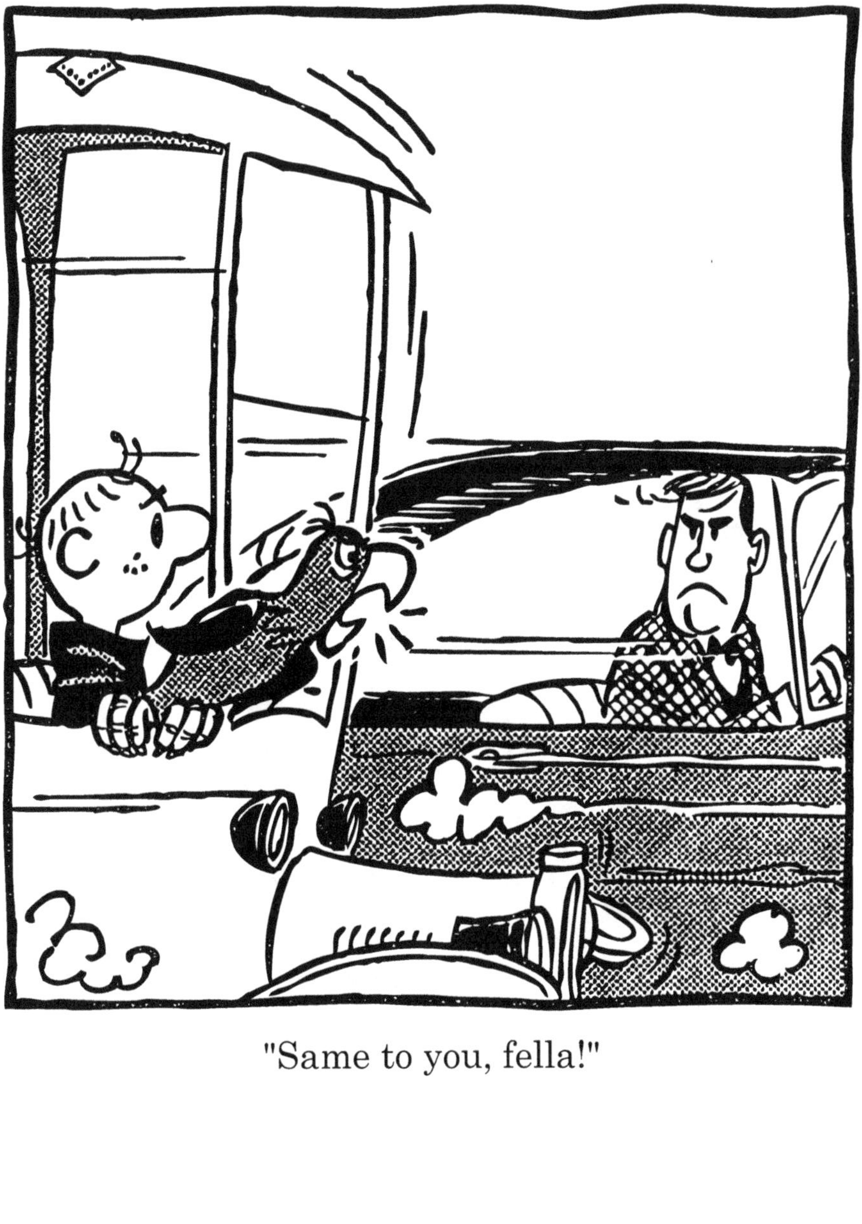

"Same to you, fella!"

"I don't think he quite made it."

"...But that wasn't your BIGGEST mistake."

"I've enjoyed meeting you. Now, about that dime..."

"Brother Juniper's approach
to spring-cleaning is very direct."

"It's from the man upstairs."

"Is something troubling you? Even your coat hangers seem to be sagging today."

713

"...But don't you believe in giving
credit where credit is due?"

"Why not? It's EDUCATIONAL, isn't it?"

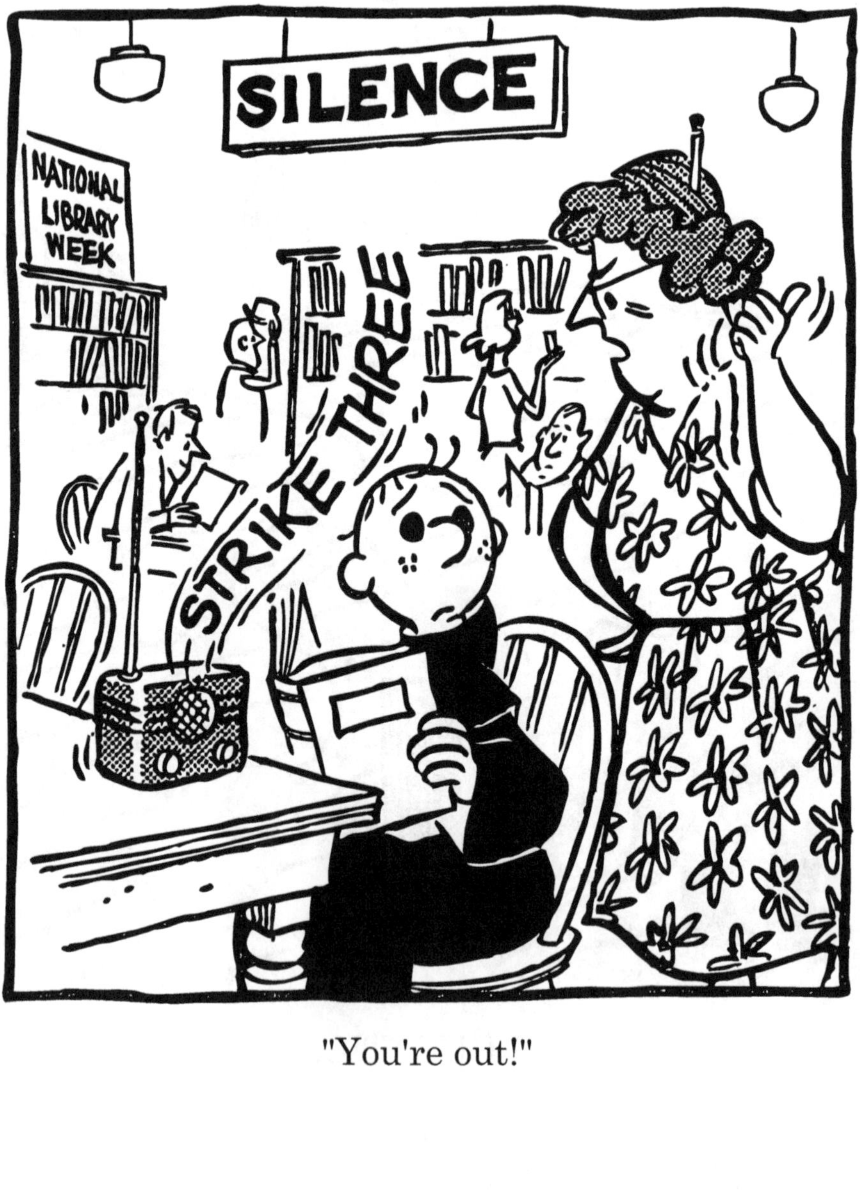
SILENCE
NATIONAL LIBRARY WEEK
STRIKE THREE

"You're out!"

"But they say they don't WANT to
go back to Capistrano."

"...But, my dear sir, shrimps are
SUPPOSED to be small."

"You spend so much time with those pigeons, you're beginning to walk like them!"

"This'll never work. He has a vow of poverty."

CHURCH
PLAY
REHEARSAL
SCENE I
CASTING
DIRECTOR

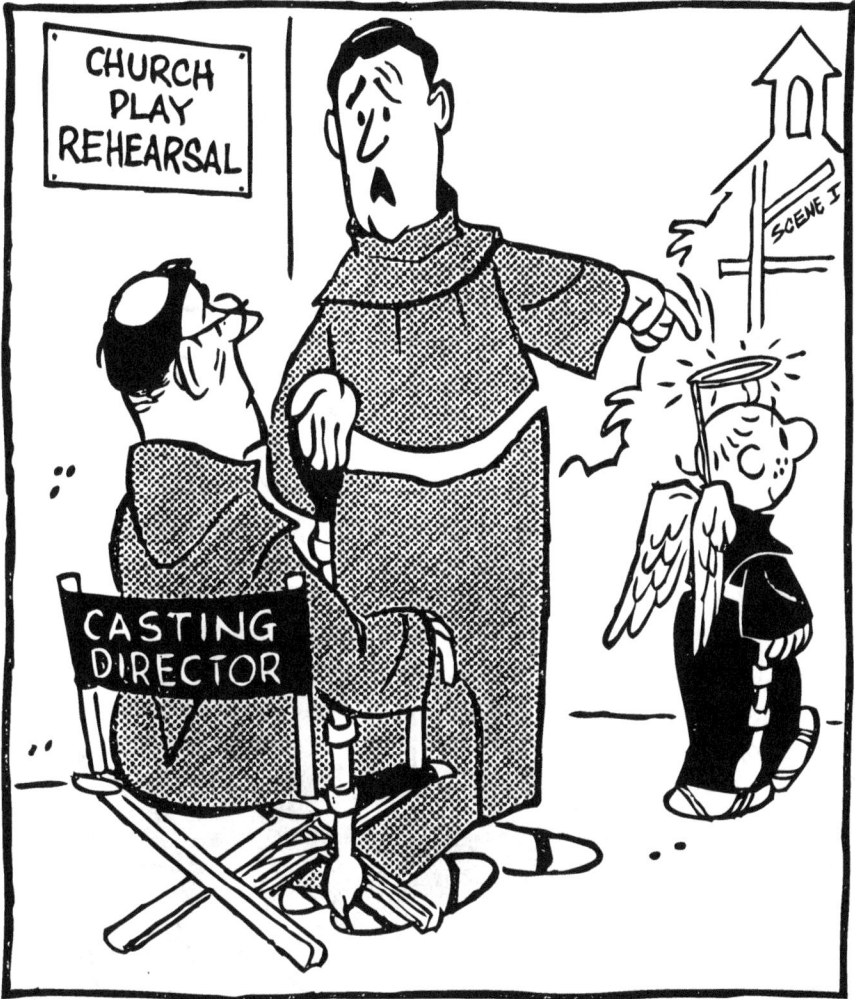

"Are you out of your mind?"

"There, but for the grace of God, go you!"

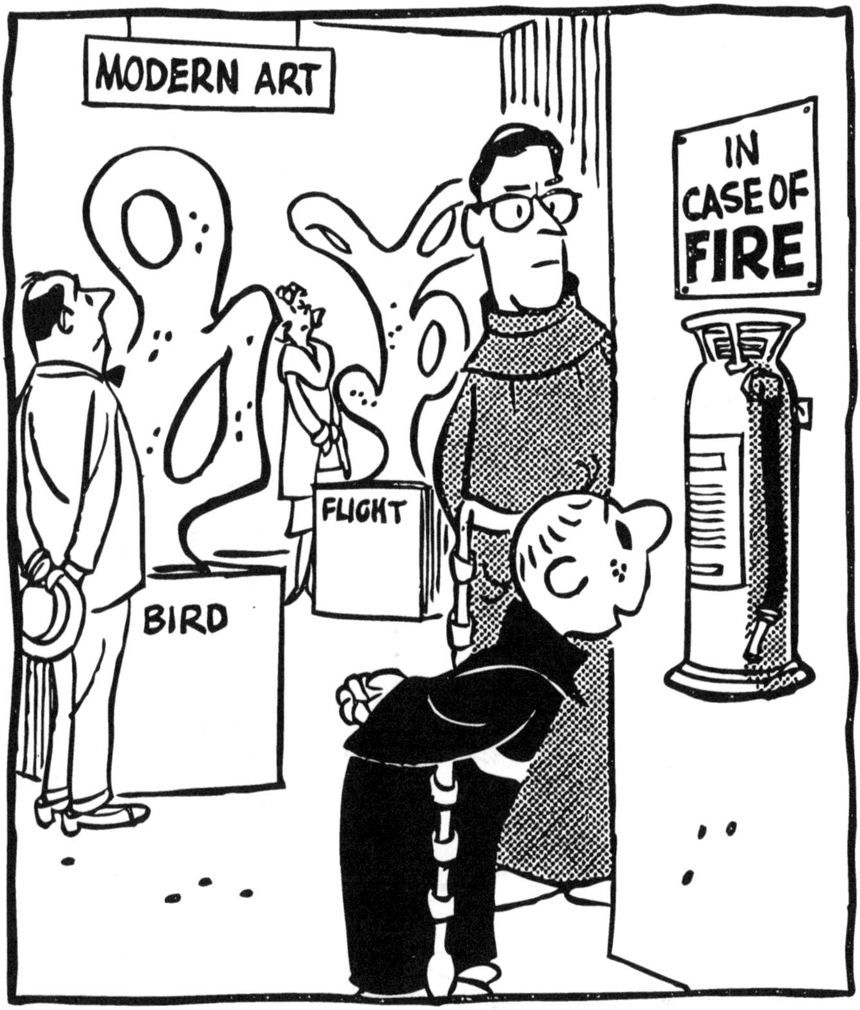
MODERN ART
IN CASE OF FIRE
BIRD
FLIGHT

"Now, THIS I understand."

"Want to see where I was
vaccinated? Right in there."

"This is where I do my status-seeking."

"What's so miniature about $1.50?"

"Okay, you can sing 'Whippoorwill,' but nobody asked for an encore!"

"Time heals all wounds, they say!"

"...But why did God make little rocks if he didn't want little kids to throw them?"

"Please limit your echo to three minutes."

"On second thought do you think we SHOULD
chop down this big beautiful work of nature?"

"Trouble spot? The whole ROOM's a trouble spot!"

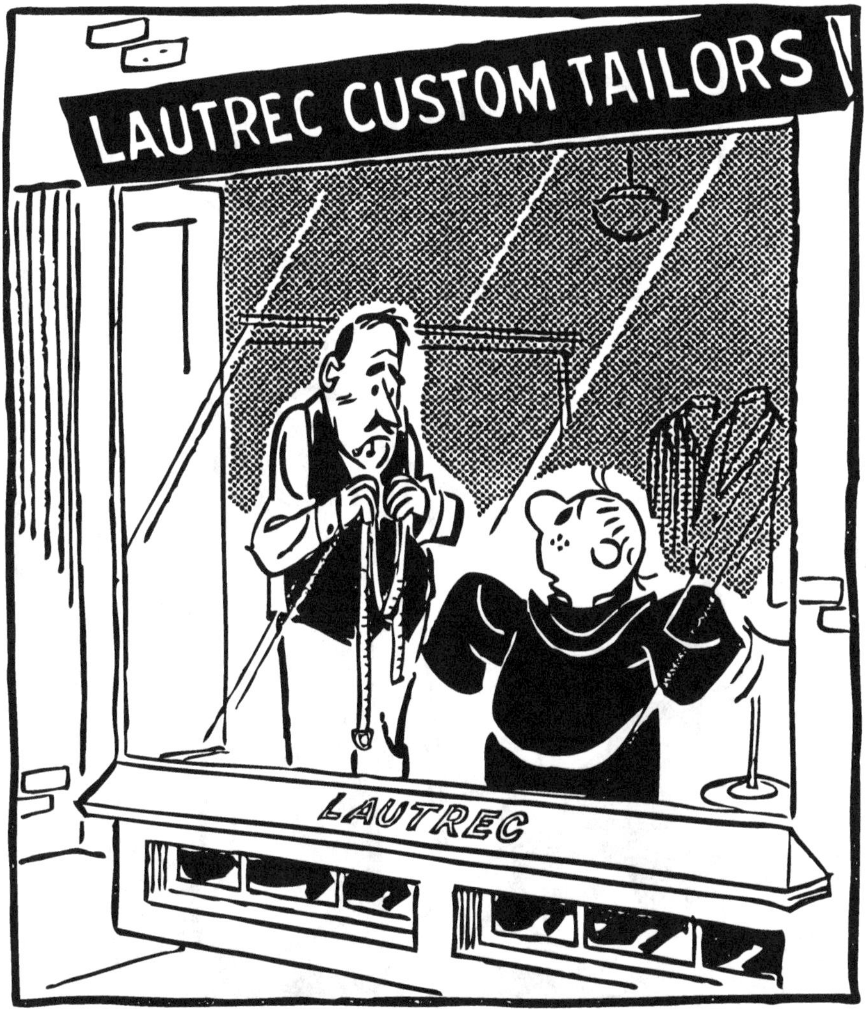
LAUTREC CUSTOM TAILORS
LAUTREC

"Too loose, Lautrec!"

"...But if it was my rugged constitution that pulled me through, how come you sent a bill?"

"If the paint job starts to fade,
come back and I'll touch it up."

"What message? I didn't send any message."

"All right, EVERYBODY out of the pool."

"They say: When you SEE the
moth, it's already too late."

"The children would like to express
their thanks. Now, if you'll just
accompany me to the police station..."

"If you have to ASK how much, you can't afford it."

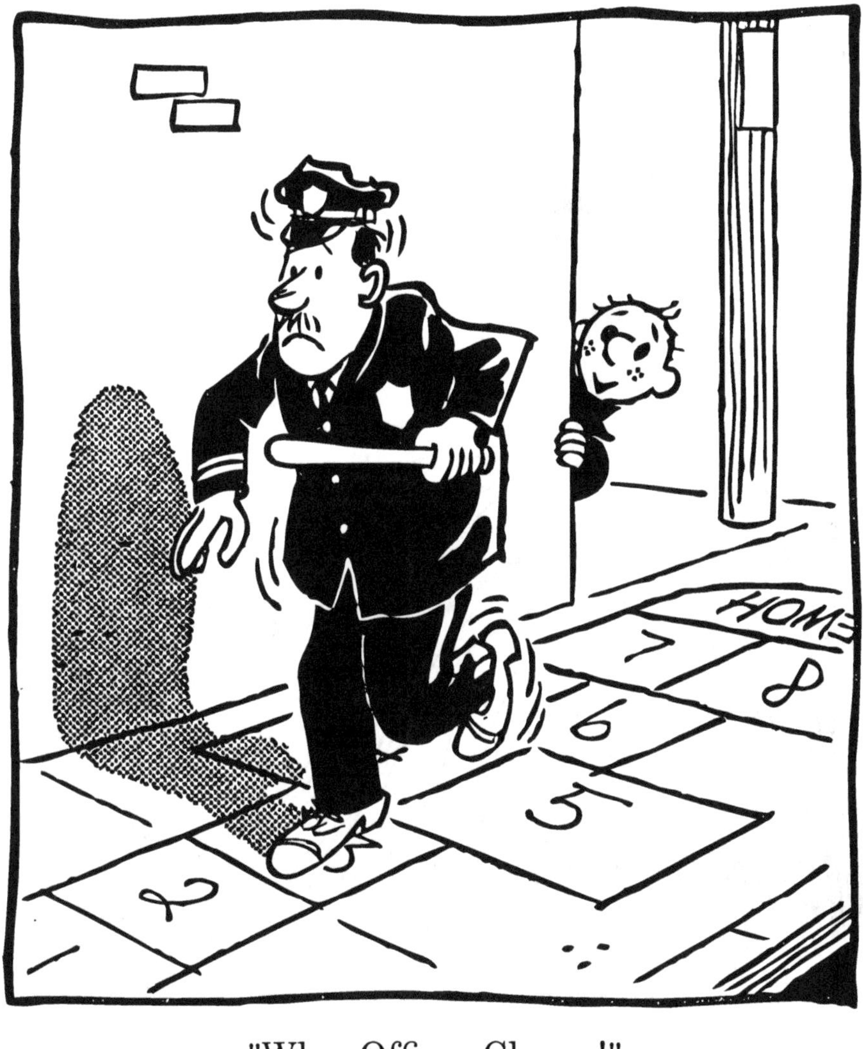

HOME

"Why, Officer Clancy!"

"All right, all right! So you found
a needle in a haystack!"

"Carry it in your mouth...like this, see?"

"Human nature is the same all over, only it seems like there's a lot more of it on buses."

"Beetles have the advantage.
They can work Sundays."

"How about that? Wall-to-wall attendance!"

"Have you been playing with the mailman again?"

"Are we good losers? Sonny, we're perfect."

"Run for it, men. Here comes
the eye of the hurricane."

"All in favor, say, 'Yea, verily.'"

"Look, if you don't cultivate a taste
for music on earth, you'll have a miserable
time when you get to heaven."

"...First, you beat up two eggs."

"Third floor, Miss...if it isn't out of your way."

"Personally, I don't go much
for these spectator sports."

"If this is a restaurant chain, I'll bet we're
eating in the WEAKEST LINK."

"Would you mind saying something inspirational to help me through this morning's run?"

"All right, so how would YOU spell it?"

"The sugar? Oh, I hid it in the creamer so the ants wouldn't know where to look for it."

"Out of gas...what a coincidence."

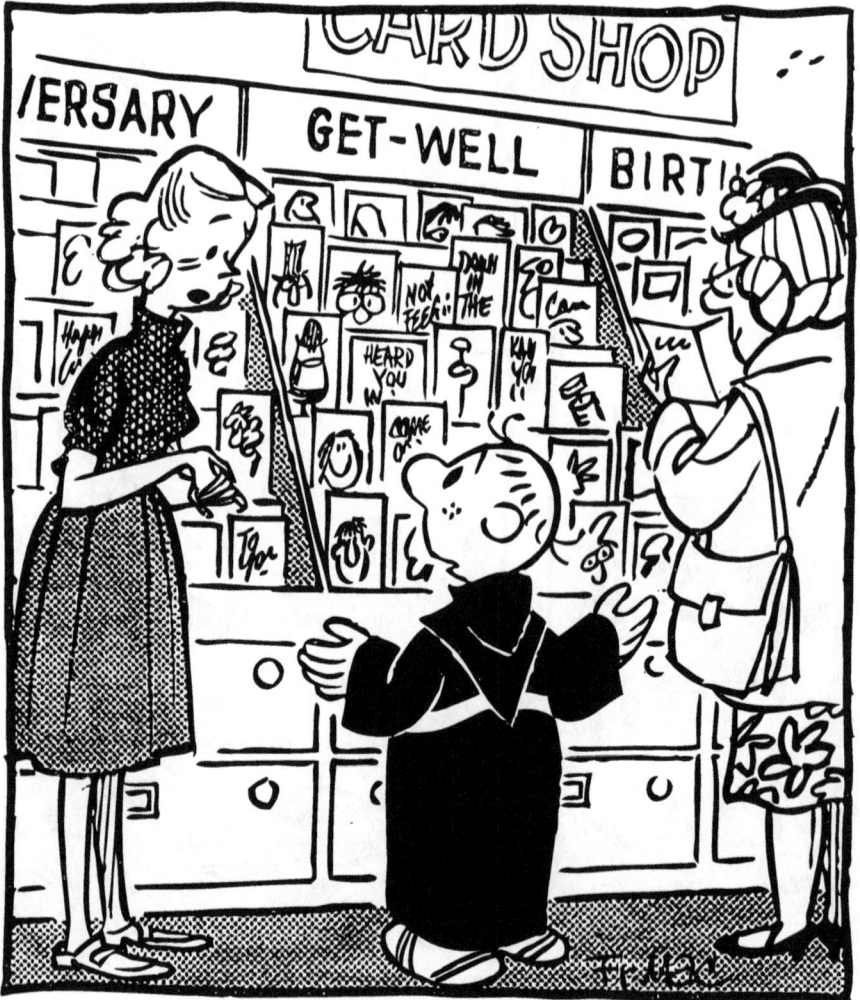

"How come all the get-well
cards are sick-sick-sick?"

"It's for you."

"Say, this is the best idea I've had all week,
and here it is only Monday."

"Did you starch this hammock?"

"It's the biggest check we ever received,
but it's made out to God alone."

"If he says 'Business is picking up' one
more time, I'm asking for a transfer."

"Psst, not there! On the ROOF!"

"Now, what kind of talk is that: 'Bah, humbug'?"

"Stop me if you've heard this one."

"You and your big welcome mat!"

"Don't tell me I forgot to turn you back an hour?"

"Take an epistle."

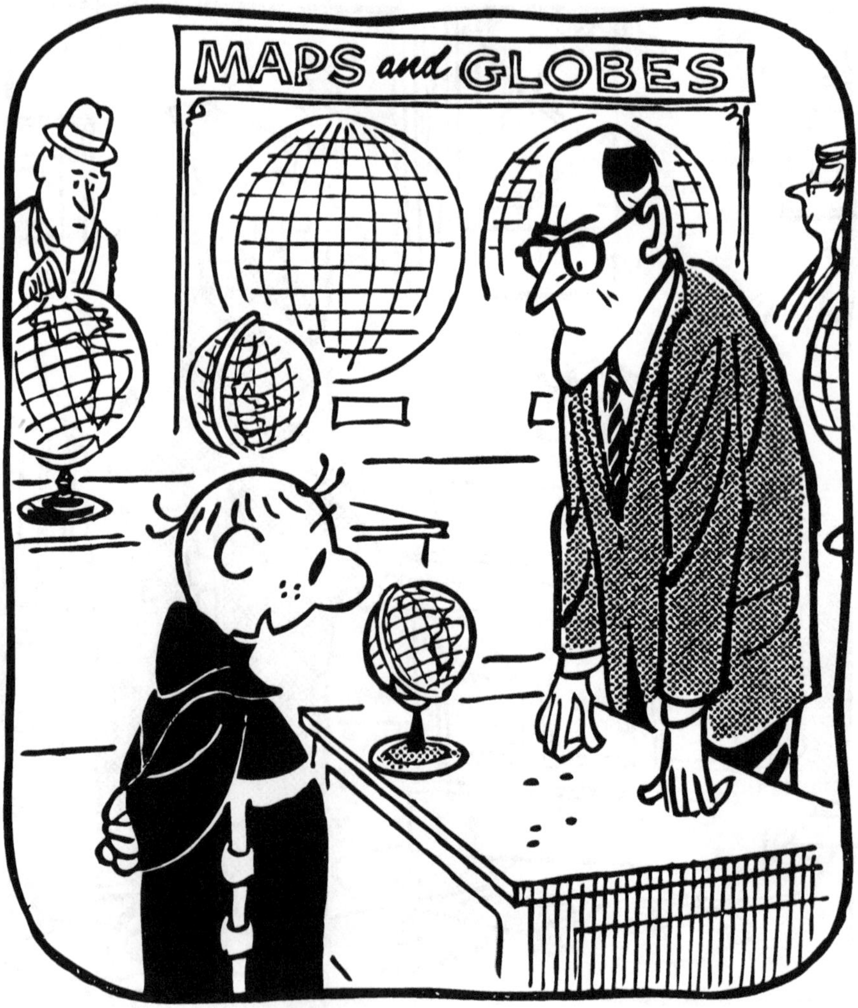
MAPS and GLOBES

"Small world, isn't it?"

"...Guess I'll go home and hang myself...in effigy."

"Neatness COUNTS, you know!"

"Now the other foot."

"I thought we agreed to keep
the Guardian Angels out of this."

"Nature abhors a vacuum - and
I can't say I blame her!"

"Will you kindly stop crunching
that acorn while I'm putting?"

"I just hope you didn't learn to cook
where you learned to spell."

779

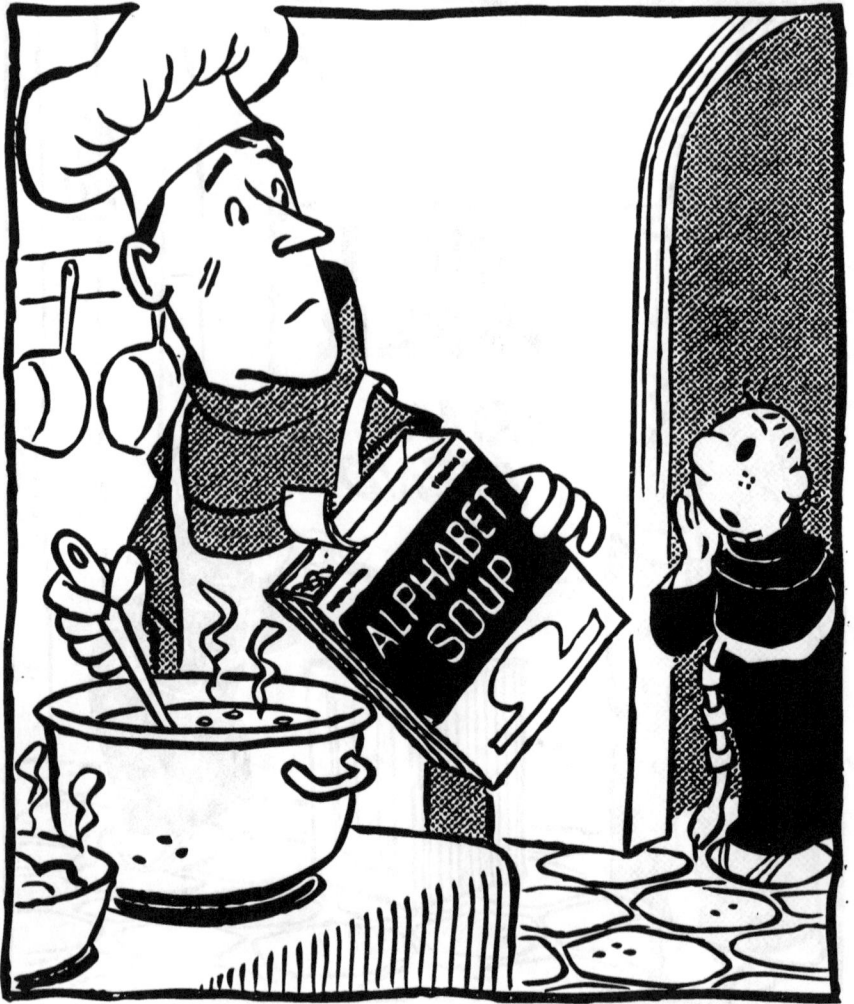

"There's only a few in for supper. You
won't need more than a paragraph."

"Comes in three stunning shades:
jet black, ink black, and midnight black."

"Sure, he's a very nice guy, if you
happen to LIKE very nice guys."

"See you people next week: Same time,
same place, same sermon!"

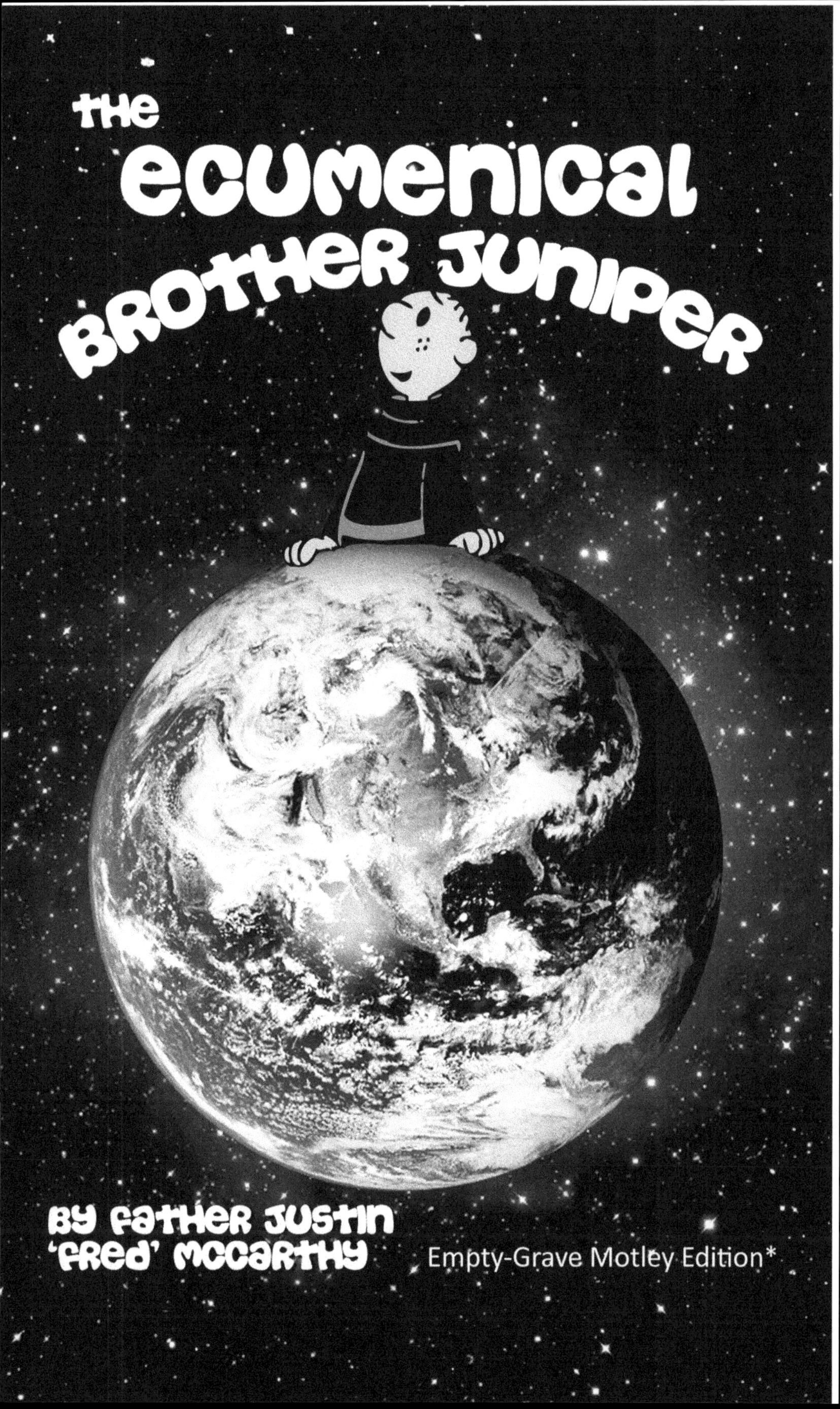
THE
ECUMENICAL
BROTHER JUNIPER
BY FATHER JUSTIN
'FRED' McCARTHY
Empty-Grave Motley Edition*

"The road to WHERE is paved with WHAT?"

"Oh no! Not another sing along with Wagner?"

"All right, Hans Brinker, off with the
skates and let's get supper!"

"Last of the ninth. Three men on...two men out...
three and two on the batter. Too bad we're eighteen
runs behind."

"Oh boy, SEVEN HUNDRED years bad luck."

"I'll bite. Is it animal, vegetable, or mineral?"

"Saturday night, Bernard. Hop in."

"I send him out for a package of zinnia seeds,
and look what he brings back."

"So that's where our hot water goes!"

"On your toes, girls. Here comes the ol' egghead."

"Did you just hear a voice say: 'Don't mumble'?"

"I can't figure it out. We use the same type razor blades they use."

797

"Aw, c'mon, Officer Clancy,
where's your spirit of romance?"

"But if we said it was any good you'd
give us the same thing tomorrow."

"Get out there and SAVE somebody.
We're not running a dude ranch!"

"C'mon, GROW!"

"We ought to do better next week.
No game is scheduled."

"I SAID: Can you spare a couple of quarts?"

"Greatest invention since the wheel:
it's called 'the siesta'."

"Thatsa right, the stones are free...
after you pay for the peach."

"The butcher and the baker will give us credit, but the candlestick maker wants his dough."

"There's no substitute for experience."

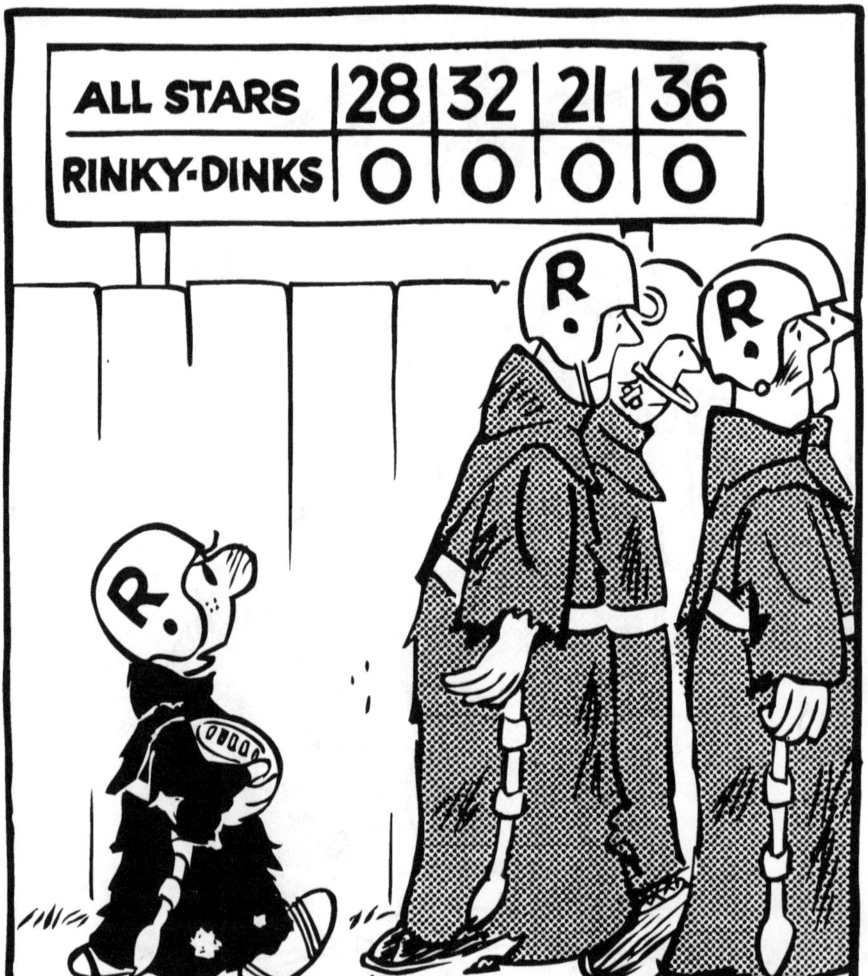
ALL STARS 28 32 21 36
RINKY-DINKS 0 0 0 0
R
R
R

"Of all the sorry exhibitions!"

"Something tells me there's been a terrible mix-up."

"Why'd you let him take your hat?"

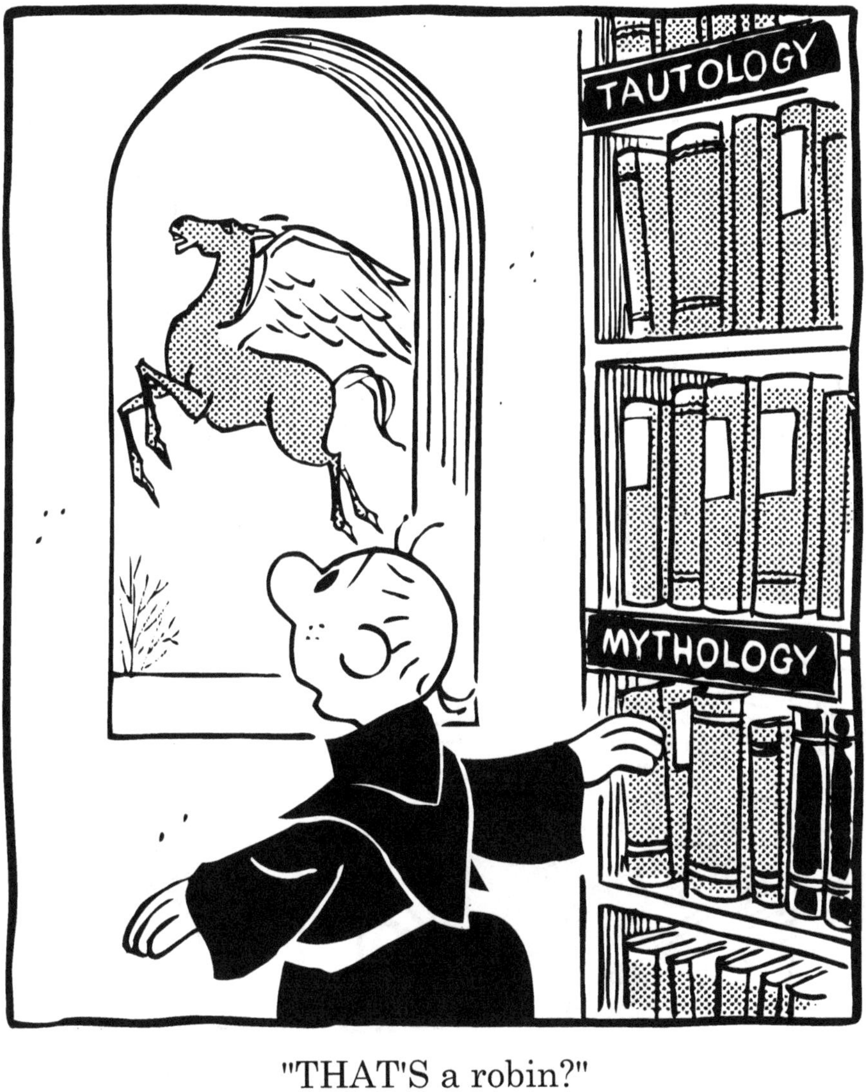
TAUTOLOGY
MYTHOLOGY

"THAT'S a robin?"

"...but are you SURE this Count Basie
studied under Giuseppe Verdi?"

"At us, the Cleveland Browns have
no need to tremble."

"Think of church as a baseball game, Pete. That way you'll never miss the opening pitch."

"...But, Doc, I can't go back and tell 'em I have 'housemaid's knee'! Couldn't you make it 'athlete's foot'?"

"Pack your prayer book.
You've been traded to Saint Swithins."

"We are poor little lambs who..."

"I'm not sure this is the right road, but as long as it's here we may as well take it."

"He just stepped out. He'll be sorry he missed you."

"Looking for a good lyricist, man?"

"You the one that gives the non-fat milk?"

"Wait a minute! I just scrubbed the kitchen!"

"I notice that, like Rudolph the red-nosed reindeer,
you went down in history."

"Do you go anywhere near
St. Swithins-in-the-Meadow, sir?"

"What do you mean 'It won't start'?"

"All right: one more time!"

"Twenty years of this should qualify us
as collectors of Internal Revenue."

"Humpty-Dumpty rides again!"

"Aha, about to cast the first stone, eh?"

"Tell Thoreau to stop communing with
nature and get to work."

"Say, that's quite a follow-through you have there!"

"It started out as fudge, but if I can't make taffy
out of it, I'm gonna try for pudding."

"We ran out of postal stamps so I used trading stamps...but only on the supermarket bills!"

"Ahah, just as I suspected."

"...Does a man good to work in the soil."

"You the one who belongs to the
Manuscript-of-the-Month Club?"

"This'll cost you a bundle,
but that's only an estimate!"

"Back up faster. He's gaining on us!"

"Remember, it's just temporary—
till we get the pipe fixed."

"Personally, I hate liver, but I serve it five times a week 'cause it just happens to be good for you!"

"I do MOST of my praying in pajamas."

"Man, that's REAL coffee!"

"You just add sand and...bang!—instant time!"

"Unaccustomed as I am to public speaking..."

"Give me ten good reasons why we couldn't
join a Cook-of-the-Month Club."

"In a fair fight, who do you think would win:
Friar Tuck or Friar Lawrence?"

"If this keeps up, we'll have the Sunday golfers."

"Now hear this: three dozen extra-large, eight dozen medium, twelve dozen small..."

"May not look like much, sonny, but there's a ton of popcorn on the way."

"Bronx Zoo, April 25, 1935, 2 p.m., wasn't it?"

"Well, if it isn't the Durango Kid and his
faithful mount, back at the old corral."

"Look at him...trying to get a nice, even tan,
when he should be out rescuing people!"

"I won't volunteer, but I'll accept a sincere draft."

"Why don't we send them to the World's
Fair—as OUR exhibit?"

"It's exactly 6:37, but I'm not sure what day it is."

"Is it a nationally advertised label?"

"No, no! You can't take it back after you roll it!"

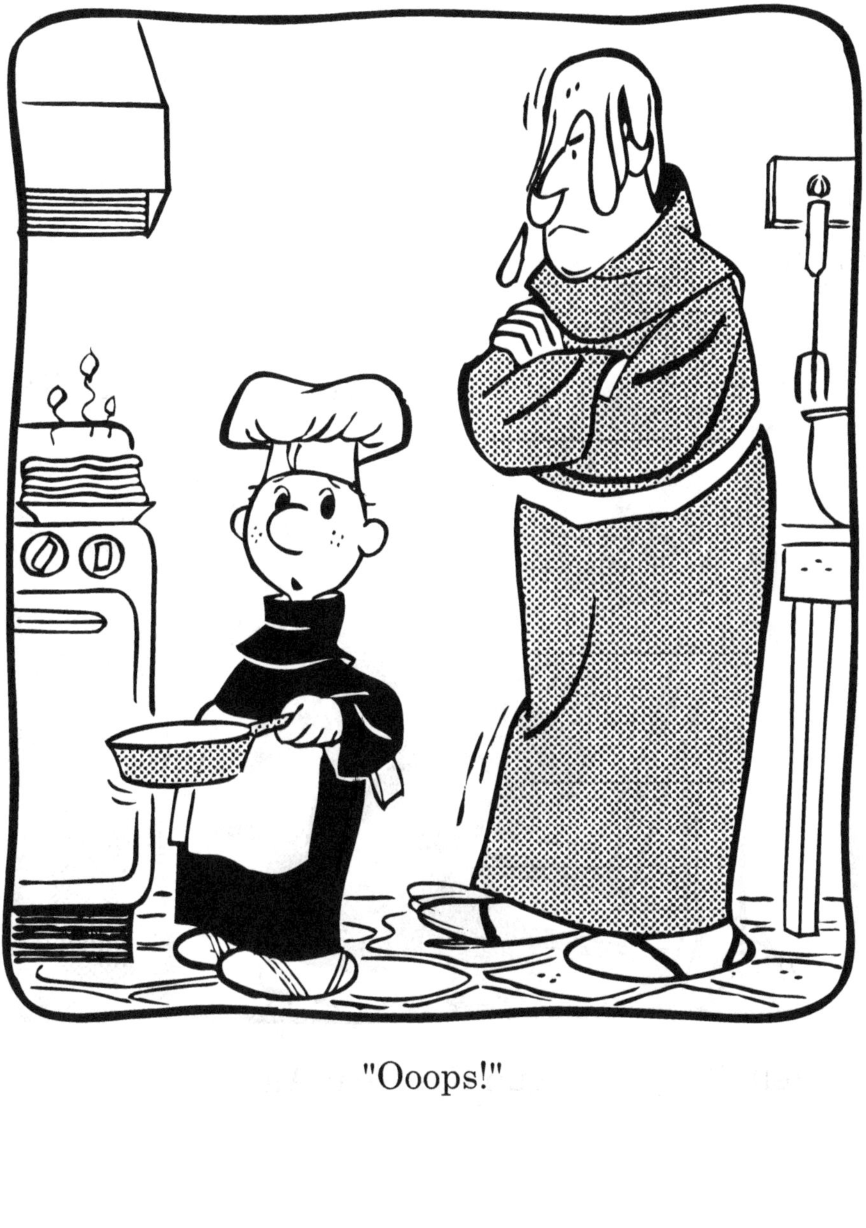

"Ooops!"

"Well, I've just begun the great American novel."

"The only reason I panhandle, sir, is
because I don't like being broke."

"...And how did things go at the office today?"

"Well, here we go—off to another
disastrous road trip."

"That one was REALLY grim, wasn't it, kiddies?"

"You're not using MY console to tune
that ol' guitar!"

"...So I said to him...What was that noise? ...I said:
'Are you afraid to meet your Maker?'"

"You just aren't the REGAL type, that's why."

"Oops!"

"Yes, but you'll never have a hit without a guitar."

"For his opening selection, Brother Juniper
will render Debussy...limb from limb!"

"Just a minute. Is that MY electric
toothbrush you're using?"

"You are slowly becoming better and better."

"The defense rests."

The Cartoonist

Father Justin 'Fred' McCarthy *(1918 - 2009)* expertly doodled his way through childhood in Boston. As a student at Boston College he felt the call of religious service. He heard and acted on that call by transferring to St. Bonaventure College in Buffalo. It was there that his cartooning hobby flowered and drew the attention of his peers - which resulted in the appearance of a nameless little monk in college flyers and posters. In 1942, he dubbed this cheery, pint-sized creation, "Brother Juniper."

McCarthy was a member of the Secular Franciscan Order for seventy-one years. He served as art director of the national Franciscan magazine, *Friar*. He also taught classes about the art of comics and humour at numerous universities and colleges; and networked with fellow comic artists by playing street football out in front of New York's Waldorf-Astoria Hotel. Rumour has it that, at eighty-four, he could still punt a football forty yards.

Father McCarthy retired to southern Florida with his wife Lilly and continued to create new material for the well-travelled Brother Juniper. In a 2004 interview he is quoted as saying:

> *I hope that my 'little sunbeam in burlap' will serve as an exemplar of Catholic good humor while providing us with a chuckle a week.*

The Cartoon

Brother Juniper began as a nameless sketch for personal amusement but over thirty years he grew into an international superstar. Brother Juniper ran in over 100 American daily newspapers and a number of international ones as well. It is the only religious-themed comic to be internationally syndicated in dailies. It was met by a readership of over 15,000,000 in the US alone.

In 1959 the comic won "The Brotherhood of the Year" award from the National Conference of Christians and Jews.
McCarthy on the appeal of Brother Juniper:

> *Take someone from the Middle Ages, put him in a modern setting and you have something funny right there. He's Catholic with a small 'c'. He's always trying to help people but always slipping on a banana peel. Characters like Brother Juniper, and Charlie Brown, lose the battle but win the war.*

Bibliography

Brother Juniper - 1957
Brother Juniper Strikes Again - 1958
Brother Juniper at Work and Play - 1959
More Brother Juniper - 1958
Inside Brother Juniper - 1960
Well Done, Brother Juniper - 1963
The Whimsical World of Brother Juniper - 1963
The Ecumenical Brother Juniper - 1965
The Definitive Brother Juniper - 2012

History of the Real Brother Juniper

Saint Juniper (~1210 AD - 1258 AD) was one of the original followers of Saint Francis of Assisi and was received into the order by St. Francis himself. St. Juniper was also known as, "the renowned jester of the Lord." Of St. Juniper, St. Francis quipped, "Would to God, my brothers, I had a whole forest of such Junipers."

St. Francis tasked Juniper with expanding the order in Gualdo Tadino and Viterbo, which he did with great success. St. Juniper is buried at Ara Coeli Church in Rome. The day of his feast is January 29th. Several stories of Saint Juniper are recounted in *the Little Flowers of St. Francis* (1390 AD)

The Little Flowers of St. Francis (Excerpts)

Here Beginneth the Life of Brother Juniper

How Brother Juniper Cut Off The Foot Of A Pig To Give It To A Sick Brother: Chapter I

One of the most chosen disciples and first companions of St Francis was Brother Juniper, a man of profound humility and of great fervour and charity, of whom St Francis once said, when speaking of him to some of his companions: "He would be a good Friar Minor who had overcome the world as perfectly as Brother Juniper." Once when he was visiting a sick brother at St Mary of the Angels, he said to him, as if all on fire with the charity of God: "Can I do thee any service?" And the sick man answered: "Thou wouldst give me great consolation if thou couldst get me a pig's foot to eat." Brother Juniper answered immediately: "Leave it to me; thou shalt have one at once." So he went and took a knife from the kitchen, and in fervour of spirit went into the forest, where many swine were feeding, and having caught one, he cut off one of its feet and ran off with it, leaving the swine with its foot cut off; and coming back to the convent, he carefully washed the foot, and diligently prepared and cooked it.

Then he brought it with great charity to the sick man, who ate it with avidity; and Brother Juniper was filled with joy and consolation, and related the history of his assault upon the swine for his diversion. Meanwhile, the swineherd who had seen the brother cut off the foot, went and told the tale in order, and with great bitterness, to his lord, who, being informed of the fact, came to the convent and abused the friars, calling them hypocrites, deceiver, robbers, and evil men. "Why," said he, "have you cut off the foot of my swine?"

At the noise which he made, St Francis and all the friars came together, and with all humility made excuses for their brother, and, as ignorant of the fact, promised, in order to appease the angry man, to make amends for the wrong which had been done to him. But he was not to be appeased, and left St Francis with many threats and reproaches, repeating over and over again that they had maliciously cut the foot off his swine, refusing to accept any excuse or promise of repayment; and so departed in great wrath. And as all the other friars wondered: "Can Brother Juniper indeed have done this through indiscreet zeal?

So he sent for him, and asked him privately: "Hast thou cut off the foot of a swine in the forest?" To which Father Juniper answered quite joyfully, not as one who has committed a fault, but believing he had done a great act of charity: "It is true, sweet Father, that I did cut off that swine's foot; and if thou wilt listen compassionately, I will tell thee the reason. I went out of charity to visit the brother who is sick." And so he related the matter in order, adding: "I tell thee, dear father, that this foot did the sick brother so much good, that if I had cut off the feet of a hundred swine instead of one, I verily believe that God would have been pleased therewith." To whom St Francis, in great zeal for justice, and in much bitterness of heart, made answer: "O Brother Juniper, wherefore hast thou given this great scandal? Not without reason doth this man complain, and thus rage against us; perhaps even now he is going about the city spreading this evil report of us, and with good cause. Therefore I command thee by holy obedience, that thou go after him until thou find him, and cast thyself prostrate before him, confessing thy fault, and promising to make such full satisfaction that he shall have no more reason to complain of us, for this is indeed a most grievous offence."

At these words Brother Juniper was much amazed, wondering that any one should have been angered at so charitable an action, for all temporal things appeared to him of no value, save in so far as they could be charitably applied to the service of our neighbour. So he made answer: "Doubt not, Father, but that I shall soon content and satisfy him. And why should there be all this disturbance, seeing that the swine was rather God's than his, and that it furnished the means for an act of charity?" And so he went his way, and coming to the man, who was still chafing and past all patience, he told him for what reason he had cut off the pig's foot, and all with such fervour, exultation and joy, as if he were telling him of some great benefit he had done him which deserved to be highly rewarded.

The man grew more and more furious at his discourse, and loaded him with much abuse, calling him a fantastical fool and a wicked thief. Brother Juniper, who delighted in insults, cared nothing for all this abuse, but marvelling that any one should be wrath at what seemed to him only a matter of rejoicing, he thought he had not made himself well understood, and so repeated the story all over again, and then flung himself on the man's neck and embraced him, telling him that all had been done out of charity, and inciting and begging him for the same motive to give the rest of the swine also; and all this with so much charity, simplicity, and humility, that the man's heart was changed within him, and he threw himself at Brothers Juniper's feet, acknowledging with many tears the injuries which by word and deed he had done to him and his brethren.

Then he went and killed the swine, and having cut it up, he brought it, with many tears and great devotion, to St Mary of the Angels, and gave it to those holy friars in compensation for the injury he had done them. Then St Francis, considering the simplicity and patience under adversity of this good Brother Juniper, said to his companions and those who stood by: "Would to God, my brethren, that I had a forest of such Junipers!"

An Instance Of Brother Juniper's Great Power Against The Devil: Chapter II

The devils could not endure the purity of Brother Juniper's innocence and his profound humility, as appears in the following example: A certain demoniac one day fled in an unaccustomed manner, and through devious paths, seven miles from his home. When his parents, who had followed him in great distress of mind, at last overtook him, they asked him why he had fled in this strange way. The demoniac answered: "Because that fool Juniper was coming this way. I could not endure his presence, and therefore, rather than wait his coming, I fled away through these woods."

And on inquiring into the truth of these words, they found that Brother Juniper had indeed arrived at the time the devil had said. Therefore when demoniacs were brought to St Francis to be healed, if the evil spirit did not immediately depart at his command, he was wont to say: "Unless thou dost instantly leave this creature, I will bring Brother Juniper to thee." Then the devil, fearing the presence of Brother Juniper, and being unable to endure the virtue and humility of St Francis, would forthwith depart.

How, By The Contrivance Of The Devil, Brother Juniper Was Condemned To The Gallows: Chapter III

Once upon a time the devil, desiring to terrify Brother Juniper, and to raise up scandal and tribulation against him, betook himself to a most cruel tyrant, named Nicholas, who was then at war with the city of Viterbo, and said to him: "My lord, take heed to watch your castle well, for a vile traitor will come here shortly from Viterbo to kill you and set fire to your castle. And by this sign you shall know him: he will come in the guise of a poor beggar, with his clothes all tattered and patched, and a torn hood falling on his shoulders, and he will carry with him an awl, wherewith to kill you, and a flint and steel wherewith to set fire to the castle; and if you find not my words to be true, punish me as you will." At these words Nicholas was seized with great terror, believing the speaker to be a person worthy of credit; and he commanded a strict watch to be kept, and that if such a person would present himself he should be brought before him forthwith. Presently Brother Juniper arrived alone; for, because of his great perfection, he was allowed to travel without a companion as he pleased.

On this there went to meet him certain wild young men, who began to mock him, treating him with great contempt and indignity. And Brother Juniper was no way troubled thereat, but rather incited them to ill-treat him more and more. And as they came to the castle-gate, the guards seeing him thus disfigured, with his scanty habit torn in two - for he had given half of it on the way to a begger, for the love of God, so that he had no longer the appearance of a Friar Minor - recognizing the signs given of the expected murderer, they dragged him with great fury before the tyrant Nicholas.

They searched him to find whether he had any offensive weapons, and found in his sleeve an awl, which he used to mend his sandals, and also a flint and steel which he carried with him to strike a light when he abode, as he often did, in the woods or in desert places. Nicholas, seeing the signs given by the devil, commanded that a cord should be fastened round his neck, which was done with so great cruelty that it entered into the flesh. He was then most cruelly scourged; and being asked who he was, he replied: "I am a great sinner." When asked whether he wanted to betray the castle to the men of Viterbo, he answered: "I am a great traitor, and unworthy of any mercy."

Being questioned whether he intended to kill the tyrant Nicholas with that awl, and to burn the castle, he replied that he should do greater things than these, should God permit him. This Nicholas then, being wholly mastered by his fury, would examine no further, but without delay condemned Brother Juniper, as a traitor and murderer, to be fastened to a horse's tail, and so dragged on the ground to the gallows, there to be forthwith hanged by the neck. And Brother Juniper made no excuse for himself, but, as one who joys to suffer for the love of God, he was full of contentment and rejoicing.

So the command of the tyrant was carried into effect. Brother Juniper was tied by the feet to the horse's tail, and dragged along the ground, making no complaint, but, like a meek lamb led to the slaughter, he submitted with all humility. At this spectacle of prompt justice, all the people ran together to behold the execution of so hasty and cruel a judgment, but no one knew the culprit. Nevertheless it befell, by the will of God, that a good man, who had seen Brother Juniper taken and sentenced forthwith, ran to the house of the Friars Minor, and said: "I pray you, for the love of God, to come with me at once, for a poor man has been seized and immediately condemned and led to death. Come, that he may at least place his soul in your hands, for he seems to me a good man, and he has had no time to make his confession; even now they are leading him to the gallows, yet he seems to have no fear of death nor care of his soul.

Oh, be pleased to come quickly!" Then the guardian, who was a compassionate man, went at once to provide for the salvation of this soul; and when he came to the place of execution, he could not get near for the crowd; but, as he stood watching for an opening, he heard a voice say: "Do not so, do not so, cruel men; you are hurting my legs!" And as he recognised the voice of Brother Juniper, the guardian, in fervour of spirit, forced his way through the crowd, and tearing the bandage from the face of the condemned, he saw that it was indeed Brother Juniper, who looked upon him with a cheerful and smiling countenance.

Then the guardian with many tears besought the executioners and all the people for pity to wait a little space, till he should go and beseech the tyrant to have mercy on Brother Juniper. The executioners promised to wait a few moments, believing, no doubt, that he was some kinsman of the prisoner. So the devout and pious guardian went to the tyrant Nicholas, weeping bitterly, and said: "My lord, I am so filled with grief and amazement that my tongue can scarcely utter it, for it seems to me that in this our land has been committed to-day the greatest sin and the greatest evil which has been wrought from the days of our fathers even until now, and I believe that it has been done through ignorance." Nicholas heard the guardian patiently, and inquired: "What is this great sin and evil which has been committed to-day in this land?" And the guardian answered: "It is this, my lord, that you have condemned - and, as I assuredly believe, unjustly - to a most cruel punishment one of the holiest friars at this time in the Order of St Francis, to whom you profess a singular devotion." Then said Nicholas: "Now tell me, father guardian, who is he; for perhaps, knowing him not, I have committed a great fault?" "He," said the guardian, "whom you have condemned to death is Brother Juniper, the companion of St Francis."

Then was the tyrant amazed, for he had heard the fame of Brother Juniper's sanctity; and, pale with fear, he hastened together with the guardian to Brother Juniper, and loosed him from the horse's tail and set him free, and in the presence of all the people he prostrated himself on the ground before Brother Juniper, and with many tears confessed his fault, and the cruelty of which he had been guilty towards that holy friar; adding: "I believe indeed that the days of my wicked life are numbered, since I have thus without reason cruelly tortured so holy a man. For, in punishment of my evil life, God will send me in a few days an evil death, though this thing I did ignorantly."

Then Brother Juniper freely forgave the tyrant Nicholas: but a few days afterwards God permitted a most cruel death to overtake him. And so Brother Juniper departed, leaving all the people greatly edified.

How Brother Juniper Gave All That He Had To The Poor For The Love Of God: Chapter IV

Brother Juniper was so full of pity and compassion for the poor, that when he saw anyone poor or naked he immediately took off his tunic, or the hood of his clock, and gave it to him. The guardian therefore laid an obedience upon him not to give away his tunic or any part of his habit. A few days afterwards, a poor half-naked man asked an alms of Brother Juniper for the love of God, who answered him with great compassion: "I have nothing which I could give thee but my tunic, and my superior has laid me under obedience not to give it, nor any part of my habit, to anyone. But if thou take it off my back I will not resist thee." He did not speak to a deaf man; for the begger forthwith stripped him of his tunic, and went off with it.

When Brother Juniper returned home, and was asked what had become of his tunic, he replied: "A good man took it off my back, and went away with it." And as the virtue of compassion increased in him, he was not contented with giving his tunic, but would give books, or clocks, or whatever he could lay his hands on, to the poor. For this reason the brethren took care to leave nothing in the common rooms of the convent, because Brother Juniper gave away everything for the love of God and to the glory of his name.

How Brother Juniper Took Certain Little Bells From The Alter, And Gave Them Away For The Love Of God: Chapter V

One Christmas-day Brother Juniper was in deep meditation before the altar at Scesi, the which altar was right fairly and richly adorned; so, at the desire of the sacristan, Brother Juniper remained to keep guard over it while he went to his dinner. And as he was absorbed in devout meditations, a poor woman came asking an alms of him for the love of God. To whom Brother Juniper made answer: "Wait a while, and I will see if I can find anything for thee on this grand altar."

Now there was upon the altar an exceedingly rich and costly frontal of cloth of gold, with silver bells of great value. "These bells," said Brother Juniper, "are a superfluity"; so he took a knife and cut them off the frontal, and gave them to the poor woman out of compassion. The sacristan, after he had eaten three or four mouthfuls, bethought him of the ways of Brother Juniper, whom he had left in charge; and began exceedingly to doubt whether, in his charitable zeal, he might not do some damage to the costly altar. As soon as the suspicion entered his head, he rose from the table, and went back to the church, to see if any of the ornaments of the altar had been removed or taken away; and when he saw that the frontal had been cut, and the little bells carried off, he was troubled and scandalised beyond measure.

Brother Juniper, seeing that he was very angry, said to him: "Be not disturbed about those little bells, for I have given them to a poor woman who had great need of them, and here they were good for nothing but to make a pompous display of worldly vanity." When the sacristan had heard this, he went with all speed to seek the woman in the church, and throughout the city; but he could neither find her nor meet with anyone who had seen her. So he returned, and in great wrath took the frontal, and carried it to the general, who was at Assisi, saying: "Father general, I demand justice on Brother Juniper, who has spoilt this hanging for me, the very best I had in the sacristy. See how he has destroyed it by cutting away all the silver bells, which he says he has given to a poor woman!" And the general answered him: "It is not Brother Juniper who has done this, but thine own folly; for thou oughtest by this time to have known his ways: and I tell thee, I marvel only that he did not give away the whole frontal. Nevertheless, I will give him a sound correction for this fault."

And having called the brethren together in chapter, he sent for Brother Juniper, and, in the presence of the whole community, reproved him most severely concerning the said bells; and, waxing wrathful as he spoke, he raised his voice till it became hoarse. Brother Juniper cared little or nothing for these words, for he delighted in reproaches, and rejoiced when he received a good humiliation; but his one thought in return was to find a remedy for the general's hoarseness. So when he had received his reproof, he went straight to the town for flour and butter, to make a good hasty-pudding, with which he returned when the night was far spent; then lighting a candle, he went with his hasty-pudding to the door of the general's cell and knocked. The general came to open it, and seeing him with a lighted candle and a pipkin in his hand, asked: "Who is there?"

Brother Juniper answered him: "Father, when you reproved me to-day for my faults, I perceived that your voice grew hoarse, and I thought it was from over-fatigue. I considered therefore what would be the best remedy, and have had this hasty-pudding made for you; therefore I pray you eat of it, for I tell you that it will ease your throat and your chest." "What an hour of the night is this." said the general, "to come and disturb other people!" And Brother Juniper made answer: "See, it has been made for you; I pray you eat of it without more ado, for it will do you good." But the general being angry at the lateness of the hour, and at Brother Juniper's persistence, answered him roughly, bidding him go his way, for at such an hour he would not eat. Then Brother Juniper, seeing that neither persuasions nor prayers were of any avail, said: "Father, since you will not eat the pudding which was made for you, at least do this for me: hold the candle for me, and I will eat it."

Then the general, being a devout and kindly man, seeing the piety and simplicity of Brother Juniper, and how he had done all this out of devotion, answered: "Well, since thou will have it so, thou and I will eat together." And so the two of them ate this hasty-pudding together, out of an importunate charity, and were refreshed by their devotion more than by the food.

How Brother Juniper Kept Silence For Six Months: Chapter VI

Brother Juniper once determined with himself to keep silence for six months together, in this manner. The first day for love of the Eternal Father. The second for love of Jesus Christ his Son. The third for love of the Holy Ghost. The fourth in reverence to the most holy Virgin Mary; and proceeding thus, each day in honour of some saint, he passed six whole months without speaking.

THE

BROTHER

JUNIPER

REJUVENATION

PROJECT

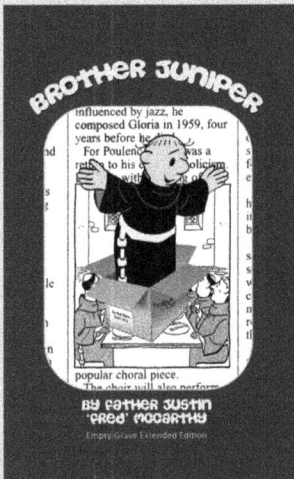

BROTHER JUNIPER

influenced by jazz, he composed Gloria in 1959, four years before he...
For Poulenc...was a re...to his...olicism...with...age of...popular choral piece. The choir will also perform...

BY FATHER JUSTIN 'FRED' MCCARTHY
Empty-Grave Extended Edition

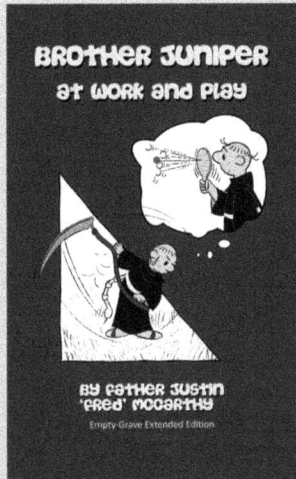

BROTHER JUNIPER
at work and play

BY FATHER JUSTIN 'FRED' MCCARTHY
Empty-Grave Extended Edition

BROTHER JUNIPER
STRIKES AGAIN

BY FATHER JUSTIN 'FRED' MCCARTHY
Empty-Grave Extended Edition

MORE BROTHER JUNIPER

BY FATHER JUSTIN 'FRED' MCCARTHY
Empty-Grave Extended Edition

The DEFINITIVE
BROTHER JUNIPER

Fr. Justin 'Fred' McCarthy

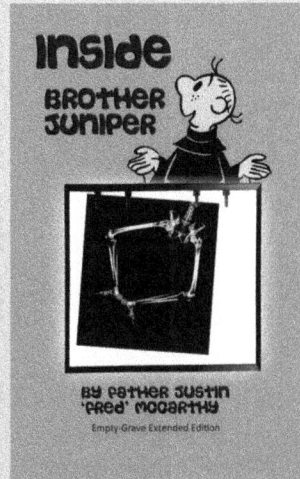

INSIDE BROTHER JUNIPER

BY FATHER JUSTIN 'FRED' MCCARTHY
Empty-Grave Extended Edition

Well Done
Brother Juniper

BY FATHER JUSTIN 'FRED' MCCARTHY
Empty-Grave Extended Edition

THE WHIMSICAL WORLD OF BROTHER JUNIPER

Father Justin 'Fred' McCarthy
Empty-Grave Extended Edition

THE ecumenical BROTHER JUNIPER

BY FATHER JUSTIN 'FRED' MCCARTHY
Empty-Grave Motley Edition

www.ingramcontent.com/pod-product-compliance
Lightning Source LLC
Chambersburg PA
CBHW060424100426
42812CB00030B/3303/J